Also by Bill O'Reilly

Confronting Evil

Confronting the Presidents

Killing Lincoln

Killing Kennedy

Killing Jesus

Killing Patton

Killing Reagan

Killing the Rising Sun

Killing England

Killing the SS

Killing Crazy Horse

Killing the Mob

Killing the Killers

Killing the Legends

Killing the Witches

The United States of Trump

Old School

Legends and Lies: The Civil War

Legends and Lies: The Patriots

Legends and Lies: The Real West

Pinheads and Patriots

A Bold Fresh Piece of Humanity

Culture Warrior

The O'Reilly Factor

Who's Looking Out for You?

Keep It Pithy

Those Who Trespass

The No Spin Zone

Hitler's Last Days

Lincoln's Last Days

The Day the World Went Nuclear

The Day the President Was Shot

Kennedy's Last Days

The Last Days of Jesus

Give Please a Chance

Kids Are Americans Too

The O'Reilly Factor for Kids

CONFRONTING AMERICA

CONFRONTING AMERICA

WHAT HAS TO CHANGE

BILL O'REILLY

and

JOSH HAMMER

ST. MARTIN'S PRESS
NEW YORK

First published in the United States by St. Martin's Press, an imprint of
St. Martin's Publishing Group

EU Representative: Macmillan Publishers Ireland Ltd., 1st Floor, The Liffey Trust Centre,
117–126 Sheriff Street Upper, Dublin 1, D01 YC43

www.stmartins.com

Credit for image on page 155: Courtesy of the author, rephotographed by Robert Jude Puglisi

Credit for image on page 205: Courtesy of the author, rephotographed by Robert Jude Puglisi

Credit for image on page 209: Courtesy Barack Obama Presidential Library

The Library of Congress Cataloging-in-Publication Data is available upon request.

ISBN 978-1-250-37407-3 (hardcover)
ISBN 978-1-250-37408-0 (ebook)

First Edition: 2026

This edition was printed by Lake Book.

10 9 8 7 6 5 4 3 2 1

Confronting America *is dedicated to my children, Madeline and Spencer O'Reilly, that they may use their skills and intellects to make America a better place. I am a proud father.*

Contents

CONFRONTING AMERICA

Introduction

Welcome to a book that is likely to infuriate, amuse, enlighten, and challenge you. It's like a Disney theme park experience but much less expensive. But all of our readers are treated the same, unlike the Disney deal, which shuts out poor families in the name of corporate profits. That should change. You Mouse pinheads can ladder some pricing. Get on it!

That's my first salvo, and there will be many more to come. But, on balance, this is a pro-America book. Having visited almost ninety countries, I believe the United States offers more opportunity than any other. But I'm not a blind patriot, a person who evaluates life emotionally. Not me. I scrutinize, criticize, sometimes lionize. Out of that comes a vivid truth: We Americans need to get better. We must "wise up," as my naval officer father told me perhaps ten thousand times.

Let's start at the beginning. The *Mayflower* people were largely loons. Too nutty for Holland and England. So, few spectators waved goodbye as they sailed out of King James land. Massachusetts, here we come! Uh-oh.*

---

* King James I was the reigning monarch of England when the *Mayflower* set sail in September 1620. The Pilgrims (or "Separatists") left Britain specifically to escape religious persecution under his government, which forced them to conform to the Church of England, a Protestant sect created by James's great-uncle, Henry VIII. We chronicle the brutality of King Henry in my book *Confronting Evil*.

Many on the rickety ship were religious zealots who, once they made landfall, began hanging alleged "witches" from trees. Nineteen of them. Today, Salem makes big money showcasing this. While we were researching my book *Killing the Witches*, Salem's mayor told me to get lost when I asked about the "morality" of cashing in on historical atrocities. You see how charming I can be.

At least I avoided a show trial.

Four hundred years after the Massachusetts Bay insanity, the United States has evolved into the most powerful nation the world has ever seen. Throughout this book, we will spotlight exactly how that occurred. But we'll also explain that power does not always translate to equal justice. All Americans can improve in the fairness arena. That is imperative if this nation is to secure *lasting* greatness.

Notice I am talking about the folks, of which I am one, not politicians. They come and go. Some are honorable, some craven. But they can't significantly improve this country. We the people have to do that ourselves. Strong leadership is great, but in a republic, the citizens should be calling the shots. Too many of us don't understand that. It's on us to *demand* positive change.

That requires discipline. You must pay attention, think outside yourself, put down the stupid cell phone, and stop consuming rank media propaganda, which will suck the life out of a person. The purveyors of public deceit should be the ones swinging from trees. I want to talk to Salem about that. Maybe the city council would like to pivot.

So, who am I to demand "change" in the good old USA? Well, thanks to you, I'm the best-selling historical author in the world, and I'm also the creator of the "No Spin" concept, which has prospered on television, and now social media, for about thirty years.

Pretty good resume, right?

Here's the kicker. I couldn't have done that in any other country. In China, I'd disappear. Putin would have poisoned me a long time ago. The Mexican drug cartels would have me hanging from a bridge, and even in Europe, the governments would never allow a public exposition like mine. In certain EU countries, they continue to block my website, BillOReilly.com.*

Yes, it's true that some American miscreants have tried to silence me. I have a list. We will deal with a number of those people in these pages. However, the honest folks have saved me time after time. It's not "Power to the People," as the Black Panthers said. It's power *from* the people.

Now, before we proceed further, it's important to know that we do not peddle ideology in this book. Both political parties are struggling at this point in history, and we should all admit it. From the beginning, there has always been strife in the political arena. Thomas Jefferson wanted the states to have the most control, Alexander Hamilton the Feds.

George Washington was kind of wishy-washy about the whole thing. The general was essentially a warrior, not an office jockey sitting around debating the Whiskey Tax. That might move him to grab a bottle, much to the displeasure of Martha, who pretty much ran George's social life.

One important caveat for our era. The American far left has grown more powerful, and that is a direct threat to our country. The crazy right-wingers have largely been marginalized, but the Socialists currently have media approval and big money behind them. The Soros family and others. Danger here. We'll deal with it.

Let's wrap this intro by getting back to me, your humble correspondent. Of course, my detractors say, "It's all about you, O'Reilly." But it's not. I am simply your guide. Here's why. No soothsayer in the world could have predicted the life I have led. I will relate some of that to illustrate what has to change in the US. There's no better teacher than real life.

Eons ago, my third-grade teacher, Sister Mary Lurana, called me a "bold fresh piece of humanity," and that's the title of my autobiography,

* Many European countries charge what they call "defamation insurance." The fees can run $150,000 a year. It's a total scam designed to keep out independent social media organizations.

in case you care. Apparently, the nun was not much concerned about my self-esteem, but she was dead-on accurate about my childhood profile.

Little has changed for me demeanor-wise after all these decades. And listen to this. About thirty-eight years ago, the good sister actually wrote me a letter while I was working for ABC News. Her opening line was, "Billy, you still have the same expression."

Probably true. Not much evolution here. Let's get on this journey.

Bill O'Reilly
Tokyo, Japan
May 2025

CHAPTER ONE

Money Matters—A Lot

If I hear Senator Bernie Sanders say the word *oligarch* one more time, I'm going to print and distribute directions to his "rustic" lake house in Vermont. Sanders is a one note Communist: "The folks are getting screwed by rich people, so the federal government should pay all your bills!" With about 340 million people running around the US, that's impossible.

Unless.

The federal government imposes a "wealth tax" and begins seizing private property and assets. Bernie desperately wants that to happen. It would start small and then . . . boom. Washington would dictate what Americans can and cannot have financially. And after we die, the confiscation would kick in big time. We'll be lucky to have a coffin to lie in.*

Bernie Sanders calls himself a "Democratic Socialist," but that's a ruse. He's a hardcore Leninist, appealing to American voters who

* In March 2026, Sanders and Congressman Ro Khanna, a Democrat representing Silicon Valley, California, introduced legislation aiming for a 5 percent annual wealth tax on US billionaires, estimated to raise substantial revenue over a decade. The proposed legislation, I believe, is unconstitutional because it "seizes" private property. But the Communists have begun the process.

don't believe they can succeed in the marketplace because the "system" exploits them. Fidel 101. Sanders should have been exposed a long time ago.

But here's the thing. The money factor is *not* being dealt with honestly in this country. Many Americans have no blankin' clue what it takes to achieve prosperity in our very competitive capitalist marketplace. And our educational system does not level with them largely because of political correctness.

✪ ✪ ✪

Your humble correspondent, me, has worked since the age of ten. Lawn cutting, snow shoveling, painting houses—you name it. Many Americans have the same experience.

After graduating from college, I took a job teaching high school in a tough neighborhood north of Miami, Florida. Opa-locka. Don't go there! The school was diverse before that word became a Harvard cliché. About half the students were Cuban, 35 percent Anglo, 15 percent Black. Even though I was inexperienced in the classroom, it quickly became clear that some of the kids were in deep trouble. They were disinterested in learning, disrespectful in demeanor, and, most tragically, disregarded warnings about the future.

Some teachers wrote these students off as hopeless. That bothered me because I understood the failure dynamic. Awful parents are the primary reason children crash and burn. Very tough to develop intellectually when your drunk father is beating the hell out of you, or your parents could not care less about your well-being.

At Pace High School, I taught a course on current events and one day put together a slide show on some lavish properties abutting Biscayne Bay. The class perked up. "Want to live there?" I asked. Unanimous assent.

Suddenly, the video changed to scenes of slum housing right outside the school property. Terrible images. The class went silent. Some of the students lived in these hovels.

I then addressed the "income inequality" situation that Bernie

Sanders loves to exploit. "All of you can succeed," I said. "But many of you will not. Your lives will be chaotic, maybe violent. But you have the power to avoid that because you're Americans."

I then told them the crucial truth. You must develop a skill and work hard at it. You have to be honest and respectful of others. You cannot abuse drugs and alcohol. If you do, you will debase yourself and slide into depravity. No bay house, no prosperity.*

"Life is hard," I continued. "Few will help your cause. Some will deceive and hurt you. Most won't care at all. You must be smart enough to evaluate people in order to protect yourself. This country will provide options. But it's up to you to embrace them. And when you fail, which you will, you bounce back hard. Never accept personal defeat."

Some of the students got it. Others were frightened by my blunt presentation. After receiving a few phone complaints from misguided parents, the principal, a corrupt nitwit, called me in and demanded an explanation.

"I told them the truth," I said, looking hard at the guy. "Problem with that?"

Mr. Charm, always.

✪ ✪ ✪

Later in the semester, I attended a faculty meeting where a discussion of "hot pants" was underway. This was the early 1970s, when "short shorts" were cool for girls. Some of the teachers and administrators were appalled by the garment. I was amazed that this was actually a topic in a faculty meeting when drugs, bullying, and general chaos enveloped the school. So, I decided to take some action. I would destroy the assembly.

Picture this: about twenty-five teachers, most of whom were middle-class folks, sitting in a room looking at the principal and assistant principal who were standing before them. It was about

---

* A study from the federal government's "Substance Abuse and Services Administration" finds more than 30 percent of people living beneath the poverty line abuse drugs and alcohol on a regular basis.

equal in terms of men and women. The faculty meeting was held after school, so most people were annoyed, wanting to go home. I would accelerate that process.

The assistant principal was obsessed, then she threw the discussion open and asked the faculty, "What do you think is the appropriate dress at football games?"

My hand shot up like an Elon Musk rocket. At this point in the school year, most of the teachers knew this was not a good sign.

I was sitting in the back of the room next to my college roommate Joe Rubino, who was also a teacher at the school. Rubino put his head in his hands. He knew what was coming.

I addressed the assistant principal directly. "I know something about attire at football games, having played the game in college." I then paused for dramatic effect. "The proper dress is shoulder pads, a helmet, spiked shoes, and a long jersey."

My few admirers on the faculty actually burst out laughing, humiliating the woman. Which is exactly what I wanted to do. While some seniors were headed for prison, these poltroons were talking about short pants. It was absurd.

That pretty much ended any kind of "hot pants" discussion going forward. The daggers coming out of the eyes of the administrators and a few other faculty lackeys were sharp and pronounced. I did not care. At this point, my job was to focus these pinheads on trying to save as many children as we could. If I had to mock some of the faculty in order to do that—let the mocking begin.

✪ ✪ ✪

Unfortunately, it's the same today. Many educators want to avoid real life. Money, success, failure, behavior, morality are all subjects largely avoided in many schools. Especially in poor areas. But making excuses and promoting victimhood are very hot topics. Some teachers use them to justify future failure. Not your fault. Slavery, immigration, the White patriarchy. You know the drill.

This needs to change. Give the kids a fighting chance, tell them the truth. You have to compete, and you *must* have a skill set or you're screwed. A neck tattoo is not going to stimulate higher wages unless you are motivated to work in a strip club. Crude is not an attribute in securing a worthwhile job.

The United States *must* improve its educational mandates. We don't have to become South Korea, where they drive students like cattle. But schools cannot continue to accept antisocial behavior, student narcissism, and social promotion.

The "oligarchs" are not driving poverty and crime, disintegrating families are.*

Our school system is supposed to be the last line of defense for saving the socially disadvantaged. It is NOT doing the job. That's the real reason we have so much disparity of income, crime, and hopelessness.

Get it, Bernie Sanders?

* According to a 2025 study from the University of Massachusetts, 84 percent of Democrats see "oligarchs" as a direct threat to democracy. That figure falls to 49 percent for Republicans.

CHAPTER TWO

The Race Dilemma

Skin color doesn't matter. Who cares? I'm Caucasian. I had no choice with two Irish parents. That's the way it is.

The Levitt brothers, who built the massive suburbs of Levittown in Pennsylvania and on Long Island, would not sell the homes to African Americans. Bad for business after the Second World War, they thought. So, growing up there, I didn't know any Black people.*

But I *did* know Willie Mays, the New York Giants' center fielder. Magnificent athlete. Idolized him. Still have my Willie Mays model baseball glove to this day. It's sixty-five years old.

Some morons in my Levittown neighborhood used the N-word. I walked away. My parents and friends did not do that.

When I was nineteen years old, I pitched for the Brooklyn Monarchs, an adult baseball team. I was the only Caucasian in the dugout. My nickname was "White Boy," as in, "White Boy, we don't want to be standing around watching you walk people. Understand?"

---

* The Levitt brothers—William ("Bill") and Alfred—along with their father, Abraham, revolutionized American housing post–World War II by creating massive, affordable suburban developments known as Levittowns. Utilizing assembly-line techniques, they transformed construction into a manufacturing process, enabling rapid, low-cost home production that fueled the rise of modern suburbia. Unfortunately, the Levitt crew was racist, denying homes to many minorities.

Yes, I did. Perfectly.

The Monarchs were a rough crew. Some of the guys in their early twenties already had multiple kids. My teammates were working-class people who lived in all-Black neighborhoods. I listened to their banter, which was often hysterical. I said little. I threw strikes.

My radio favorite was Motown. The Four Tops were the best. Sometimes when the game got boring, the Monarchs would harmonize in the dugout. "The Tracks of My Tears" by Smokey Robinson was big. I never sang, although I loved the song.

Being an outsider on the team didn't bother me, and I did not try to ingratiate myself. I respected the guys but knew my place. The cultural gulf was just too big. I was going to college and would never see daily life in Bedford-Stuyvesant. So, even though I was curious about inner-city culture, I did not intrude on my teammates. We had a good season. See you next summer.

But that didn't happen because I was off to the University of London, where the Monarchs would *not* be going. Different worlds.

Throughout my life, I have never cared about ethnicity. I try to treat everyone in a fair way. I believe most Americans do that. Some think my opinion is naive in the extreme. On MS NOW, formerly MSNBC, you hear all the time that America is a rotten, racist place.*

In September 2007, I had dinner with Al Sharpton. I was anchoring *The O'Reilly Factor* on Fox News, and the reverend had debated me a few times. I knew his reputation as a race hustler, someone who made money stoking division. But I wanted to see his demeanor in a more personal way. Give the guy a chance.

We went to Sylvia's in Harlem, a legendary soul food restaurant. The cooking and service were excellent. During the conversation, Sharpton mentioned that his charity was having financial problems

* A 2025 survey from Gallup finds Americans' confidence in the mass media has fallen to a historic low, with just 28 percent expressing a "great deal" or "fair amount" of trust in newspapers, television, and radio to report the news fully, accurately, and fairly. This is down from 31 percent in 2024 and 40 percent in 2020.

and he didn't have enough money to distribute turkeys for Thanksgiving, as he did annually.

"How much do you spend on that?" I asked.

He said $25,000. I sent him a check from my charitable foundation the next day. I never said anything publicly about it.

One week later, I did a radio commentary about the dinner in which I spotlighted my late grandmother, who was frightened of Black people even though she didn't know any. I opined that I wished I could have taken her to Sylvia's so she could see there is no difference between a Black-owned enterprise and a White-owned one.

The hate website Media Matters immediately accused me of being a racist, taking my analysis out of context. That's what those people do—try to harm high-profile nonprogressives. No lie is beneath them.[*]

Al Sharpton said nothing in my defense, and he easily could have.

✪ ✪ ✪

In the United States right now, Asian Americans make the most money. According to the census, those households have a median income of $113,000.

For Black Americans, the number is $56,500. For non-Hispanic White Americans, $89,000.

It is not fair to compare Hispanic families because so many are new arrivals to America. The reason Asians lead the money league is education and culture. I'm generalizing, but Asian families are traditionally tight; the work ethic is paramount. Crude behavior is not acceptable, with intoxication a rarity. Children are expected to perform academically, get a good job, build a solid family unit.

There is also not much grievance going on among Asians, even

---

* Media Matters for America (MMfA) is a Washington, DC–based, progressive 501(c)(3) nonprofit organization founded in 2004 to monitor, analyze, and correct so-called conservative misinformation. It acts as a watchdog, frequently criticizing right-leaning outlets like Fox News and promoting liberal perspectives on media coverage. The group has an annual operating budget of $27 million.

though they were hammered in nineteenth-century America. Chinese immigrants endured brutal conditions working on the railroads and in the mines. In fact, the Chinese Exclusion Act of 1882 banned Chinese immigrants, even those already in the United States, from becoming US citizens.*

Today in Black communities, 64 percent of children are living without a father in the house. For Asians, the number is 15 percent.

There you go.

It angers me that the powerful in America will not tell the truth about parenting. If dad splits, the children suffer. That's not hard to understand. But is that an important message in the media or academia? No, it is not.

In addition, the so-called hip-hop culture has badly damaged the African American pathway to success. Hooligans and miscreants have been glorified even as their musical products have harmed millions of young people. This is not Motown, this is Helltown.

Vice President Kamala Harris said in 2020 that Tupac Shakur was one of her "favorite" artists.

Okay. Here's a sample of Tupac:

> *"You claim to be a player, but I F'ed your wife.*
> *We bust bad boys, (N-word) F'ed for life."*

Shakur was murdered in 1996 at the age of twenty-five. The drive-by crime in Nevada was never solved. To this day, many Americans consider him a hero. Kamala's stamp of approval got national headlines. The corrupt media, of course, endorsed her amazingly irresponsible statement about the rapper.

✪✪✪

* President Chester A. Arthur was elevated to the top job after the assassination of President James Garfield on July 2, 1881. Arthur, a machine politician from New York, vetoed the first Chinese exclusion law. But he soon succumbed to racist pressure, and the legislation passed.

The harsh truth is that a violent, permissive entertainment culture has corrupted many young minority Americans. You will not be able to compete in a capitalist society if you embrace threatening and profane speech and ruin your appearance with garish tattoos and piercings.

If Daddy's money sustains you, it doesn't matter what you look like. But if you have to make it on your own, it does.

Also, seeing yourself as a rebellious victim will not lead to happiness and stability. It's really reverse racism. Parents, teachers, and preachers are failing to state the obvious to at-risk kids of all races: You will fail in life if you don't have discipline and vision. You are doomed to poverty if you go down Depravity Road.

Where is that message? Why aren't there public service announcements everywhere countering the destructive culture? Where are public school courses on life skills and patriotism?

The whole corrupt culture thing makes me furious. This has to be confronted.

✪ ✪ ✪

Now, pot is everywhere. Idiot politicians have legalized marijuana so it's easily available to adolescents in urban centers. Walk down the street in New York City and smell the fresh air.

Uh, you can't. Marijuana smoke is everywhere. Stand outside many urban public middle schools before classes begin in the morning. Kids are toking up.*

If you smoke cigarettes in this country, you negatively stand out. The Marlboro Man has been banished. But inhale pot and somehow you're cool. How did that happen?

Two reasons: First, celebrities like Snoop Dogg and Willie Nelson widely publicize their drug intake. Second, many liberal baby

---

* New York State legalized the recreational sale of cannabis in March 2021. Legal marijuana shops in the city have proliferated significantly, offering lab-tested, New York–grown products for adults twenty-one and older. As of 2026, there are over two hundred licensed dispensaries statewide, with dozens active across the five boroughs.

boomers are still mired in the good old days of sex, drugs, and rock and roll.*

"Smoking pot didn't hurt me!" they wail. "Actually, it helps me relax!"

Give me a break with the self-obsessed stuff. Chances are you weren't a ten-year-old whose neighborhood is a street pharmacy. Not that the pot pinheads care, but once a kid gets high or drunk, his or her childhood is over.

Many dopey politicians (pardon the pun) refuse to see the devastation of drug use among children. Extremely hard to come back from that. Changes everything for the worse. Not relaxing!

✪ ✪ ✪

The fabulously wealthy rap businessman Jay-Z told Oprah he sold crack as a teenager out of the Marcy Projects in Brooklyn. Crack, of course, has destroyed millions of lives. So, Jay-Z, born Shawn Carter, owes a karma debt here.

Instead of parading around as a mogul, the aging Jay should become a spokesman *against* drugs. He could easily get his partners in the National Football League to fund TV commercials where Jay-Z and his hip pals tell young people drugs are bad. Using them, selling them, condoning them.

I bet Denzel Washington would sign up for that project after his searing portrayal of a heroin dealer in *American Gangster*. Other Black performers might cooperate as well. Beyoncé?

Drugs in America are a problem for all races, not just Black people. But combined with the abandonment of fathers on a mass scale, this is a situation the African American community must take on.

As Cuba Gooding Jr. said in *American Gangster*, "Hear me?"

---

* According to data from the National Institutes of Health, the number of Americans who identify as "regular cigarette smokers" has gone from 55 percent in 1945 to 8 percent in 2025. In the same time span, the number of "regular marijuana users" has gone from 4 percent to 20 percent.

✪ ✪ ✪

Slavery is still holding some Black people back. Not the vile institution itself, that's been wiped out. But the lingering effect of enslavement weighs upon American culture.

More than one hundred nations allowed slavery in the seventeenth and eighteenth centuries. I write about the heinous Americans who made millions in my book *Confronting Evil*. The brutality of that industry is almost incomprehensible. Director Quentin Tarantino does a masterful job of exposition in his movie *Django Unchained*.

Today, some people want "reparations" for the descendants of slaves. Cash. I understand the bitterness. Millions of Black families were harmed, and that legacy extends to modern times. Generational suffering is a real thing.

But grievance based upon historical injustice is not a remedy for success. Resentment, indignation, and the overemphasis of skin color are not positive attributes.

My own family was brutalized by the English Crown. County Cavan, Ireland. My ancestors had their farm stolen by corrupt officials. But America gave the O'Reillys a chance to prosper. I don't want reparations from the Brits. I might not be an American without the terrible injustice London did to my family.

Of course, every situation is different. The past is important, but the future is paramount. Hating America because of slavery and Jim Crow is self-destructive, even if some make a fast buck doing it. The way forward should be the focus.

✪ ✪ ✪

Stephen A. Smith is a friend of mine. He is the most successful sports broadcaster in the country and may branch out into politics. He has succeeded because of God-given talent and an amazing work ethic.

Stephen and I disagree on a few things. He's not real fond of me bloviating about the "Black experience." Like my interaction with the Brooklyn Monarchs, I understand. Perfectly.

The Smith household in Queens was basically a lower-middle-class situation. As a kid, Stephen often clashed with his father. But his background did not hold him back. Skin color had nothing to do with Smith's ability to broadcast. That is a very important point. Stephen A. made it on his own.

That's the kind of role model that should be celebrated and presented to schoolkids. President Obama, too. No father in the house for him. Two terms as the most powerful person in the world.

Get it, MS NOW?

And it is Barack Obama who understood a key element in fostering respectful race relations. I was involved. But like everything attached to race, it got very complicated.

Read on.

CHAPTER THREE

It's Criminal

President Barack Obama was a well-intentioned Chief Executive with a significant progressive blind spot. That is my assessment after covering him for almost nine years.

Our relationship began with a rocky encounter in New Hampshire. The year was 2008, and the senator from Illinois was campaigning for the Democratic presidential nomination against a very tough rival: Senator Hillary Clinton.

I traveled to the "Live Free or Die" state to get a firsthand look at both candidates who were barnstorming around. New Hampshire was the first primary, so interest was ultra-high.

Both candidates had rallies in Nashua high school gymnasiums the day I arrived. That was January 5. Senator Clinton's event was poorly attended and flat. Not much energy. She nodded in my direction but did not hold a press briefing.

Senator Obama, however, oozed charisma, and the gym was packed. He didn't say much beyond his usual "hope and change" thing, but I knew then that Hillary was toast. The Democrats in the crowd LOVED Barack.

After his prepared remarks, the senator approached the rope line for some handshaking and pleasantries. There, I waited with my camera crew. I had a few questions.

Without warning, a very large man walked over and stood directly in front of the camera. I motioned to my photographer to pivot right. The large man moved right as well, totally blocking our shots of the senator.

I asked the guy to give us a break. He would not. Although I didn't know it at the time, his name was Marvin Nicholson, and he was a personal bodyguard for Barack Obama.

As the senator got closer, I had to make a decision. We were not getting the video we needed. So, I asked the big fellow a second time to move. He ignored me.

I then shoved him out of the way. Fairly hard.

The Secret Service and Senator Obama saw the guy stumbling. They looked at me. I looked at them. Then I said this:

"Senator, Bill O'Reilly, Fox News. Might we have a few words?"

Now, I fully expected Mr. Obama to turn on his heel. He did not. The Democrat approached, put out his hand, and said, "How are you, Bill?"

How am I? Grouchy.

"Fine, Senator, but I'd very much like to ask you a few questions."

"We'll do an interview, but not here. My staff will be in touch."

As the candidate sauntered away, I thought: Cool guy. In control. His "body man" glared at me. I'm used to it.

And the senator did give me an interview a few months later in York, Pennsylvania. Marvin was there as well. I nodded at him. No point in resurrecting the past. No apologies from either of us. I suspected Barack Obama was amused.

The Wikipedia description of the New Hampshire confrontation contains this phrase: "O'Reilly and his film crew caused a commotion."

Not true. My tech guys had nothing to do with it. I, alone, was the commotion purveyor. With, of course, good reason.

No wimp zone!

Thus began my "relationship" with President Obama, which was respectful and challenging. A few years later, in Washington, DC, I encountered him at another rope line. This time, I wanted him to help a charity for severely wounded Iraq and Afghanistan vets by signing a number of pictures. He agreed. We raised about $30 million for the Independence Fund in that campaign. The plan was to auction off ten pictures signed by all five living presidents. After President Obama signed, the others agreed. Except one.

Jimmy Carter refused. I personally called his office in Plains, Georgia, and was given the runaround by his chief of staff. There was no explanation of why the former president could not sign ten pictures. It would take him less than a minute. I strongly suspect he loathed me and that's why he wouldn't cooperate.

So, I threatened Carter. I told his chief of staff that I would show the pictures on television, signed by the other four presidents, and explain how he had refused to help the wounded veterans.

All the money raised was to get them high-tech wheelchairs. So, this would have been devastating to Jimmy Carter's legacy.

In addition, I told the woman in Plains that I was sending Fox producer Jesse Watters down to personally hand the pictures to President Carter. In the face of all that, the thirty-ninth president of the United States capitulated, and we got the signatures.

One footnote: I take no delight in writing this account. But Carter made the play himself. The other four presidents, Clinton, Bush the Younger, Bush the Elder, and Obama, eagerly helped.

Carter had no excuse.

And, there was another righteous cause involving President Obama and your humble correspondent. But this one fell short, and it should not have.

✪✪✪

Every criminology study you will ever see says the same thing: Young African American men commit a disproportionate amount of violent crimes and fill our prisons.

Most folks know this but are fuzzy on the primary reasons why. However, it's not that complicated. The main reason is lack of parental supervision in a poverty environment. That situation continues to plague Black America.

Picture this. You are twelve years old. You rarely see your father. Your mom works a low-paying job; she's exhausted much of the time. Maybe your grandmother watches you. Maybe not. Many conflicts you see on the street lead to violence.

Your house is basic, your neighborhood dangerous. Drugs and alcohol instantly available. Crude behavior on display around the clock.

Your friends are in the same circumstance. Your school is a madhouse: little discipline, teachers who are routinely threatened and demeaned in the classroom.

On the street, gangs that sell drugs offer you money to join and do what they do. You might be threatened or beaten if you decline. Your entire life is watching chaos and violence unfold. Temptation a constant.

What chance does a boy like that have? And it doesn't matter what color he is. Cliché alert: The deck of life is stacked against him.

But there is a pathway out. It's called mentoring.

✪✪✪

In the late 1970s, I was working in Denver, Colorado, doing quite well as a reporter and weekend anchor. But I was becoming selfish in pursuit of success. So, I signed up to become a "Big Brother."

That organization is nationwide. It's now known as Big Brothers Big Sisters. Volunteers help young kids from broken homes. They set up fun recreation and help with problems. Many of the mentors become surrogate parents. Hundreds of thousands of at-risk kids are helped.*

I was assigned a family with three children and a beleaguered mother. The husband/father had taken up with a younger woman and moved to Milwaukee, abandoning his offspring. Irish guy. I never met him, and that was fortunate, because assault and battery would have arisen.

---

* Big Brothers Big Sisters of America is the largest and oldest youth mentoring organization in the United States, founded in 1904 to create and support one-to-one mentoring relationships that nurture the creativity of youth. The organization pairs volunteers ("Bigs") with children ("Littles") ages six to eighteen.

I helped the three kids and am still in touch to this day. They survived a brutal ordeal. They all attended college.

That should happen nationwide: mentoring on a grand scale. Knowing he considered personal assistance important, I discussed the situation with President Obama, mainly through his top adviser, Valerie Jarrett. Tough lady. But we got along.

On February 27, 2014, I was invited to the White House for the rollout of the My Brother's Keeper program. I was seated up front near Colin Powell and other prominent Black leaders. After the president's address outlining how successful Keeper had been in Chicago, he walked over to me for a short chat. Some in the crowd were stunned.

The next day, Valerie Jarrett appeared on *The O'Reilly Factor* to discuss the Keeper program. Again, the concept is simple: An army of successful men try to help boys who are deprived. No downside whatsoever. We just have to get the mentors to sign up.

✪ ✪ ✪

Politics is often destructive. Essentially, I am a problem solver and have no use for empty rhetoric and power seeking. I firmly believed that Barack Obama understood and cared about at-risk Black youth. His own father ran out on him, and his mother was a mess.

In Honolulu, young Barry was primarily raised by his maternal grandparents.

Despite all that, the man succeeded on a historic scale. Harvard Law, elected a senator from Illinois, two-term president of the United States. Incredible story.

So, after a lot of thought, I set out on a remarkable quest to dramatically assist the My Brother's Keeper program.

Move over, Don Quixote.*

---

* *Don Quixote* (published in two parts, 1605 and 1615) by Miguel de Cervantes is considered the first modern novel and a cornerstone of Western literature. It is a satirical, humorous, and tragic tale that explores the clash between idealism and reality.

✪ ✪ ✪

Establishing momentum for any worthy cause that depends on volunteers is exceedingly difficult. The plan for Keepers, as stated, was to have successful men all over the country agree to help kids in difficult circumstances. That takes enormous marketing and coordination.

The key to establishing the mentorship situation was money. Big money. The government was not going to pony up, even though it should. The funds had to be raised privately.

After a few weeks, I devised a plan. Perhaps the best perk of being a successful journalist is that you get to meet very influential people. You have "access" to the wealthy and powerful.

I wanted to raise $1 *billion* for the Keeper program. That kind of money would establish an endowment whereby funds would continually be available forever. You want to get the word out in America, you need cash.

My vision, which I kept largely to myself, was a worldwide pay-per-view concert. And there was only one act that could command the global attention needed: The Beatles.

At least the two surviving ones, Paul McCartney and Ringo Starr.

Here's the scenario: a ninety-minute show at MetLife Stadium in New Jersey featuring all The Beatles' hits. In addition to McCartney and Starr, the two sons of the late John Lennon, as well as Ringo's kid, Zak, would be in the band.

Rounding out the crew: Billy Joel and Bono—I knew both and knew they would sign on because they're good guys who do a lot of charity work. Other musicians might also help out, but you get the idea. Everyone on the planet would buy a TV ticket to watch this show. At least that was the hope.

I went to work.

First, I talked to my boss at Fox News, Roger Ailes, about convincing Fox Entertainment to run the concert on television. Network bureaucracies are awful, but this pitch was easy. If some nitwit at Fox turned it down, the other three networks would line up.

Then, I spoke with Woody Johnson, the owner of the New York Jets, about getting the stadium almost gratis. It would have happened. Woody, who later became the US Ambassador to Great Britain, is a good guy, and he saw the potential societal benefit immediately.

Next, I put together a list of Fortune 500 companies that would underwrite all marketing and logistical expenses in return for being attached to the show. They would also donate some cash. That's called "putting the arm on you" in mob parlance.

Then, we researched the best pay-per-view outfits to make sure Antarctica and everywhere else on the planet could access the concert for a $100 watch fee.

In addition, we'd make a deal with record companies to sell the live album.

On and on and on. Ka-ching, ka-ching, ka-ching.

The talent would work for free because the promotional opportunities for them would be record breaking. I had it all covered. But then reality set in.

✪ ✪ ✪

The key to the entire project was Paul McCartney. Once he signed on, everything would fall into place. I had encountered Ringo Starr at Radio City Music Hall, and he seemed to be an affable fellow. Billy Joel and Bono, as mentioned, are both altruistic men.

I had met McCartney once. He is married to a cousin of Barbara Walters, and the late ABC icon was a friend of mine. Barbara threw a party in Midtown Manhattan for the couple and demanded that I show up.

Parties are not my strong suit, but I accepted the invitation. Big, rich crowd. Paul arrives wearing a black leather jacket. Barbara grabs my arm and pulls me over, saying, "Don't forget to call him 'Sir,'" as he had been knighted by the Queen of England.

Which, of course, an Irish American working-class guy like me would never do.

So, there I am looking down at the "cute Beatle." Bear in mind that this was a few years before the Keeper project. I can usually tell if people recognize me, and McCartney did. Barbara Walters then said, "Sir Paul, I'd like to introduce you to Bill O'Reilly."

It was a bit noisy in the room, and McCartney paused before saying, "Nice to meet you, PHIL!"

Nonplussed, I replied, "Good meeting you, RINGO!"

Good line, right? Barbara Walters didn't think so. She gave me a look that would sink a freighter.

The rest of the evening was uneventful, and I don't think I offended anyone, but who knows. Social gatherings confuse me.

✪ ✪ ✪

Years later, remembering the Walters introduction, I had to find a way to convince Paul McCartney to help at-risk kids. The concert concept was good, but presentation is everything. I researched. One name kept appearing: John Eastman.

Paul McCartney married Linda Eastman in March 1969, about the same time John Lennon married Yoko Ono. There was major tension as the ladies were always around, especially when the Beatles recorded *Abbey Road*. I chronicle that in my book *Killing the Legends*.

John Eastman was Linda's brother and a sharp businessman. An attorney, he represented a number of big-time musicians like Elton John, David Bowie, and Andrew Lloyd Webber. Almost immediately, he began advising his new brother-in-law.

That did not sit well with John Lennon and George Harrison.

By 1970, the band was in disarray. Yoko Ono controlled Lennon, Linda and John Eastman had enormous influence on McCartney. Then the bomb dropped.

On December 31, 1970, John Eastman filed legal papers in London to dissolve The Beatles' partnership agreement. There was much bitterness. In fact, John Lennon directed a song at Paul McCartney titled "How Do You Sleep?"

Eastman then took over McCartney's business dealings, resulting in the musician becoming a billionaire. Linda McCartney died from cancer in 1998 at the age of fifty-six. Her brother continued to manage Paul McCartney's musical empire until Eastman himself passed in 2022.

So, it was John Eastman who, in 2014, I had to win over. I thought he'd like the idea as the benefit that would come from this charitable concert would ensure goodwill everywhere. Everyone wins! And Barack Obama is involved! A dreamscape for liberals like John Eastman.

✪ ✪ ✪

It wasn't easy getting to Eastman. I suspected he was not a fan of mine, a situation that is "not unusual," as Tom Jones once sang.

Eastman had helped Billy Joel out after the Long Island singer's first manager took extreme advantage of him. So, I asked Bill to put in a good word, which I think he did.

Finally, weeks later, John Eastman was on the telephone line. I did not sense instant bonding.

I kept my pitch tight, although I dropped big business names like crazy. But the headliner in my spiel was President Barack Obama. That should do it, right?

Wrong.

After listening to me for about five minutes, Eastman spoke. He had no questions, never a good sign in a conversation. In fact, he sounded bored.

"You do realize that *creators* are special people," Eastman intoned.

"Sure," I replied.

"And *creators* have to decide what is right for them. No one else."

"Of course."

"Therefore, this is a process, and I cannot guarantee anything. We'll get back to you."

That was it. Ice had formed on my office phone. I had more chance of vacationing with Hillary and Bill Clinton than I had with this arrogant guy "getting back to me," which, of course, he did not.

But I wasn't done.

A woman named Antoinette Bush worked at Fox. People call her Toni. She was the executive vice president and global head of government affairs for News Corporation, which owned Fox News.

She is also a cousin of Valerie Jarrett, who was the most powerful person in the White House, outside of the Obamas.

So, I met with Antoinette Bush.

Essentially, I suggested that if the president himself would call Paul McCartney and his gatekeeper, Eastman, the concert would happen. I also said that I did not want any mention of my role in the Keeper project so politics would not be an issue. I wasn't in this for publicity.

I emphasized the *billion-dollar* payday and how much that would help the kids. I tried to be charming, not confrontational.

I swear.

Antoinette Bush said she "would get back to me." Unlike John Eastman, I thought she actually would.

Never heard from her.

✪ ✪ ✪

It would be unfair of me to speculate here. An enormous opportunity to do good evaporated for no reason that I can see.

Maybe Eastman didn't even tell McCartney about the project. That's possible. As for President Obama, he was a busy guy.

The My Brother's Keeper organization still exists, but few have ever heard of it. Crimes committed by African American young men continue to plague the land.

Paul McCartney and Ringo Starr, both in their eighties, still do shows. Barack Obama has a bunch of nice houses and gives speeches at $250,000 a pop, more for overseas engagements.

So, conceivably, a big My Brother's Keeper concert could still happen. But it won't. And that's part of what must change in America.

When you can do some good, do it. Especially if you are rich and powerful.

Pretty blankin' simple.

CHAPTER FOUR

Are You a Patriot?

Some Americans despise their own country. They have the right to do that. Others object to some aspects of the United States. They want significant change.

This book fits into the change category, but I am writing from a patriotic point of view, not a destructive one. We can be better. Let's at least try.

That's a tough sell in a very selfish time. "Where's mine?" is a common refrain. "I'm entitled because I'm a victim. I want more from the government. I deserve more. Give me what I want and I'll vote for you."

That's the opposite of patriotism.*

✪✪✪

Dissent is often worthy but almost always comes with a price. Colin Kaepernick, for example, got hammered. You may remember that in

* As of 2026, America is marked by historically low levels of patriotic pride, particularly among younger generations, while a deep partisan divide remains, with Republicans expressing significantly higher levels of national pride than Democrats. In 2025, a record-low 58 percent of US adults reported being "very" or "extremely" proud to be American. National pride has been gradually declining since 2001, when 87 percent of Americans expressed high pride.

2016, the San Francisco 49ers quarterback led a movement to kneel before the national anthem. The issue was institutional racism. The display was obviously disrespectful and even hurtful to some Americans.

Kaepernick didn't care. He was angry. He carried grievance against a country where he made millions throwing a football. He sincerely (in my opinion) believed he was doing something noble by embracing protest, but I believe he was misguided and his actions were not well thought out.

And then there's this: For his protest, Colin K was blackballed by the National Football League.

That was wrong. Canceling people without due process is a terrible abuse of freedom. Kaepernick was absolutely canceled. If I were the NFL commissioner, I would have explained to him that his protest was out of context at an entertainment event and the alienation it caused hurt his team financially. There are other forums available to vent political displeasure. Kaepernick should have been guided to them.

✪ ✪ ✪

During the Vietnam War era, a terrible hate wave swept across our land. The conflict was a disaster for America engineered by a corrupt president, Lyndon Johnson.

I was in college, where the vibe was ridiculous. The United States was the villain, the heinous Communist dictator, Ho Chi Minh, the hero.

Geez.

Many college students bought into that insane scenario, but I never did. I was smarter than Jane Fonda and John Kerry. I understood there was a reason the brutal regimes in China and the Soviet Union were supporting Uncle Ho and his savage totalitarian movement.

But I also knew something else. Friends in my Levittown neighborhood who were drafted and sent to Southeast Asia came back to their country completely changed for the worse. One committed suicide.

Others became heroin addicts. None of them returned to their families carefree; almost all had been damaged emotionally.

I saw that. Something was very wrong. But at age twenty-one, I was unable to understand the situation completely. So, I didn't protest, but there was no "my country right or wrong," either.

In the 1990s, long after the war ended, I reported from Vietnam. Awful country back then. No freedom, little prosperity unless you were a pimp or dope dealer. In Saigon (now called Ho Chi Minh City), people approached me with letters addressed to relatives in the US asking if I would mail them when I returned to the States, which I did. Street hustlers tried to sell me the dog tags of dead American soldiers.

By then, I knew that the US's motivation in Vietnam was to blunt the oppressive Communist movement that emerged internationally after the Second World War. Our power accomplished that in South Korea, but America could not defeat Hanoi by fighting a political war. The US military won just about every engagement, but President Johnson would not defend his own troops with overwhelming power. He was afraid of a so-called wider war with the Soviets and possibly China. That's what happened. Sorry to contradict the Woodstock propaganda condemning America's motives.

My late cousin Dickie Melton was a hero who fought in Vietnam. But he rarely spoke of his personal sacrifice participating in brutal combat. The memories were simply too disturbing. I have his dog tags framed and mounted on the wall.

Looking back with sadness, I deeply respect Vietnam vets, especially those who were forced into dangerous situations beyond their control. They are overwhelmingly brave men and women who did what their country asked. However, I remain angry at the stupid politicians who drove that conflict, failing to do what was necessary to win. Yes, we should never have gone to Vietnam. But that was impossible to calculate in the 1950s when the Communists began mobilizing to rule Southeast Asia.

The truth is that once again America was fighting to keep faraway people free. Is that not noble? Of course it is.

✪ ✪ ✪

It was a bit different in Iraq and Afghanistan. Yes, politicians miscalculated, but here the USA had been attacked by Muslim terrorists. Emotions were incredibly high. Many of us remember the scene in a Florida elementary school when President George W. Bush got the word from his aide Andrew Card that the 9/11 slaughter was underway.

Bush is a good man. Unlike Lyndon Johnson. But his insecurity led him to depend on Vice President Dick Cheney and Defense Secretary Donald Rumsfeld, who did not completely understand the jihadist movement or tribalism in Iraq.

In the winter of 2005, Secretary Rumsfeld invited me to his Washington home for a dinner party. Secretary of State Condoleezza Rice and other Bush administration heavyweights were there. The Defense Secretary was ecstatic that almost two years after Saddam Hussein had been deposed, "free elections" were taking place in Iraq. Secretary Rice, while supportive, was a bit more skeptical about the "free" part.

Sitting at the dinner table, I had no blankin' idea.

As Clint Eastwood's character Dirty Harry said in *Magnum Force*, "A man has got to know his limitations."

In 1991, I had covered the first Gulf War for *Inside Edition*. Your humble correspondent stood on the aptly described "Highway of Death" surrounded by burned-out Iraqi tanks and vehicles. After foolishly invading neighboring Kuwait, Saddam Hussein had been humiliated by an international coalition of forty-two nations, the largest since World War II. The dictator's troops were quickly routed, retreating in panic back to Baghdad.

However, President Bush the Elder did not finish Saddam off. He allowed the Iraqi Army to survive. He could have wiped it out on that highway because it was the only road back to Iraq and there was no cover. But some Muslim nations opposed what would have been a slaughter, and Bush acquiesced. Big mistake.

About fourteen years later, President Bush the Younger was in charge of Iraq. I did not know enough to formulate a strong opinion as that is an insanely complex country. Sunni/Shia, Iran-backed militias, hidden terrorists. One gigantic mess.

Bush and his advisors believed the evil Saddam possessed "weapons of mass destruction." Colin Powell was the point man who warned Americans that this was true and that the vile dictator could hand the WMDs off to jihadists. Iraq had refused to allow United Nations weapons inspectors into the country. Saddam, himself, told his top generals he had hidden biological weapons. *The New York Times* put that story on page one. *Times* reporter Judith Miller, an honest journalist, lost her career because her anonymously sourced story turned out to be false.

Saddam had lied to his own generals.

From my perch on *The O'Reilly Factor*, I supported the US invasion of Iraq after hearing British Prime Minister Tony Blair back up President Bush's assessment. The WMD evidence seemed to be overwhelming. I am a fact-based journalist who believes the US is essentially a noble nation. That's the basis of my patriotism. But in the case of Saddam Hussein, everything went south.

Eventually, the Iraq War descended into daily chaos. The local people were afraid. They would not fight for democracy. They had little idea what it actually was. The violent Saddam regime had imposed so much fear that, to this day, Iraq remains one of the most unstable places on earth.

As Americans began dying over there, I knew I had to see for myself what was going on. So, Baghdad, here I come.

✪ ✪ ✪

In December 2006, the fighting in Iraq was brutal. Various terrorist groups, some armed and funded by neighboring Iran, were targeting American soldiers.

Eventually, about six thousand US personnel were killed in that awful place and thirty-two thousand wounded.

My crew flew into Kuwait, where I visited some American troops, then took a military plane to Baghdad. I sat in the back of the cockpit, watching the pilots do all kinds of evasive maneuvers before landing.

My vision was to drive from the airport to the relatively safe "Green Zone" in Baghdad so I could get a feel for the landscape. Not happening. Too dangerous.

Ambushes and hidden roadside bombs made the short ride perilous. So, we flew into Baghdad on Blackhawk helicopters. I sat behind the left-door machine gunner. Quite an experience.

My visit to Iraq lasted three days. I signed books, talked with the troops, and took it all in. Menace was in the air. The terrorists were organized and obeyed no rules of engagement. Identifying murderous jihadists in the middle of the general population was impossible.

The second night in country, I stayed at one of Saddam's palaces. Before he was deposed on April 9, 2003, the dictator had about one hundred "luxury residences" so he could furtively move around the country.

I commandeered the tyrant's bedroom, a large, tacky space painted sky blue. The bathroom had faux gold fixtures but no shower. Our guides told us Saddam rarely bathed, believing his enemies could poison him through running water.

There was no sleeping for me. Too much bad karma in that room. I spent much of the night on the palace rooftop watching the sky light up with flares and ordnance. This went on for hours.

I think I did some good in the Iraqi theater, meeting with the troops and listening to their stories. We were well protected and somewhat coddled. But I learned a lot. Generally speaking, US forces believed in the mission called Operation Iraqi Freedom. Of course, I consider them patriots. Once again, America attempted to bring a besieged people some relief. Once again, many of those we tried to help didn't care or even worked against the United States.

Not our fault. But lessons should be learned. Thousands of dead and wounded Americans demand that.

✪ ✪ ✪

Almost one year later, I found myself in Afghanistan. This was a totally different situation—one that angers me to this day.

For years, Osama bin Laden organized and trained his al-Qaeda brigades in Afghanistan with the approval of the Taliban government there. After the 9/11 atrocity, President Bush demanded the Taliban destroy or capture these killers led by bin Laden. The Taliban gave America the proverbial finger.

Okay.

In October 2001, US forces attacked Afghanistan. On December 1, the Taliban were overthrown. There were relatively few casualties on the American side.

With some NATO help, we then began rebuilding that forlorn country. Despite twenty years of effort and trillions spent, it didn't work. The primitive Afghan society cared about freedom and justice almost as much as Putin does.

Because my Iraq trip had gone well, I decided to visit the Afghan war zone in November 2007. My flight from Istanbul was calm. After about five hours, the pilot announced our landing approach. I looked out the window. Complete darkness. I asked the pilot if we were over water. No, he said, few Afghans have electricity. So there's no light after dark.

Welcome to the nineteenth century.

We landed at Bagram Air Base, a huge facility that reminded me of Tan Son Nhat airport outside of Saigon. We bunked with the troops as the hotels in Kabul were routinely firebombed.

The next morning, I wanted to drive into town, again to get a feeling for the area. Unlike Iraq, my bodyguards agreed. However, one soldier whispered to me, "They know you're here."

They?

Taliban terrorists.

After a quick visit to the massive American embassy complex, I suggested a ride out of town.

No.

But this time I won. We visited a marketplace, allowing me to ask everyday Afghans about the possibility of freedom.

Few answered. Spies were everywhere, they whispered. Fear ruled.

Once again, the United States military did its job providing some security and protection in the larger cities. But, after two decades, it was clear the Afghan people were not going to modernize. We had to get out. But that was complicated.

President Trump began the process by making a deal with the reconstituted Taliban, who controlled major parts of the countryside. The US would leave Afghanistan, but, in the meantime, violence against our people must stop.

And it did. For eighteen months.

But before Trump could complete a withdrawal, he lost the election of 2020. Joe Biden became president. Eight months later, Mr. Biden shocked the world by completely surrendering to the Taliban, which gleefully took possession of Bagram and billions of dollars' worth of American weapons.

That was a stunning capitulation that directly led to panic and the deaths of 13 Americans as well as 160 Afghans at the Kabul airport. Did you hear President Biden explain that? I didn't. Terrible.

Today, the Taliban are back abusing their own people and protecting terrorists. Thus, Joe Biden joins Lyndon Johnson in the war Hall of Shame.

But the Americans who served in Afghanistan should be honored. It's not their fault politicians screwed up. It's not entirely the country's fault, either. It's totally on poor leadership. Every country on earth experiences that. We are no exception.

✪ ✪ ✪

If you've watched me on television over the years, you know I deeply respect my country. The US has freed billions of oppressed people all over the world. Individual Americans have accomplished that.

My father was a naval officer on his way to the Japanese theater when Truman dropped the atom bomb. If old Harry had not ordered the extreme action, my dad would have been killed in the planned US invasion. Thousands of kamikaze pilots awaited American ships.

My grandfather, John O'Reilly, was a hero in the World War I battle of Meuse-Argonne. His Brooklyn outfit took 75 percent casualties. He escaped injury.

Well, physical harm, anyway. Like my cousin Dickie Melton, my grandfather would never talk about his war experience. But it changed him, according to family members.

My sense of patriotism extends beyond words. I cannot associate with people who denigrate America. Criticism is fine, often needed. Loathing, no. I will call that out. Black Lives Matter, Antifa, Communists, they are the enemy. Enough with those people.

All loyal Americans have a duty to their country. Simply celebrating the Fourth of July is not going to cut it. So, in the next chapter, we'll get into that. A caution, however: You might not like reading what I have to say.

I know. What else is new? But fair warning.

CHAPTER FIVE

Loyalty

Remember these song lyrics?

> *"Where have you gone Joe DiMaggio?*
> *Our nation turns its lonely eyes to you."*

That was Paul Simon and Art Garfunkel back in 1968 singing about the decline of tradition in America, the loss of purpose and innocence.*

Loyalty. Fidelity. Honesty. All were under heavy pressure in the late 1960s when many Americans were angry over the Vietnam War. Today, again, we see traditional attributes under stress as millions of us embrace social media habits that diminish our awareness of what's going on in our country, as well as in the personal relationships we might have. High tech without discipline erodes important values.

Examples. We owe America allegiance if we are living here because

---

* "Mrs. Robinson" is a 1968 folk-rock song by Simon & Garfunkel that became an iconic anthem of the era, reaching number one on the Billboard Hot 100. Written for the film *The Graduate*, it features famous lyrics referencing Joe DiMaggio and Jesus to explore themes of hypocrisy, nostalgia, and lost American innocence.

the US is a place that provides more opportunity than any other nation the world has ever seen.

If, that is, you are willing to pay the personal price it takes to succeed. Many are not willing. The sad truth is that more and more of us don't even think about helping the nation. We don't twiddle thumbs anymore, we use them constantly to stimulate the cell phone.

Big change is needed here. Far too many Americans are ignorant and/or apathetic.

✪ ✪ ✪

Let's get specific. Voting is a patriotic act. So is giving to charity and helping your fellow citizens. Paying fair taxes, obeying the law, showing respect for American traditions—all positives.

Sometimes Americans are asked to do more. Joining the military, volunteering to improve your neighborhood, comforting the afflicted, sacrificing for the public good.

Conversely, you damage your country if you are dishonest, irresponsible, frequently intoxicated, apathetic to a degree where you do not seek knowledge. You are content to be foolish and self-absorbed.

Promoting destructive behavior insults your country. You buy illegal drugs, you are helping the enemies of America. You steal, cheat, lie, hurt others, you are weakening the social fabric of the US.

You've heard it before: It's not all about you. There is nobility in doing good things for others. As uttered in the movie *Fast Times at Ridgemont High*, "Learn it. Know it. Live it."

When an opportunity to help arrives, and it will, seize it.

✪ ✪ ✪

The call came into my assistant about four weeks after Donald Trump won reelection in November 2024. The National Security Chief under President Biden, Jake Sullivan, wanted a favor from me. VERY unusual.

My dealings with the Biden administration were straightforward: I thought the president and his people were disastrous for the country.

I had published a book called *Confronting the Presidents* labeling Joe Biden the second-worst president in history—the pre–Civil War coward James Buchanan being number one.

I backed up my Biden opinion with facts about the open border, massive inflation, chaos overseas, and the president's dithering demeanor. In four years, what did he accomplish? I asked the question over and over. Never received a cogent answer.

It isn't personal, strictly based on his performance. I only met Mr. Biden once. That was back when he was vice president. We were at the White House Correspondents' Dinner in Washington. I politely asked him for an interview, citing President Obama's three chats with me, which were generally well received.

Looking amused, Biden said it straight: "There's no way I'm going to do an interview with you, O'Reilly. You don't need me."

It was a smart play. Biden was going to run for president, and his strategy was just to do interviews with "friendly" journalists. No shortage of them if you're a Democrat.

Little did the vice president know at the time, but his boss had already made a deal to support Secretary of State Hillary Clinton for the Democratic nomination in 2016.

Anyway, back to the phone call.

I never spoke directly to Jake Sullivan. Instead, an "intermediary" asked if I could set up a call with President-elect Trump to talk about the hostages being held by Hamas in Gaza and a possible release. Of course, I said I would try, and then I asked why Sullivan was coming to me.

The reply: Things needed to move quickly and quietly. The Biden people did not want any publicity that might derail negotiations. They felt that if I brought it to Donald Trump directly, that was their best shot. Sullivan did not want to go through administrative channels.

Made sense. But these things are never easy. However, Donald Trump has known me for more than three decades, and if I flag him with the word *important*, I can usually get his attention.

Which I did. My efforts quickly put the two administrations

together on the phone but also resulted in me stepping out of my role as a journalist and into a diplomatic position.

So, why did I do that?

First, it is my duty as a Christian to help people, and obviously innocent kidnapped hostages desperately needed assistance.*

Second, President Trump is a longtime friend of mine, and if the Biden administration had information about an important situation, he needed to know about it.

And third, President Biden was the elected leader of the country. Respect for that demanded my attention no matter what I thought of his acumen.

One week later, the requested call took place. I didn't have to convince Donald Trump, he understood the importance immediately. Once again, Mr. Sullivan did not directly speak on the phone but was in a room relaying information through the "intermediary," whom I am choosing to protect. I moderated the call.

The gist of it was this: Hamas was signaling that it might release a few hostages as a gesture of goodwill. However, both the terrorists and the Israeli government needed the newly elected president, Trump, to get involved and sign off on it.

If that were made public, it might embarrass Joe Biden, and who knew how the Israeli leadership would react. Thus, the caution and extremely unusual routing through me, your humble correspondent.

For thirty-five minutes, Donald Trump asked incisive, well-informed questions that Sullivan answered by proxy. I followed up on some of them but did not offer an opinion (I know, hard to believe).

The conference call ended with the president-elect giving Jake Sullivan some direct contact information.

I did not report any of that to my viewers, radio listeners, or readers. It was too undefined and delicate. Lives were on the line.

* One hostage in question was taken on October 7, 2023, from the Nova Music Festival, which was underway in the northwest Negev Desert when the terrorists struck. The other two were kidnapped from the Kfar Aza Kibbutz, a small farming community near Israel's border with Gaza.

I agreed to get involved to help the suffering victims as well as my country. I didn't need self-aggrandizement. Just like the Paul McCartney situation.

On January 19, 2025, one day before President Trump's inauguration, three hostages were released by Hamas: twenty-eight-year-old Emily Damari, thirty-one-year-old Doron Steinbrecher, and twenty-four-year-old Romi Gonen. All the women believed they were going to die.*

Looking back, a few things stand out. First, President Trump was always personally engaged in rescuing the hostages. Second, my long association with him has been extremely positive, and that's just one example. And third, I remain proud that I may have helped the three young women as well as my country.

✪ ✪ ✪

Another call. About four weeks after the hostage discussion, I was summoned to Mar-a-Lago. Late December 2024. Here's what happened.

My twenty-one-year-old son and I were in California visiting friends and zooming around. While driving in Los Angeles, my cell phone buzzed.

"Donald Trump wants you to go to Palm Beach," my assistant said.

"When?"

"Now."

"Why?"

"They didn't say."

Which was entirely appropriate. When a president asks you to show up, you show up. No clarification needed for patriots.

"Isn't it New Year's Eve?" I asked.

---

* Emily Damari returned to her family at the Kfar Aza Kibbutz near Israel's border with Gaza. She has since undergone months of psychological care as well as physical rehabilitation for gunshot wounds to her left hand and right leg. Doron Steinbrecher spoke publicly on behalf of the remaining hostages held by Hamas. Romi Gonen is still receiving medical treatment for a gunshot wound to her arm.

"Yes, but there's an evening flight to Miami."

"Will there be canapés?"

Greetings, South Florida. There are worse places in January.

On New Year's Day, President-elect Trump and his team were working. I walked into his office to find a wide-ranging discussion underway.

To say the room was surprised to see me is a vast understatement. So, I immediately knew Mr. Trump had requested my presence because he wanted to shake things up a bit. You may have noticed, he's fond of doing that.

In every case where I am in proximity to a president, I do not offer an opinion unless asked by the Chief Executive. That's simply protocol, and I respect it.

Topics on this day included Greenland, Canada, and Panama. I listened.

After about five minutes, President Trump looked at me and said, "Where's your son?"

"In the outer room with the ladies." (Trump's assistants, all of whom are excellent.)

"Bring him in."

So here comes a college senior majoring in political science to join a high-level discussion about United States policy. Economics advisor Peter Navarro immediately and generously offered his seat.

Now, not only was President-elect Trump kind to summon my son, but the fact he even THOUGHT of him is extraordinary.

About two minutes later, Donald Trump looks at me and says, "We may invade Panama. They've been ripping us off for years. What do you think?"

"Not good."

"Why?"

"The hemisphere will hate us."

"I don't care."

"Here's a better way," I said, pausing for effect. "Write down what you want from Mulino [Panamanian President José Raúl Mulino], give it to me, and *I'll* go to Panama City tomorrow and get everything. He'll never stand up to you."

Picture the room. All of the advisors looking at the floor. My son staring at me with a slight shake of the head. Is my father actually doing this?

Donald Trump shook his head as well. In amusement, I believe, because that's what I want to believe.

The discussion then turned to Greenland. I asked if Don Jr. was buying a condo there. Eyes rolled, and the meeting wrapped up. The president was hungry.

A relatively short time later, Panama gave Mr. Trump nearly everything he wanted.*

I may be delusional, but perhaps I might have helped my country in that meeting. If you were Presidente Mulino, would you want me coming down there?

✪ ✪ ✪

Summoned again. St. Patrick's Day, 2025. This time to the Oval Office. Advisors all over the place. I'm sitting next to Elon Musk, who's making headlines with the Department of Government Efficiency. DOGE.

My first time meeting Mr. Musk. He's brilliant. But not in the public relations area. Not my business. I support stopping government waste. That is a patriotic thing. However, loyalty to the country cuts both ways. Citizens and leadership both have a responsibility to make the nation stronger. Wasteful spending is not a way to do that. So right on, Elon Musk.

When I entered the Oval Office, President Trump was in an expansive mood. Things were cooking, his energy a stark contrast to his predecessor. Immediately, I gave him a folder on "Kate's Law," which

---

* After in-person negotiations with Secretary of State Marco Rubio, Panama's government agreed to cease the operations of two Chinese-owned companies that were providing security for the canal. The Panamanians also agreed to free transit for US Navy vessels and other discounts for commercial shipping. In addition, the Mulino government has allowed US Special Forces to operate inside Panama.

would harshly punish criminal aliens who defy deportation and return to the US illegally. Ten years in the federal pen upon conviction.

The Kate's Law concept began in 2015 after thirty-two-year-old Kate Steinle was shot dead while walking with her father on a San Francisco waterfront promenade. The perpetrator was a Mexican criminal migrant named José Inez García-Zárate, who had been deported FIVE times.

Yet American authorities would not incarcerate him for any length of time, leaving García-Zárate to sell dope on the street and carry a deadly weapon.*

Obviously, that failure to protect Kate led to her death. What a travesty.

So, ten years ago, I designed Kate's Law and promoted it heavily on *The O'Reilly Factor*.

Harry Reid, the late senator from Nevada, blocked it, saying it "demonized" migrants. President Trump supported Kate's Law after winning in 2016. So did powerful senators like Ted Cruz and Chuck Grassley.

But the Republican leader in the Senate, Mitch McConnell, refused to put it up for a standalone vote, citing the usual political gibberish.

In my opinion, McConnell and Reid are responsible for thousands of crimes committed over the years by illegal aliens who were allowed to roam free even after defying deportation. Remember, Kate's Law only deals with undocumented criminals. How could any patriotic American not support it?

On March 17, 2025, President Trump again stated he wanted the law passed. But it has yet to be passed, despite being reintroduced several times.

In the middle of that Oval Office conversation, Mr. Trump had to

---

* José Inez García-Zárate was eventually acquitted of murder and manslaughter in 2017. His defense attorney said he accidentally dropped the gun, causing it to fire and kill Kate Steinle. As preposterous as that sounds, the San Francisco jury bought it. On March 1, 2024, García-Zárate was deported to Mexico for the sixth time.

take a call from British Prime Minister Keir Starmer, so I got a chance to speak with Elon Musk.

He asked me how he was doing with the DOGE thing.*

I told him the project was badly needed. American workers don't deserve to have their tax dollars wasted. But I also said the "chainsaw" display hurt his efforts.

You may remember Mr. Musk waving the cutting machine in front of a camera to symbolize his attempts to slash ridiculous federal expenditures.

Elon Musk kind of agreed with my assessment. The chainsaw scene empowered the administration's enemies, especially the anti-DOGE media. As usual, I was pretty direct answering the tycoon's questions. Not sure he often gets that kind of presentation.

The meeting continued for a few more minutes, and then we all departed. For me, all of this remains hard to process. The White House! The Oval Office!

I never use this word, but it was truly *awesome*. But then another unbelievable thing happened.

I was summoned by the Chinese!

---

* The Department of Government Efficiency was a temporary US advisory initiative established by President Donald Trump on January 20, 2025, aimed at reducing federal spending, downsizing bureaucracy, and cutting regulations. Led by Elon Musk and Vivek Ramaswamy, it aimed to restructure federal agencies by targeting a 5 percent reduction in employees and major budget cuts. DOGE faced criticism for lack of transparency and potential conflicts of interest. The agency was disbanded in November 2025.

CHAPTER SIX

Always Faithful

This time the call came from Harvard, deeply enmeshed in a bruising feud with President Trump over the university's staunch leftist policies.

The fuse for the Trump conflict was student demonstrations against Israel and alleged mistreatment of Jewish students and faculty. The issue was stark and urgent, with one survey saying 40 percent of Jews on the Cambridge campus believed they were targets of discrimination.

Having secured a master's degree in public administration from the Harvard Kennedy School, I am a presence there. Well, a phantom presence. The school has rarely invited me to speak or promoted my work as the most successful nonfiction author in the world.

There's no doubt that the people who run the place are well aware of my media profile. I don't think most of them approve, as more than 80 percent of the administration is liberal, according to the *Harvard Crimson* newspaper.

That's not surprising because the culture in Cambridge, Massachusetts, is ardently left. It was that way when I was there in the mid-1990s but not nearly as exclusionary as it is today.

On the other end of the phone call was Graham Allison, the dean emeritus of the Kennedy School. Perhaps the most brilliant American analyst of modern China, Allison is a fair man whom I have stayed in touch with over the years. The dean was passing on an invitation.*

Members of the Chinese power structure wanted me to give a presentation at the Beijing Club. The focus would be on President Trump. The Communists knew I had written a book on him (*The United States of Trump*), and they watched my television analysis on YouTube. They had many questions about the president and wanted an independent correspondent to address them.

The powerful Chinese merchant who put the invitation on the table does a lot of business with Harvard medical research, that kind of thing. He is a Communist but operates very successful enterprises around the world. He wants détente with the US. So, he approached Graham Allison.

The seminar would be off the record, mostly questions and answers, and a free supper would follow.

The gratis supper thing always gets me.

But I hesitated. This was *very* unusual. We researched and could not find anything similar in the past: a private American citizen showing up in a foreign country and speaking with a regime somewhat hostile to the United States.

Before World War II, the extremely misguided aviator Charles Lindbergh hung around with Adolf Hitler's henchmen. As it turned out, Charlie knew little and was used as a propaganda tool by the Nazis, to his shame.

Also, this was no interview thing. It was simply me bloviating about ultraserious issues outside the United States. Dicey scenario.

There was only one person with whom I discussed the situation: Donald Trump himself. I made it clear to the president—respectfully, of course—that if I did the event, I would be representing only myself. No talking points from anyone. No honorarium, no travel expenses, no anything. I'd even hire my own translator.

---

* Graham Allison (born 1940) is a distinguished American political scientist, academic, and national security expert best known for his analysis of crisis decision-making and nuclear policy and his work on US-China relations. He has spent over five decades at Harvard University.

Having known the president for thirty-five years, I anticipated his first question: "Why do they want to talk to you?"

"Because I'm a special guy," I replied.

He ignored the comment and then said something like, "Well, if they throw you in a Gulag, we're not bailing you out!"

"Thank you, Mr. President. I'll bring extra clothes."

✪✪✪

The Air China jet from Osaka, Japan, touched down in Beijing at 4:15 p.m. on Tuesday, May 27, 2025. On board was your humble correspondent and my twenty-one-year-old son, who had just received a political science degree from Salve Regina University in Newport, Rhode Island.

An adventure was about to begin.

I decided to make the trip, hoping to pass on some information to influential Chinese about the Trump administration. Maybe my point of view could bring something positive. Big maybe. I fully realized the environment would be tough. This was no junket.

First off, we did not bring our cell phones. I knew they would be hacked. We used burners. Second, the driver who picked us up at the airport was not a cabbie; he was "security." Third, the young woman at the customs gate had a conniption when I took a picture of a China Passport Control sign.

Hello, police state.*

Our room at the lavish Four Seasons Hotel was most likely bugged. So, I snooped around like Sean Connery in *From Russia with Love*, but didn't find anything.

Outside, the streets of Beijing were crowded, but not with tourists. Everyday Chinese folks bustled around, few making eye contact. Cops and security officers were everywhere.

---

* China operates the world's most extensive and sophisticated digital police state, characterized by ubiquitous, AI-powered surveillance, mass data collection, and a "stability maintenance" apparatus that extends beyond its borders. Under President Xi Jinping, this system has evolved into a twenty-first-century network designed to monitor citizens, suppress dissent, and ensure ideological conformity, utilizing tools that can predict and label individuals as suspicious.

Nobody misbehaved.

That's because all antisocial displays are considered "crimes against the people." Littering can get you hauled in. Take drugs, long vacation, far away. No earrings on men, no piercings. I saw no tattoos. They are associated with "bad elements."

The Chinese "justice system" is fascinating and simple: You're guilty. In fact, 99 percent of those criminally charged are convicted. That may be because the alleged miscreants can't have a lawyer or even see the state's evidence. Pleading not guilty is madness as it angers those who would judge you.

Lots of capital punishment in China. In fact, according to Amnesty International, there are approximately forty "execution vans" that roam the country. You can get the death penalty for "corruption," drug dealing, fraud, and the two big ones: crimes against the Communist Party and crimes against the state.

Don't ask. I have no idea what the difference is. All I know is if Robert De Niro were operating in China, his life experience would have ended a long time ago.

Anyway, if you get sentenced to death in a rural area, the "execution van" rolls up, guys jump out, tie you to a gurney, and give you a lethal injection.*

Mao would love this.

Right now, there are approximately 2 million prisoners being held in China. The overall population is 1.5 billion. Relatively few Chinese *ever* get out of line. And there are so many rules you can't absorb them all.

Upon entering the "Forbidden City," you must go through a metal detector. I was carrying two pens. Instantly confiscated. I asked my translator why.

---

* China's execution vans are specialized, police-designed vehicles introduced around 2003 to carry out death sentences via lethal injection. These mobile chambers, often described as looking like ambulances, allow for executions to occur in local areas without transporting prisoners to central facilities, enhancing efficiency and reducing costs compared to traditional shooting methods.

"Pens are forbidden in Forbidden City."

Oh.

✪ ✪ ✪

My son was a bit worried that his father might easily commit a variety of capital crimes in the first ten minutes of the Beijing Club presentation. He knows his dad.

I told him no sweat.

But there was a bit of perspiration as we were outnumbered 1.5 billion to 2.

Heavy odds.

We rolled up to the Beijing Club venue in a black Mercedes sent to deliver us. "Oddjob" was driving. That's a James Bond *Goldfinger* reference for you Generation Zers.

My son and I were politely ushered inside and seated at a long table surrounded by ten men and one woman, who was probably the most powerful person in the room.

About half the crew spoke English, the other half used headphones for instant translation. All the Chinese were exceptionally polite. They wore simple clothing, no jewelry or other material displays.

After my introduction, the questions began. But not before I made a brief opening statement.

Expressing my gratitude for the invitation and kind reception, I told the group that the "No Spin Zone" had arrived in Beijing. They all got the reference, nodding politely. I then said that although I would not quote anyone specifically when I returned home, a debriefing with the president would happen out of respect.

More nodding.

Finally, I briefly mentioned that my pens were now the personal property of the Chinese government and asked if I could borrow one.

A few confused nods. Then the questioning began.

✪ ✪ ✪

Before I get into the Q and A, it's important to understand the mindset of the Chinese leadership. They are true believers. China has been a country for about four thousand years and has never known a day of freedom. Not a moment. Authoritarian governance always.

For three thousand years, various dynasties ruled. Then the always amusing Mongolians took over. Then more dynasties and cruel emperors. Finally, a brutal civil war between the Kuomintang military government and various dissenters, including a fanatical Communist movement.

In 1949, the Communists led by Mao Zedong prevailed, defeating Chiang Kai-shek, who, fleeing for his life, retreated to the island of Taiwan, 110 miles from the mainland.

As chronicled in my book *Confronting Evil*, Mao was perhaps the worst mass murderer in human history. Estimates say the dictator was responsible for about twenty million of his own countrymen dying. Many perished from starvation as the dictator redesigned the economy, forcing farmers into communes where mismanagement and incompetence depleted food supplies.

Millions of Chinese ate vermin to survive, then died from disease and malnutrition. The world had no idea because reporting was banned by the Communists.

Today, Mao Zedong remains a hero in China, his picture publicly displayed everywhere. Mao's "Little Red Book" is compulsory reading. The Chinese people have been taught to revere him. In my opinion, that will never change. The state and party dominate all aspects of life. Everything else is suspect.*

✪ ✪ ✪

* Mao's "Little Red Book" remains one of the most popular published works in human history after the Bible and the Quran. Compiled in 1964, it was designed as a pocket-sized, easy-to-carry "ideological weapon" to strengthen Mao's cult of personality and standardize ideology within the People's Liberation Army (PLA) and later the general public. More than 6.5 billion copies have been printed to date.

Against that backdrop, a confirmed capitalist, Roman Catholic, and staunch promoter of individual freedom was about to engage the opposition at the Beijing Club. It was late afternoon on Wednesday, May 28. My son sat three seats away from me looking a bit tense. Although the questioners were exceedingly polite, it was obvious they were tough boys. And a tough girl!

As mentioned, these privileged Chinese often saw me opine on YouTube, which is only available to the elite in China. The regular folks don't have access to much outside information.

The questioning began with the topic of Taiwan, by far the most important issue in the room. What does Donald Trump think of Chinese sovereignty over the prosperous island? Does he understand that China must eventually rule there?

My answer was vague: "Yes, the president understands the emotional and nationalist issues involved."

Some nodding. "So, what would he do if a military conflict arises?"

Carefully and slowly I replied, "There would be American, Australian, Japanese, and South Korean warships in the Straits [of Taiwan]. A huge conflict would begin."

"Why?" a bureaucrat asked.

"Because President Trump is not going to allow weakness." I kept my answer terse.

But then I surprised the group by saying this: "I think diplomacy can work this problem out; 2049 is the one-hundredth anniversary of the Communist takeover in China. It is certainly possible to craft a deal where Taiwan retains some autonomy, while the Chinese flag flies over it. If China and America enter into a 'Partnership for Peace and Prosperity,' that will likely happen.

"But, if force is used, President Trump will respond in kind."

Silence.

There was an acceptance of my answer. No pushback. Another question rolled in.

"We want your president to come here," said an elderly Mandarin. "Will he?"

"You would have to give him an incentive to do that."

Frowns.

Then the director of "security," a small but ultrapowerful guy with life-and-death authority, looked up and said, "What might that be?"

"You've got to get out of the fentanyl business," I said slowly.

The security czar replied in perfect English, "We don't make fentanyl. We only make the precursors."

Whereupon, I straightened up in my chair, looking down at the Standing Committee member, and said, "Do you really *need* to be in that business?"

I caught sight of my son looking pale. More silence. It needed to be said, so I said it. With me you get what you don't pay for. Don't ask if you don't want to know. I can't say that in Mandarin, but, believe me, the room got the message.

Then I pushed it: "You might consider getting out of the Putin business as well. You don't need him."

I looked around the room, and there was no reaction at all. Everyone there knew the Russian leader was despicable, and certainly nobody was going to defend China's relationship with him in the presence of an American.

A lifeline. Our host for the evening, a powerful Shanghai businessman educated in California, quickly asked about President Trump's dealings with the media. Relief. We all had a few laughs over that. At least I did. The Chinese are grinners, not laughers.

The rest of the three-hour event flew by, and the private dinner for five, including a surprise guest, the former Chinese ambassador to the US, went smoothly. And get this: As we were walking out the door, a small man stopped us and handed me two very nice pens!

As we were riding back to the hotel, I asked my son how he thought the event went. We hadn't conversed much throughout the evening. But now he said the most important thing I could possibly hear.

"Proud of you, Dad."

✪ ✪ ✪

A little more than four months later, President Trump met with Chinese leader Xi Jinping in South Korea. The headline from that meeting was that the Chinese government would cooperate with the US to stop the fentanyl trade.*

✪ ✪ ✪

I did my best for a noble cause. My country. All Americans have an obligation to help the nation if they can. That's no longer a national theme even though President Kennedy immortalized it with the words "Ask not what your country can do for you, but what you can do for your country."

We must get back to that wise command.

One final footnote. A short time after returning to New York, I received a text from Dean Allison. It was from the Beijing Club organizer saying my appearance was "a triumph."

Much better review than I usually get back in the good ol' USA.

* In 2025, China agreed to cooperate with the United States to counter the flow of fentanyl and its precursor chemicals, a major development in bilateral relations aimed at mitigating the US opioid crisis. As of late 2025 and early 2026, this agreement has evolved into targeted actions by Beijing to restrict the export of specific chemicals used by drug cartels, particularly in Mexico, to produce fentanyl. China has moved to schedule (control) specific fentanyl precursor chemicals that are banned internationally, aligning with the 1988 UN Convention.

CHAPTER SEVEN

A National Dereliction

Enough with these drugs. No more excuses for pursuing inebriation ("getting high," for you nitwits). It's not cool or positive in any way. Substance abusers hurt their families, their friends, their country, and, of course, themselves. You buy drugs, you reward evil drug merchants. You abuse and debase yourself.

So, we need to confront American substance abusers with this slogan: "Get clean or get lost."

Misguided people whine about drug and alcohol addiction being a disease. Maybe. There is a predisposition to addiction in some folks, but no germs infect your body. You have to actively *seek* intoxication (the disease) over and over and over.

Here's the most important point about America's failure to mitigate its substance abuse problem. A sane society does not let someone with Ebola walk around a grocery store. Health officials would physically stop that. This country should provide "treatment" for addiction. The problem is that many, perhaps most, substance abusers *reject* treatment. They want to get high. All the time. And they generally don't care who their lifestyle might hurt.

In addition, there are legions of people who enable and even encourage addiction. Example: In 1968, Sly and the Family Stone had a hit record called "I Wanna Take You Higher."

Fabulous. And the kicker is that Sly Stone (no pun intended) followed his musical guidance. His life became a hellish nightmare that destroyed him and his group. The singer's severe addiction to crack cocaine rendered him pretty much useless.

Higher, Sly? You squandered everything.*

✪✪✪

It is my belief that many powerful people in this country could not care less about drug and alcohol addiction. It's not *their* problem. The drug world in particular is gross and intransigent. As the racist mobster said in *The Godfather*, "They're animals anyway. Let them lose their souls." That's a terrible sentiment but not uncommon.

However, it's not simply irresponsible solo behavior we're examining. What about all the innocent people these addicts hurt?

Right now, the National Institutes of Health estimate that about fifty million Americans intoxicate themselves at least once a week. In 2023, 12,500 people were killed on the roads by impaired drivers.

At least twenty million American children live with a parent who has a "substance abuse disorder." Imagine that horror. Defenseless kids constantly witnessing degenerative behavior by their own parents. And what does society do? Drag the kids away, funneling them into foster homes?

My God. I'm sorry, but any parent who puts getting high before the welfare of his or her own children deserves severe punishment. I mean severe. No civilized nation should allow that.

And then there's death.

In 2004, there were thirty thousand fatal drug overdoses in the US. Ten years later, close to one hundred thousand—a 166 percent increase.

Two reasons for this. First, the rise of deadly fentanyl as well as the

---

* Sly Stone, the legendary frontman of Sly and the Family Stone, struggled with severe, long-term addiction to cocaine and PCP, which escalated rapidly after 1969. His addiction caused erratic behavior, and he missed numerous concerts and had severely damaged his musical career by the late 1970s. He frequently carried drugs in a violin case and, despite rehab, battled dependency for decades. Sly Stone died on June 9, 2025, at the age of 82.

failure of the courts to punish both narcotics dealers and users. Many urban areas like New York City and Chicago allow drug addicts to openly inject themselves in public view. Kids watching, who cares? In fact, under the demented policy of "harm reduction," these cities will actually *give* abusers drug paraphernalia. Make it easy for them to destroy themselves. Meanwhile, medications like methadone are dispensed for free. That prescribed substance blocks the effects of opioids. However, most addicts reject methadone because getting high is their goal. If they would ingest the drug, the opioid problem would drastically decline.

But they don't want it. Get the picture? That's the truth. And it is imperative that America handle the truth.

According to FBI data, 80 percent of incarcerated Americans have a history of substance abuse, 60 percent of all those arrested have illegal drugs in their bloodstream when taken into custody. Almost one million miscreants a year are caught possessing illegal drugs.

That means that many addicts commit burglary, robbery, assault, and muggings at an alarming rate. They also push narcotics on the street, creating more stoned zombies. So, how about some "harm reduction" for crime victims?

Is that too much to ask?

Apparently, it is. And there's much more.

According to the data, 65 percent of homeless people are drug addicts. In addition, 40 percent of the unemployed are substance abusers. This out-of-control problem affects everyone as billions of taxpayer dollars are spent every year to confront drug damage in some form. The situation has plagued our land for decades. Americans buy and consume more illegal narcotics than any other country on earth.

But there is a solution.

✪ ✪ ✪

Before we get to protecting innocent people against the drug scourge, let me say with certainty: There is no *will* in Washington or in your state capital to stop the substance abuse madness. Sorry, Nancy Reagan, but "just say no" is not going to cut it. In addition, you progressives running around screaming "treatment" are poltroons. Voluntary rehabilitation does not work. About 60 percent of the participants relapse. In addition, many addicts won't even consider getting clean no matter how deleterious their circumstance.

But there is a treatment scenario that could crush America's drug problem, and it's fairly simple. However, it would require a realistic assessment of the narcotics problem, something that seemingly terrifies our leadership.

The solution is on display right now in South Asia.

✪ ✪ ✪

When you land at Singapore's Changi Airport, you enter a fantastic facility. There are butterfly gardens, a rooftop swimming pool and spa, a movie theater. Free beds are available in quiet rooms called "snooze zones."

You don't want to leave.

But when you do, a far different society from America is on display. Singapore is a nation of six million people where capitalism rules. However, individual freedom is constrained by an authoritarian government. As Buffalo Springfield once sang, "Step out of line, the man comes and take you away."*

There is no drug problem in Singapore. The Central Narcotics Bureau makes sure of that. Its mandate is clearly stated: "Singapore's focus is on building a drug-free society, not a drug tolerant one. As a small nation, we can ill afford the societal devastation that can be caused by widespread drug addiction, as witnessed in other countries."

Top of the list: the good ol' USA.

Singapore executes drug dealers. On November 27, 2025, two heroin merchants, Mohammed Rizwan and Samiwathin Selnaraju, left this world with ropes around their necks. Singaporean authorities will

---

* The lyric comes from the 1966 Buffalo Springfield protest song "For What It's Worth." The single, written by Stephen Stills and Neil Young, was inspired by anti–Vietnam War protests in Los Angeles.

not release exact data on the country's use of capital punishment. But let's just say it is not rare.

However, it is how drug *users* are treated that is the key to controlling addiction and making society safer.

Police in Singapore do not need probable cause to drug test anyone. And if you come up positive, say hi to mandatory incarceration. Pot users are included in this equation.

Drug-involved individuals are placed in the custody of the Drug Supervision Program. Many are quickly sent to rehabilitation facilities, where they are confined up to twenty-two months, depending on their addiction profile.

The centers do provide therapeutic treatments, but these are not comfortable places. And if you relapse, hard prison time awaits.

The combination of harsh punishment for dealers and temporary banishment for users takes the risk/reward drug situation off the chart. Pushers have far fewer customers willing to chance confinement.

Two further things. Caning, a physical beating with a blunt stick, is employed as punishment in some drug situations. Second, if a person is even caught hanging out with a drug user, but does not actually test positive for narcotics, he or she is punished as well.

I walked the streets of Singapore after midnight in a few poor neighborhoods. Not a problem. No menace, no urban blight.

The hangman's specter has something to do with that.

✪✪✪

Obviously, the United States cannot duplicate Singapore's drug policy because we have a Constitution that guarantees due process, limits cruel and unusual punishment, and curbs police power. However, there are measures our society *can* adopt.

If a person is convicted of a crime, any crime, and is found with drugs in his or her bloodstream, the sentencing judge should have the option of sending the criminal to confinement at a therapeutic drug rehabilitation facility. Take the drug-involved person off the streets. Rehab required—not optional. States could easily pass laws mandating that. In fact, I believe voters would support it enthusiastically in many places that are not named San Francisco.

Of course, the ACLU would challenge, but so what? Fight them on the legal front. It is clear *that* group promotes dangerous behavior. That's not a difficult argument to make.

Forced rehab guts the narcotics marketplace. Combine that with tough prison sentences for dealers, and the nation's drug horror would considerably diminish. Millions of Americans would be spared pain and death. Millions.

So why is this not being done?

✪ ✪ ✪

The answer to that question is depressing and rarely discussed with honesty. Here's the truth across the political spectrum.

Many on the Right simply don't care about the drug issue. They sometimes feel drug-involved people deserve their fate. And it's true that those who succumb to the selfish world of intoxication are responsible for their awful behavior. But, again, so many innocents are hurt, you would think conservatives would get actively involved to tamp down collateral damage.

President Trump is using military power to destroy drug smuggling operations in foreign countries. I support that. But the campaign will not wipe out the narcotics market in America. Far too much money is made by the drug traffickers.

On the other side, the leftists refuse to acknowledge reality. Optional rehab and "harm reduction" are their mantras. False world, as I have explained. Only consequences can mitigate substance abuse. No other way.

Therefore, the drug scourge continues to get worse in America because both political parties operate without urgency or even conviction. The narcotics situation is entirely man-made, so the solutions to it must fall in the same category. But there is little will to diminish the scourge.

Apathy and false premises concerning substance abuse allow for death and destruction. The United States needs to wise up on this and take bold action. Drug addicts can be saved, at least many of them, by intense therapy, job skill instruction, as well as the fear of punishment. We should combine those things into a plan of action.

That is, *if* this country really cares about protecting the innocent.

Which, at this point in history, it does not.

CHAPTER EIGHT

Fake News

Benjamin Franklin originated phony news reporting in America. The mischievous genius figured out how the press could be manipulated to distort and distract. Bet you didn't know that.

As a young man in Boston, Franklin worked an apprenticeship at the *New England Courant* newspaper. At night, when all employees were gone, he would slip essays under the editor's door using the pseudonym Silence Dogood. Some were published, causing a sensation, as "Silence" specialized in salacious gossip as well as mocking politicians. This was in 1722, when the Puritan lifestyle suppressed anything that might be considered entertaining.

Sixty years later, in 1782, Old Ben created a fictional newspaper called the *Supplement to the Boston Independent Chronicle*. Franklin was ensconced in Paris at the time, but it didn't matter; the made-up articles were used to malign King George and the colonists who supported him.*

So, Benjamin Franklin is the architect of the "fake news" controversy that America is dealing with today.

---

* In 1782, Benjamin Franklin resided in the French capital, serving as the chief American diplomat. He was deeply involved in negotiating the Treaty of Paris to formally end the Revolutionary War with Great Britain. That treaty was signed in 1783.

Most of the other Founding Fathers didn't have much use for a free and honest press, but understood it was necessary to challenge, and even control, authority. However, there was an exception. As president, John Adams signed the Sedition Act, which criminalized "false, scandalous, and malicious" writings against the government. Dozens of scribes went to jail.

After Thomas Jefferson defeated Adams in 1800, the Sedition Act was repealed even though Jefferson himself was not a fan of newspapers. A number of them attacked Old Tom for his treatment of slaves on his Virginia estate.*

Nevertheless, President Jefferson understood the big picture, saying, "Our Liberty depends on the freedom of the press, and that cannot be limited without being lost."

✪ ✪ ✪

The colonists themselves mostly didn't care what was printed because many of them could not read. Also, there was absolutely no free press tradition in England and Europe, whence they came. Write something bad about the king, there's a cell waiting for you in the Tower of London.

In the 1800s, pamphlets called "penny dreadfuls" appeared in England focusing on lurid and scandalous tales. The folks loved them just as many Americans revere tabloid stuff today. But serious reporting in the new republic was directed solely toward the wealthy and powerful.

✪ ✪ ✪

Donald Trump has forever altered the free press in the United States. At first, the establishment media mocked his entry into politics, but,

---

* Thomas Jefferson enslaved more than six hundred human beings over the course of his lifetime, most on his Monticello plantation. Despite writing that slavery was an "evil," Jefferson freed only seven people—two during his life and five in his will, most of whom were members of the Hemings family. Following his death in 1826, his remaining enslaved property was sold to pay off his extensive debts. We chronicle Jefferson's history in *Killing England* and *Confronting Evil*.

in 2016, things drastically changed. Trump's insurgent populist presidential campaign became a direct challenge to the liberal press barons. They were appalled that a real estate mogul could achieve political power. They considered Donald Trump a vulgarian.

I was right in the middle of that. In fact, some believe I changed American journalism for the worse. Simply by giving Trump a fair shake. As you can imagine, there was much angst about that in the corporate boardrooms.

Here's the setup. The Fox News Channel (FNC) began in 1996 as a cable enterprise giving some voice to conservative Americans who were long denied access by the three liberal networks, CNN, and powerful urban newspapers, specifically *The New York Times*, *The Washington Post*, *The Boston Globe*, and the *Los Angeles Times*.

Under the leadership of Roger Ailes, FNC quickly gathered a large audience and eventually broke the leftist media stranglehold that had been in place for decades.

Donald Trump recognized the power of Fox News early, even as the establishment media turned on him with a vengeance. A column in *The New York Times* spelled it out: Trump was such a danger that the standard rules of journalism no longer applied. The only responsible way to cover Trump was to batter him.

That analysis was written by Jim Rutenberg in August 2016. It quickly became the standard rationalization allowing press people to brutalize the Trump campaign and the candidate himself while ignoring all objective standards.

However, the liberal media's disenchantment with opposing points of view had been on display for years. A few months before Rutenberg's "Get Trump" column, I welcomed ABC News icon Ted Koppel on *The O'Reilly Factor*.

Having worked as a correspondent for ABC during the Peter Jennings years, I respected Koppel's intelligence and journalistic skill. But his program *Nightline* was run by a brutal producer named Rick Kaplan, and Koppel allowed awful things to happen, in my opinion. Kaplan often treated people with stunning contempt.

However, the Trump phenomenon was just beginning, so I wanted Ted's take.

And I certainly got it.

O'REILLY: Let's assess Donald Trump. I've interviewed him a number of times, not an easy interview. How would you do it?

KOPPEL: You know something, Bill, you and I have talked about this general subject over the years, it's irrelevant how I would do it. And you know who made it irrelevant? You did. You have changed the television landscape over the last twenty years. You took it from being objective and dull to being subjective and entertaining. And in this current climate, it doesn't matter what the interviewer asks him. Mr. Trump is going to say whatever he wants to say, as outrageous as it may be.

O'REILLY: Okay, but ABC does interview Mr. Trump on a regular basis. And our job, whether as a commentator or reporter, is to get as much information, number one, and number two, show the viewer who he really is. So, again, I'll go back to he's sitting on *Nightline* opposite you—how do you [interview] him?

KOPPEL: Well, the first way you do it is not in the interview, you do it with some reporting. It's an old-fashioned concept, but I think demonstrating who and what Mr. Trump is and what his policies really amount to is something you don't do in an interview. He doesn't answer questions.

Which is true to some extent. But certainly not unique to Donald Trump. Every modern president with the exception of Harry Truman practiced the art of spin and evasion. It's easy for politicians to filibuster, evade hard questions. I shut that down, but most television interviewers do not.

But there is a major problem with Koppel relying on old-fashioned "reporting" to get the truth. The *real* truth is the corporate news industry leans left and has for decades. It routinely skews news presentations against the Right, ignoring facts in the process.

Historically, there have been a few traditional news anchors, like Eric Sevareid, John Chancellor, David Brinkley. But beginning with Dan Rather replacing Walter Cronkite at CBS News in 1981, the network culture turned dramatically left. The Vietnam War had a lot to do with that, as it shaped many TV journalists who were caught up in the anti-establishment culture of the late 1960s.

In the Trump era of today, the corporate television news networks actively despise the populist, with three exceptions: NewsNation, Fox, and Newsmax. Therefore, reporters are expected to highlight Donald Trump's negatives and avoid his positives. Don't follow that path, your job is in peril.

You will also become a social outcast, especially in Washington, DC.

That analysis is undeniable, and Mr. Koppel, as smart as he is, has to know it.

So how can "reporting" done by partisans be taken as "truth"?

In addition, I certainly understand the accusation that I "changed" television news for the worse. Before *The O'Reilly Factor* emerged as a dominant force in America, daily political commentary was almost exclusively seen on the op-ed pages of newspapers. The television news networks often took their coverage cues from *The New York Times* and *The Washington Post*.

I offered a different view that respected traditional and some conservative values. Why should the liberal point of view dominate in American journalism? That was unfair and injurious to the nation, in my opinion. News analysis should have a variety of voices.

Well, the establishment didn't like my emergence at all and came after me with a vengeance that was actually shocking. People were paid to smear me. At times, I had to have private security living on my property.

Ted Koppel did not participate in that, but my feeling is he sees me as a barbarian who not only got to the gate but kicked it in—ransacking the once-dominant liberal view.

So be it. I paid a price but did the right thing.

✪ ✪ ✪

Presidents have long complained about how they are treated in the media, going back to the Founding Fathers and continuing today. But since the election of Ronald Reagan, the media has moved to the Left. In 1983, President Reagan wrote a letter to his friend Douglas Morrow in Los Angeles. I have the message in which the president complains bitterly about unfair media coverage. In the letter, Reagan addresses a bill to tax those who received unemployment insurance payments, which was in fact introduced by Democrats in Congress, but which the media blamed on Reagan.

✪ ✪ ✪

To be fair, presidents from both parties consistently lodge complaints against the media. President Obama felt Fox News was deeply unfair to him. Nevertheless, Mr. Obama granted me three interviews, to his credit. Joe Biden deep-sixed me entirely.

But, as stated, the press has moved to the Left since Ronald Reagan's election in 1980. Anyone who denies that has no relationship with honesty.

✪ ✪ ✪

By far, the best presidential critique I've seen about the press comes from President Harry Truman, a Democrat who loathed the media. Writing to an acquaintance named Rufus Burrus on April 16, 1951, "Give 'em hell Harry" opined:

> *In going over the history of various Presidents I find that [press dishonesty] is nothing new. Washington was abused in the press of his time and there never was a more thoroughly misrepresented President than Thomas Jefferson. Of course, you are familiar with how they treated Andrew Jackson but they did not get away with it in his case like they did with some of the others. The two Presidents after Jackson's time who have been most thoroughly misrepresented are Grover Cleveland and Woodrow Wilson. They almost hounded Cleveland to his grave. It is interesting to read the lies they published about him and Mrs. Cleveland.*

Of course Lincoln was thoroughly misrepresented and it took fifty years to get at the truth.

To provide perspective, President Truman saw the media of his time as enemies. In fact, he publicly threatened to punch out a Washington newspaper critic who gave his daughter Margaret, a singer, a poor review. The pro-FDR press at the time considered the Missouri haberdasher a bumpkin. And they let him know it.

It is conceivable that Harry Truman and Donald Trump would have gotten along based on their mutual contempt for the press.

✪ ✪ ✪

So how can the American media be changed? Unlike most problems, this one is unsolvable because there is big money to be made in hating or loving individual presidents. And TV news, especially, is ALL about profit.

In addition, this cash flow is protected by the First Amendment, and that will not change. So, media corruption will continue unabated.

✪ ✪ ✪

I wish it were not so. I've spent fifty years in journalism and understand that an honest media is a cornerstone of freedom. But the romance is gone and will never return. Money and fanatical ideology have killed the once-golden news-reporting goose.*

✪ ✪ ✪

One final story. In August 2025, I sat in the Guild Hall of East Hampton listening to Bob Woodward and Carl Bernstein reminiscing about their triumphant reporting during the Watergate ordeal.

---

* A Pew poll published in October 2025 says that nearly half the country does not trust the media and that television news ratings have cratered. When I left Fox News after the first quarter of 2017, *The O'Reilly Factor* was averaging 4,187,000 viewers at 8:00 p.m. No national television news agency even approaches the size of that audience today.

I decided on a career in journalism because of these two guys: tough reporters who pursued the truth. But on that night, the boys were not very interested in rehashing the past. Nope. What lit them up was bashing President Trump in front of a largely liberal audience.

Mr. Woodward has made millions hammering Trump. He has written three negative books on the man. It was an easy sell to the publishing industry and to the "hate Trump" public.

Mr. Bernstein spent years as a paid CNN "contributor" vilifying Trump. Again, nice money doing that. No sweat denigrating just about everything Trump did. No challenge from CNN on-air personnel. The toughest comeback Bernstein faced was "tell me more."

On this summer evening, both agreed that President Trump was destroying the Constitution and turning the US into a police state. The audience egged them on. I looked around for the Gestapo. Didn't see them.

It was a tedious but predictable spectacle. However, I was sad rather than annoyed. Woodward and Bernstein were once the gold standard in journalism. Now, they peddle Trump hatred rather than seeking perspective. There is no cash in perspective.

A shame. As is the collapse of American journalism.

CHAPTER NINE

Working for a Living

You can't get what you want,
'Til you know what you want.
—Joe Jackson

It is conceivable that I would not hire me. That's correct, there's a definite downside to employing a maverick who has no interest in currying favor. Many bosses absolutely want obsequious people around them. That's how incompetents survive.

Quick story I have already told, but it's worth a repeat. Martin Van Buren became president of the United States because he kissed Andrew Jackson's tush. As Old Hickory's vice president, Van Buren agreed with *everything* his boss said even before the words were fully formed. "The Little Magician," as Martin was called, turned toadyism into an art form and is responsible for the most used word in the world: *okay.*

How? Well, Van Buren's other nickname was "Old Kinderhook," after his New York hometown. Soon, it was shortened to OK, which became slang for "fine with me."

Today, in every part of the planet, *okay* is understood.

In 1836, Van Buren won the presidency off the incredibly popular Jackson's endorsement. He was a one-term disaster because vexing problems are not often solved by sycophants.

Anyway, office politics haven't changed very much in two hundred years; kissing up remains very prevalent.

But not with me.

The counter to my defiant workplace attitude is that I have always labored extremely hard. If you pay me, I never phone it in. I've made money for every company or person who's ever hired me.

The O'Reillys are workers. In County Cavan, Ireland, my ancestors had a two-acre farm that supported a growing family until the dastardly British overlords stole the land. These thieves raised taxes so high, most small farmers couldn't pay. Confiscation followed. In 1868, my people packed it in for Brooklyn, where they worked anywhere that would hire them. Twin sixteen-year-old boys made the voyage from Galway on a "coffin ship." They were given free passage in return for tossing dead bodies overboard into the Atlantic Ocean.

Obviously, life was a struggle back then. There were few safety nets other than personal generosity. You worked for food and shelter. Very basic. My ancestors always labored. On my mother's side, three sisters took jobs in a hat factory for paltry wages. My grandfather was a porter on trains to Canada. My other grandfather was a cop. Money was always tight.

In fact, I am the first member of my family to become affluent. After 150 years of working-class status in America, I left that status behind. But it was a very difficult climb.

✪✪✪

Here's what has to change today. The work ethic in America is on the decline. That's what the socialism thing is all about. Statistics say half of US homes receive some kind of means-tested welfare. Millions of these folks feel they are entitled to government-funded programs. Free stuff. Food, shelter, childcare, healthcare, transportation. Give me, give me, give me.*

---

* As of March 2026, approximately 104 million Americans aged sixteen or older were not in the labor force. These individuals are classified as "not in the labor force" because they are neither employed nor actively looking for work, a category that in-

There's something wrong with that attitude. It erodes ambition, crushes spirits, creates massive dependency.

It's not everyone. Some individuals, through no fault of their own, need help. It would be cruel to turn away from them.

However, grifters abound. Venal politicians goad and patronize the less fortunate. Votes are cast. Bernie Sanders is the worst. The Communist Senator from Vermont runs around vilifying successful Americans, positing that the system should take things away from them for "redistribution."

Sanders knows communism and socialism have never worked. Human nature runs contrary to punishing achievement. The only way to impose forced redistribution is by the gun. Totalitarianism. The Chinese model.

Old Bernie doesn't care. He sets up class warfare. He panders to the jealous. He sells victimization. The American way is responsible if you fail—not *you*. The intellectually dishonest Elizabeth Warren does the same thing. Here's her take. Fail, it's a racist society's fault. The US is a corrupt country catering to wealthy, White men. They are evil. Socialism is good. Don't depend on yourself, depend on a government that has debt approaching $40 trillion.

I once asked the very liberal actor Warren Beatty if he supported income redistribution. Of course, he said he did. We were having dinner in Santa Monica, California. His wife Annette Bening was in attendance, as was Al Pacino. Annette loathes me. I believe I amuse Pacino.

Anyway, as we ate expensive appetizers, the conversation centered on how seizing assets from the affluent through onerous taxation or other means can be justified. I questioned Beatty: Why should my (and his) hard-earned tax money be given to layabouts and substance abusers? How can you justify that?

I thought Annette was going to throw some calamari at me. Warren didn't really have an answer other than helping people is good.

---

cludes retirees, students, stay-at-home parents, and discouraged workers. Each year, the federal government pays out $4 trillion in welfare and other subsidies.

And it IS good. As long as some phony power seekers don't impose it and the money is responsibly spent.

Here's what should be taught in every school: Hard work and honesty are the keys to economic success. You are not "entitled" to other people's stuff. You are compelled to develop skills so you can compete in a capitalist society.

Dependency is bad. Self-sufficiency is good. The United States offers more opportunity and options than anywhere else, which is why millions of foreign nationals are trying to get in here.

If schools would pound home those themes to the urchins, America would be a stronger country and an overall better place.

Or am I wrong?

✪ ✪ ✪

My father never gave me a dime. A child of the Great Depression, he believed another economic disaster was inevitable. So, he harbored his money. Big time. We lived extremely modestly in Levittown, Long Island, and so did everyone else in that gigantic community. But when the Good Humor man showed up in the summer, I needed cash for a toasted almond bar.

My mother usually came through.

But I didn't like asking her for the twenty-five cents. Or matinee movie money to see *House on Haunted Hill* at the Westbury Theater (still there). So, at age ten, my work life began.

My friends and I shoveled snow in the winter (no global warming then). Cut lawns in the summer. When I turned twelve, babysitting became an option. If there was work to do in the neighborhood, we were up for it.

At seventeen, I got a job at a Carvel ice cream stand. I made $1.30 an hour. Free malts and hot fudge sundaes. But I had to pay some small tax. Money was not piling up.

At eighteen I passed the lifeguard and water safety instructor test. Better money teaching little kids to swim and sauntering around the pool like a big shot. But gassing up my old Nash Rambler and buying lunch was a drain. I needed to move up salary-wise.

So, I started a house painting business.

Here's the scenario. There were hundreds of houses in Levittown that needed fresh paint every few years. Most husbands in said houses worked their butts off during the week, and the absolute last thing they wanted to do during their time off was stand on a ladder sloshing paint around.

These guys couldn't afford the pros, but I, already a junior capitalist, undercut the professional painting estimates by a significant amount.

The work poured in.

Unfortunately, I had to hire four friends to do the labor. One was an excellent painter. I was so-so. The other three were certified menaces.

However, we mostly did a decent job, and word got around. Big money for the soon-to-be college student. My father loved the whole thing. I paid my way.

Painting is hard work. My kids wouldn't even think of it, and they are not lazy. But back then, we were willing to put those ladders up, fight the wasps, and get two coats down fast. Another job awaited.

There were always problems. One guy did not like ladder work and was so shaky, he dropped his paint on a bush. An expensive bush. I immediately draped a drop cloth over the green growth, which was now white.

The house was completely dark when we came back around 11:00 p.m. armed with small axes. The shrub quickly disappeared.

Two days later, the job was finished. I always did a walk around with the customer before payment was made. The house itself looked good. Shining white shingles, dark-green trim.

The guy turns to me and says, "Looks okay, but there's something different."

Whereupon I replied, "People always tell us that because fresh paint really changes things."

He handed me a check made out to "cash." We shook hands. I'm going to hell.

✪ ✪ ✪

As mentioned earlier, my first "real" job after graduating from college was teaching high school.

Monsignor Edward Pace High is a Catholic institution designed to educate working-class students. The rich kids attend Christopher Columbus High School down the Palmetto Expressway.

Pace is in a bad neighborhood six miles north of Miami—which is another world. Young teachers at the school were paid next to nothing, but the administration did secure a place to live for a couple of guys arriving from the North.

"You'll like the apartment complex," the principal told me on the phone. "It has a pool."

And it did. One problem. When we pulled up to our new quarters, there was a refrigerator at the bottom of said pool. And our neighbors looked like they had just been paroled from Raiford Prison.

We quickly sought other accommodations.

At twenty-two years old, I was a good teacher of History and English. The original Mr. Kotter, if you can remember the *Welcome Back* guy. But a reoccurring theme began to emerge. I did it my way.

Pace was a rough-hewn place. Students sniffing glue was big in 1972. So was bullying kids who were different. I did not brook any of that.

"Mr. O'Reilly" was a tough guy. My senior class learned that in a hurry. One day a student named Annette called me Bill. She was three years younger than me.

Looking stern, I asked Annette to stand up. The class was mesmerized. A confrontation. A test of the inexperienced teacher. I was calm.

"Ms. Brown [not her real last name], you know it's against class rules to address me by my first name. Why did you do it?"

The young lady blushed heavily, the class now totally silent. "I don't know," she finally answered.

"Well, I do. You were displaying immaturity. I hope it doesn't happen again." I gave her my Clint Eastwood squint-eyed look. She sat down.

All over for the disrupters. Embarrassing teenagers in front of their peers is horrific for them. That solidified my profile. Don't mess with this guy.

I felt sorry for Annette and, a short time later, spoke with her privately. She understood and did well in the class, which was run with fairness and efficiency. Every kid who wanted to learn did. There was no chaos.

✪ ✪ ✪

There's one more important point about kids learning the value of work. Throughout the school year, a few parent-teacher conferences occurred. The smart and motivated students were always represented by their family members, who wanted to hear praise.

The parents of failing kids never showed because they didn't care. No government can legislate good parenting, and most of the social problems that plague the US are driven by derelict or absent mothers and fathers. This is an unsolvable problem.

My job as a teacher was to mitigate as much parental damage as I could. Millions of other teachers do the same thing. But, sadly, we are heavily outnumbered by bad parents. A national shame.

After two years in the classroom (a miracle I wasn't sacked), I decided to use my God-given talents, writing and bloviating, in a larger way.

Hello, journalism.

✪ ✪ ✪

My first job in broadcasting was in Scranton, Pennsylvania, Joe Biden's hometown and a working-class depot. Nice folks, generally speaking, in northeastern Pennsylvania.

I had just graduated from Boston University with a master's degree in broadcast journalism and was ready to take Walter Cronkite's job on day one.

But old Walter was 120 miles east in New York City. I was twenty-five years old but understood the world. I had to work my way up. I had to sacrifice, live in a tough place, work my butt off.

I was willing to do those things. Many young Americans today are not. They want the free bus rides New York's Communist Mayor Zohran Mamdani promises.

Graduate school had methodically taken all my savings, so I was tapped. Apartments in Scranton required a deposit that I did not have because WNEP-TV was paying me $200 a week before taxes. No debit card for me. I was lucky I had toothpaste.

The station was family owned, and the general manager, Tom Shelburne, was sympathetic when I explained that I would have to live in my car unless I found some way to earn extra money. Grooming would suffer if I had to do that.

The GM had a solution; the station would pay me $25 more a week if I wrote the script for *Uncle Ted's Ghoul School*.

My reply to the offer was short: "What?"

"Uncle Ted" was a local personality in his late fifties who knew the barstool count in every saloon within ten miles. On Saturday night at 11:30, he would host a horror movie program. Think *I Was a Teenage Werewolf* or *The Wasp Woman*. It was a live production.

Ted's job was to darken his eyes with mascara and introduce the commercials with some witty banter. That's where I came in.

Uncle Ted had no sense of humor, could barely read the giant cue cards, and was nasty to boot. Lots of F-words in the brief rehearsal. After two weeks, I told Ted we needed to have a "talk."

I am six four, around two hundred pounds. Ted could have played the head "munchkin" in *The Wizard of Oz*. Again, using my Eastwood squint, I advised Ted that unless he started reading the cards energetically, three of my friends would beat him silly and tie him to a tree in the Poconos. I went on to say that although I did not want that to happen, I was powerless because my friends were not liking the show. However, if Ted improved, maybe they would start enjoying the broadcast again and not assault him.

On Monday, I was called into the GM's office.

"Did you threaten Ted?"

"Certainly not. Why would you think that?"

"Because he is refusing to come to work next Saturday."

"Oh, no."

The GM actually laughed. "Just lay off him. We're making about four hundred bucks a show no matter what he does."

I nodded. And get this: Ted's presentation improved a bit. Especially after I brought three big guys in to watch the *Ghoul School* in person.

✪ ✪ ✪

From Scranton, I moved up fast. Dallas, Denver, primary anchor job in Hartford, Connecticut. Then my agent got the call: WCBS-TV in New York wanted the big Irish guy. I came home.

Loved Channel 2. And I didn't change my style a bit. Whatever assignment they gave me, I turned in a good report. Wasn't easy. New York City is a hard place, especially when you're on the streets doing live on-camera stuff. Almost every time, a variety of miscreants would appear out of nowhere to jump around behind me, spouting gibberish.

Had to stop that without committing felonies. So, I selected the biggest guy on every location, gave him ten bucks, and put him in charge of "crowd control." Also, I gave him my business card. I had large pals all over the city.

But most of all, I did what I always did: worked damn hard. Took no guff. From anyone.

Back up for that. Shortly before St. Patrick's Day, circa 1981, I was assigned to cover Governor Hugh Carey, who was falling in the polls. Data showed that Carey's new wife, a society woman named Evangeline Gouletas, was one of the reasons why.

The governor was attending an Irish event in midtown and worked a receiving line alongside Evangeline. All were polite and deferential until the pair reached the end of the queue. Standing there was yours truly backed by a cameraman.

Now, Hugh Carey was not a man to be trifled with, and the New York City political press corps did not often confront him. But on this night, the rules of engagement changed.

"Governor, Bill O'Reilly, Channel 2. I have a question about the latest polling."

"I know who you are," Carey snarled.

I immediately sensed disenchantment.

"Your approval rating is down significantly, and some say your wife may be part of the reason." I was low-key with the statement, not accusatory. "Any comment?"

"You're rude. Can't you see my wife is right here?"

"Hi, Mrs. Carey." I thought the governor was going to hit me when I said that.

"I'm not answering your F-ing question!" Carey thundered. Then proceeded to insult me and Channel 2 (for employing me) in a four-minute bash fest. The diatribe made Donald Trump look like Mr. Rogers.

The governor finally strode away. His state trooper guards stared at me, although I think one guy grinned.

We raced back to the studio on Fifty-Seventh Street to edit for the eleven o'clock news. Lead story. But when the producer saw the footage, there was no edit. They used the whole thing! Unheard of. I went on the set with anchor Roland Smith and the confrontational tape rolled. This is it, I thought, hero reporter! Man of the hour!

Uh, no.

The next day, WCBS news director Steve Cohen summoned me to his office. Raise, I thought. No. The station general manager, Ed Joyce, wanted to see us.

Us? Never a good sign.

Joyce was a bloodless bureaucrat who resembled Heinrich Himmler right down to the glasses. Few wanted to ride an elevator with him.

Cohen had warned me not to say ANYTHING. A good piece of advice, as it turned out. Sitting behind his desk, Joyce verbally punched me out for around five minutes. Something about "decorum" at CBS News.

I just stared at him while Cohen looked at his shoes. What the deuce was this? I politely asked a legitimate question. Yes, it was a sensitive issue, but, hey, this is the news business, right?

Wrong. This is the political power business.

On the way back to the newsroom, I asked Steve Cohen, a brilliant newsman, if I had done anything wrong. He shook his head no, but clearly he did not want this fight. I didn't blame him.

A few weeks later, I found out what really happened from a "well-placed source." It seems that Hugh Carey was buddies with the guy who ran CBS, Bill Paley. So, of course, Carey called Paley to bitch about me, your misunderstood, humble correspondent.

Paley called Joyce who called Cohen who called me. President Reagan might have been involved, but I can't confirm that. I'm being facetious, but the point is that politics intrudes on journalists all the time.

The one positive in this tale is that I gained respect in the newsroom. No fear leads to that. I went back to doing my job the same way I had always done it. And then, something startling happened.

✪✪✪

Ed Joyce got promoted to the CBS national news. Goodbye, local. Hello, Dan Rather. And Joyce wanted ME to go with him.

Hard to believe, but it's absolutely true. Maybe they wanted me dead. The offer was to cover the chaos in Latin America. War in El Salvador, Sandinistas, Contras, all of that. I would be based in Miami. For one of only a few times in my life, I didn't know what to do.

By this time, I was anchoring on the weekends alongside Lester Holt! We were both considered rising stars at WCBS, but our styles were totally opposite. Lester, a good guy, was very calm. I was a bit more, shall we say, unrestrained.

The Channel 2 station manager, Ron Tindiglia, invited me to dinner to talk about the CBS offer. Ron was a television genius. He flat out told me *not* to take the national job. He wouldn't say why, but I could feel there was something brewing that I didn't yet understand. I did consider what Ron said and very much appreciated his candor.

But I took the offer. Couldn't resist the big stage.

I should have listened to Ron.

✪✪✪

I will digress a bit before we get to a terrible thing that happened to me at CBS News.

If you work for a company, you are essentially powerless. That's a significant situation. I am a member of SAG, the Screen Actors Guild, a fairly powerful union. But although I paid heavy dues, the guild could not help me or anyone else who was treated unfairly. Salary guidelines and healthcare, yes. Beefs with management, no.

That's reality in the workplace. It is far better to run your own operation, as I do now. But corporate America does provide opportunities and money. However, you will have to swallow some ill-tasting stuff. That should be highlighted in every American school.

It is not.

The absolute truth is this: It is not enough to do your job well in many places. I was naive to believe that it would be. So, I found out the hard way.

✪ ✪ ✪

The year was 1982. Ronald Reagan in the White House, Central America on fire. The civil war in El Salvador was raging with no rules of engagement. Communist guerrillas were trying to overthrow an authoritarian government that did not respect human rights. Neither did the reds.*

Activist nuns were murdered. So was Archbishop Oscar Romero. Bodies all over the place. The US backed the government but knew their supplicants were essentially gangsters. However, the "muchachos" were considered worse because of their ties to the Communist Nicaraguan Sandinistas and Cuba.

Enter O'Reilly.

* The Salvadoran Civil War (1979–1992) in 1982 was marked by escalating violence, heavy US support for the right-wing military government, and major Communist guerrilla offensives. A defining 1982 event was the El Calabozo massacre in August, where government forces killed over two hundred civilians. The year also saw the Battle of Ilopango Airport in January, where guerillas destroyed significant air force assets.

✪ ✪ ✪

The Air Florida flight from Miami circled the airport at San Salvador. From my window seat, I saw tanks ringing the runway. Ninety minutes ago, I could buy a postcard with a flamingo on it in South Florida. Now a very dark scenario awaited.

After checking into the hotel, I went to the CBS suite for "orientation." Nobody was friendly. Today they call it "welcoming." Didn't bother me.

Orientation was straightforward: Don't get killed like ABC News correspondent Bill Stewart. In 1979, Stewart, thirty-seven, and his twenty-six-year-old translator, Juan Espinoza, were covering the Sandinista revolution in Managua, Nicaragua. The two stepped out of their van at a government checkpoint and were shot dead.

The horrific executions were photographed by an ABC employee inside the vehicle. The footage shows Stewart being forced to kneel down, then shot in the head.

The soldiers who killed Stewart and Espinoza were part of dictator Anastasio Somoza's brutal army. Somoza, a brutish thug, was supported by the Carter administration. But the national outcry over Stewart's murder shown to the world pretty much ended that. A short time later, Somoza fled to Miami, then to Paraguay, where he was assassinated.

After being briefed on Stewart (never go to your knees), another tape was presented. A Dutch photographer shot in the head filming a firefight in El Salvador. Journalist jargon for bullets flying is "bang, bang."

Don't know why, but the violent videos didn't scare me. However, I understood the danger. No question.

My primary assignment was quickly made clear: find out about a rumored massacre in the remote province of Morazán, a mountainous area where the rebels roamed. Who did it? How many died? Fine with me. Four of us jumped in a large van: cameraman, sound guy, driver/interpreter, and me, your very green network correspondent.

The journey was slow because bridges over streams had been blown up and we had to wade through water. Eventually, we rolled into San Francisco Gotera, the capital of Morazán. *Todo bueno*. At least, so far.

The government held a fort in town, and we drove on in. As the cab driver told James Bond in *Live and Let Die*, "I hope you make friends easy!"

Not always. A captain walked out to inspect our credentials and was respectful. But behind him were three men hanging from a scaffold, ropes tied to their wrists. "Muchachos?" I asked, using slang for Communist guerrilla fighters.

"No, señor. Mi hombres."

My men? What?

It seemed the three had fallen asleep on guard duty the previous night. The public punishment was an obvious warning to the Salvadoran garrison: Stay alert.

The captain, a short, well-dressed officer, denied knowing about any massacre. He offered lunch, explaining there was nowhere else to eat. We accepted.

When I mentioned our assignment was to locate the alleged combat zone, he smiled, shook his head. "Muy arriesgado."

Sí, dangerous.

Two hours later we rolled up to a deserted town. No trace of anything human. A few dead farm animals. No idea what happened.

And that's what I said in my report that aired on *CBS Weekend News*. I actually called home from the hotel back in San Salvador to alert my parents to watch. My father answered the phone. "Where are you?" he asked.

"El Salvador. Remember I told you I'd be covering the war?"

"Right. Here's your mother."

I soft-pedaled everything, not wanting to worry the folks. "I'm fine, Mom, the story will be on Channel 2 at 6:30."

✪✪✪

Years later, the incredibly vicious left-wing magazine *Mother Jones* accused me of faking my war coverage. *Politico*, *The New York Times*, the *Los Angeles Times*, and CNN all picked up the lies. Their goal was to damage me, a commentator they loathed.

I was a bit disturbed. Well, maybe more than a bit.

But then an extraordinary thing happened. Out of nowhere, Don Browne, the NBC Bureau Chief in Miami, stepped up and defended me.

"I was surprised by the article," Browne said. "I was overseeing the coverage in El Salvador. It was a brutal war. [O'Reilly] was there to cover the war. He came down to get his ticket punched and he did."

Which means I did my job. Not one of the media organizations that smeared me issued a retraction. Why bother with that? Why seek the truth? We don't like O'Reilly. So, let's get him.

I will always be grateful to Don Browne. There was nothing in it for him. Honest people are hard to find. Especially in the media.

With my ticket punched in El Salvador, the CBS brass then handed me an airline ticket to Argentina. And that is where my working life changed.

✪✪✪

The Pan American jet from Rio de Janeiro to Buenos Aires landed at Ezeiza Airport in the early afternoon. I alighted, looking for the CBS driver who was supposed to take me to the Sheraton Hotel, the American media headquarters for the Falklands War.

But no driver was present. So, I hopped into a cab for the twenty-two-mile journey.

About an hour later, I strolled into the CBS News suite, a bunch of connected rooms full of tech gear, desks, TV monitors.

"O'Reilly reporting for duty," I said to Larry Doyle, the bureau chief.

"What are you doing here? Nobody told me you were coming."

This was an omen.

"Just doing what New York asked. Here's my ticket, and they did have my room reservation."

Doyle was not pleased. "Okay, find a desk."

My pal Bernie Goldberg, a CBS correspondent for twenty-two years, explained to me in 2025 what I did not understand way back when. "They didn't like you because you were a local news hotshot and the network people look down on local news. Plus, you're you."

Ah, yes, me.

A few days after being hired by the Rather crew, I rode in an elevator with *60 Minutes* commentator Andy Rooney, who, unprompted, looked way up at me and said, "You'll never make it."

Nice to meet you, too, Andy.

Anyway, I didn't know anything about Larry Doyle and the CBS squad in Buenos Aires. Correspondents Bob Schieffer and Eric Engberg, as well as radio reporter Chuck Gomez, were on site. I had no experience with any of them. That would change fast.

✪ ✪ ✪

Without a doubt, the battle over the useless Falkland Islands was one of the most foolish conflicts in world history. On April 2, 1982, Argentine military strongman Leopoldo Galtieri ordered an "invasion" of the Malvinas, which is what Argentina calls the Falkland Islands.

Why? Well, Argentina's economy was falling apart, so a diversion was needed. The old "wag the dog" strategy. One problem: The cold and windy place had been under British control since 1690, a rest port for English mariners sailing to the Pacific.

Three days after the invasion, British Prime Minister Margaret Thatcher dispatched a bunch of warships to the South Atlantic. At first, President Reagan stayed "neutral." But he wasn't really neutral. He and "Maggie" were fast friends, so US intelligence was covertly helping the Brits.

An interesting footnote. The late Pope Francis was an influential priest in Buenos Aires at the time and supported the Falklands War. If he had not, he and his fellow Argentine Jesuits would have been in grave danger—the fascist military was not above throwing dissident priests out of helicopters.

✪✪✪

For a month, nothing much happened. Argentine soldiers, based in Port Stanley, patrolled the island, frightening the sheep. There were only a few hundred British subjects living there, and they lay low.

Finally, the mini-armada arrived.

Almost immediately the Argentine cruiser *General Belgrano* was destroyed, leaving 323 dead. But there were no reporters on the islands, and the military government censored all war news anyway. Galtieri often appeared on television telling the world his forces were kicking butt.*

Then, the Argentine Air Force, armed with powerful Exocet missiles, scored a hit. The HMS *Sheffield* sank quickly, twenty Brits killed, nearly one hundred wounded, some gravely burned.

I, your humble correspondent, was dispatched to Montevideo, Uruguay, where the hurt British sailors were being taken for treatment. Harrowing scene as stretchers were unloaded from a transport ship. Uruguay was neutral but very hostile to American reporters. Sullen soldiers kept us penned up on a dock for eight hours. No food, water, or facilities. And it was cold. Tough assignment.

Finally, the scene unfolded. I spoke with two of the wounded who were ambulatory. Others were wrapped like mummies because of severe burns.

We sent our story via satellite to Buenos Aires. It was then transmitted to New York for the Rather broadcast. But when it aired that night, there was no sign of me. CBS News had "folded" my footage and interviews into another report voiced by Bob Schieffer, who had not left the hotel in Buenos Aires.

Not good. I remembered my dinner with Ron Tindiglia.

---

* Leopoldo Fortunato Galtieri (1926–2003) was an Argentine Army general who served as the de facto president of Argentina from December 1981 to June 1982 during the final, brutal military dictatorship known as the National Reorganization Process (1976–1983). A hardline anti-Communist, he is best remembered for ordering the disastrous 1982 invasion of the Falkland Islands (Islas Malvinas), which led to his downfall and accelerated the return of democracy to Argentina. He died from a heart attack in 2003 at the age of seventy-six.

✪✪✪

On June 13, 1982, Argentine troops occupying the Falklands surrendered. But remember, the people thought their country was winning. Almost immediately, street riots broke out.

I was summoned. Taking two camera crews, which I knew would be needed, we drove the short distance to the presidential palace, called the Casa Rosada (pink house). It was here, years back, that Eva Peron addressed the folks who stood listening in the Plaza del Mayo.

Now standing before the palace was a huge crowd, screaming their collective brains out. They wanted Galtieri's head. A tight line of government soldiers stood in protection mode behind a palace iron fence. Some in the agitated crowd threw rocks and coins at the soldiers, who had shields along with their automatic weapons.

I positioned one camera guy to the left and took the other with me to the right. Suddenly, a bunch of trucks pulled into the palace courtyard. Shock troops.

Tear gas was fired, then incredibly, a few of the troops fired live rounds into the mob. People dropped; most ran, trampling anyone in their path.

My cameraman, a freelance South American named Roberto Moreno, was standing on a sidewalk taping the scene when panicked demonstrators knocked him to the ground. His gear went flying. Apparently, he hit his head on the concrete because blood trickled from his ear. He was clearly concussed.

While dragging Roberto into a doorway, I shouted at the soundman to get the crushed camera and the tape—which he did.

We stood in the doorway for a short time trying to figure out an exit strategy. Then more chaos. A few young, heavily armed soldiers appeared. One lifted his rifle in our direction. Immediately, I looked him in the eye. Showing fear in Latin America can be a death sentence, as I learned in El Salvador.

Clearly, I stated, "Periodistas, no despare, por favor." Journalists, please don't shoot.

The soldier was now about ten yards away. He looked to be a teenager. He didn't fire.

To this day, I cannot describe the adrenaline flow.

We had a designated meeting place for our van, directly behind the palace. In fact, there were two CBS vehicles. I put the dazed Roberto Moreno in the back seat and told the driver to go to the closest hospital.

Then the other driver, me, and the sound guy sped back to the Sheraton. The tape was not damaged.

✪ ✪ ✪

Before we get to the conclusion of this saga, I want to clearly state why I am writing it. This chapter is about working for a living, which is imperative if you want to live a productive life. However, the workplace can be treacherous and unfair. Somewhere down the road, you are likely to be hurt. When that happens, you have to accept the situation and change course. If you don't, the bad people win.

✪ ✪ ✪

As with Governor Carey, I thought my reporting was going to be rewarded with many accolades. Perhaps a standing O when I entered the CBS suite at the Sheraton.

Not exactly.

As I walked through the office to debrief Larry Doyle, I had blood on my jacket and smelled of tear gas.

Eyeing me warily were Bob Schieffer and his lackey Eric Engberg. I did not see them at the Casa Rosada. Maybe they were undercover or something. Perhaps they remembered Bill Stewart.

I handed the video to the techs, alerted Doyle about Moreno, and sat down to write my story.

Then all hell broke loose.

Almost snarling, Schieffer, one of Dan Rather's main men, demanded that I give him my notes.

My emotional reply was succinct and began with an *F*. I certainly was not expecting this.

Schieffer said something to the effect that I would be in deep trouble if I didn't give him my notebook. And then he said, "I heard you put your cameraman in danger. Well, we'll have to look into that."

I bolted up from the chair and gave the guy a shove he'll never forget, propelling him across the room. I said something like, "Get away from me, you jerk. This is my story."

But it wasn't.

A bunch of techs saved Schieffer's butt, dragging me away from him. Shock in the bureau. I appealed to Doyle, who told me to leave and cool off.

Schieffer never got the notebook, but a few hours later, he stood on the rooftop of the Sheraton Hotel opening the Rather program. The pretense: He was on the riot scene. Again, I didn't see him. I am as angry about this today as I was forty-four years ago.*

There was absolutely nothing I could do. I was told Roberto Moreno was okay but never saw him again as CBS quickly got him out of Argentina. At least that was the rumor.

What happened to me in Buenos Aires is called "big footing." It's still around today in some news operations. It's corrupt, insidious, and there's no excuse for it. You don't steal other people's work.

✪ ✪ ✪

Bernie Goldberg worked for CBS at the time, and, of course, the incident spread like Ebola throughout the company. I pretty much knew that I was done, and, years later, Bernie confirmed it.

"You bucked the system," Goldberg told me. "CBS News doesn't

---

* Bob Schieffer (born 1937) is an American television journalist who spent over forty years at CBS News, becoming renowned as a moderator of *Face the Nation* (1991–2015) and a staple Washington correspondent. Known for covering all four major DC beats—the White House, Pentagon, State Department, and Capitol Hill—he won eight Emmys and is a Broadcasting & Cable Hall of Fame inductee. Schieffer is active in his retirement, specifically engaging in art and recently returning to Texas for a 2026 exhibit featuring his work.

care about fairness. Dan Rather wanted his pals on the air, so that's what happened. What YOU wanted did not matter to them."

All true. All horrendous.

✪ ✪ ✪

What Bob Schieffer did was outrageous. The hack Eric Engberg spread all kinds of false stories about the incident. The boys stuck together, and this time there was no honest knight like Don Browne. It was me alone against a corrupt system. But I had to make one final attempt to right this wrong: see Dan Rather himself.

✪ ✪ ✪

Before we get to that showdown, there was one other on-the-record situation that happened during the ordeal in Buenos Aries. After Schieffer stole my story, I filed my version for the CBS "feed." That is a service provided to all television stations that are affiliated with the CBS network. The story ran about two minutes. The next day the CBS bureau in Buenos Aires received a text from New York.

> CBS News New York to CBS News Buenos Aires
>
> Doyle, O'Reilly, didn't have the time last night but would like to say many thanks for the riot piece last night. WCBS-TV and WCAU-TV both took the entire piece instead of stripping it for PIX. They called me to say thanks for a fine piece.
>
> So, thanks again. Your piece made the late feed a winner last night.

That telegram did not help me at all, unfortunately. But it did back up what I was alleging. That I covered the story but did not appear in it on the Dan Rather program.

Shameful.

✪ ✪ ✪

The man who pushed Walter Cronkite into retirement sat behind an expensive desk in his office on West Fifty-Seventh Street in New York

City. He wore a freshly pressed white shirt, suspenders, and dark suit pants from Saville Row in London. His jacket, which would be pressed just before airtime, hung on a hook behind the closed door.

I had gained audience through his agent, who did not want Rather dragged into a public spat with some young punk reporter who meant nothing to anyone.

Rather had already been briefed by Schieffer, Engberg, and Doyle, so no fair hearing was possible. I knew that.

But I had something to say to the Texan who came up the hard way and actually effectively covered stories in the field.

Rather was polite, and I suspected his secretary had been given a "short time" instruction. An important call would be announced in about five minutes. Dan, of course, would have to take that call—leading to my exit. That's how this stuff works in the circles of power.

So, I looked him in the eye and began.

"What your crew did to me in Argentina was flat-out wrong. In my opinion, I should have led your program because I risked my life getting the story. Where was Schieffer? How can this be condoned?"

My tone was even. Rather's face was blank. Then I moved in.

"What if, in Dealey Plaza, where you reported the assassination of JFK, some other correspondent not on the scene stole your footage and put his voice on your story? Would you be where you are today?"

No answer. Rather just sat there.

In late November 1963, Dan Rather was in Dallas covering President John F. Kennedy's visit to a city that generally despised him. While riding in his motorcade, JFK was shot by Lee Harvey Oswald, a mentally unbalanced former marine. I spent years investigating the assassination, culminating in my book *Killing Kennedy*.

Dan Rather was first with the news that JFK had died. He monitored transmissions to Parkland Hospital. Excellent reporting. That and follow-up stories made Rather's career.

I figured the comparison to my situation in Argentina was worth a shot. Didn't work. Dan said he'd "look into the situation."

Sure.

A few moments later, Rather's secretary buzzed saying he had to take a very important call.

✪ ✪ ✪

Word got out about my confrontation in Argentina. Doom loop. Very quickly my agent got a call from Boston offering me an anchor job. Boston is a great place. The president of CBS News, Van Gordon Sauter, gave me a glowing letter of recommendation. I couldn't believe it was me he was writing about. But again, CBS News did not want a public airing of this.

Actually, what Sauter did was very kind. He knew I would be attacked down the road because of the confrontation. So, he provided me somewhat of a shield by praising my work.

✪ ✪ ✪

No parting gifts from Rather, Schieffer, or Engberg, but I'm sure there was a bit of sneering whenever my name came up. I'm also sure they thought I was gone, baby, gone. Dead and buried in the world of national news.

They were wrong because America is a great place. Opportunity abounds. If you get up from adversity and then get down doing honest work.

Which I did.

✪ ✪ ✪

Two fascinating footnotes to the CBS story. Years later, I ran into Dan Rather at some press event in New York City. I was the top-rated cable news anchor in the country and held the number one position on the *New York Times* bestseller list with, ironically, *Killing Kennedy*.

Rather approached, and our eyes met. "Bill, it's just triumph after triumph for you."

Many things could have been said. But I didn't say them. No reason to do it. I had eclipsed the man who would soon be forced out of prominence for using false documents on a story about President George W. Bush.

Karma?

✪ ✪ ✪

In 1986, I sat across from ABC News chief Roone Arledge, who was offering me a job as a New York–based correspondent. Arledge was a cold-hearted, unapproachable man who founded *Monday Night Football* and shepherded Peter Jennings to anchorman superstardom. Most were intimidated by Arledge, but I was not. Probably because I didn't particularly want the job.

I had achieved success in Boston and very much liked the beat of the city. Did I really want to return to the corrupt culture at network news? No, I did not.

The reason for Arledge's interest was that he had seen me give the eulogy at my best friend's funeral. On January 21, 1986, ABC News correspondent Joe Spencer was killed in a wintry helicopter crash in Minnesota. Recently married, thirty-one years old. I cannot describe the pain experienced by his family and friends. My son is named after Spencer, as I always called him.

Peter Jennings was also set to speak at the mass. But Jennings didn't know Joe Spencer, which was a bit awkward. So, I pulled him aside in the sacristy before the service. "How long are you going to go, Mr. Jennings?"

I didn't know Peter at all. He was wary. "I don't know," he answered.

"Well, keep it tight because there's a ton of emotion in the church. Let's honor Joe Spencer with the facts. You take the journalism, I'll do the personal."

Now, a guy like Jennings was not used to being told to "keep it tight." But he was, as I learned, a good man. He nodded assent and walked to his seat.

The priest, a middle-aged Irishman, then said to me, "Did you just do that?"

Apparently so, Father, and I hope you "keep it tight, too."

✪✪✪

Now sitting across from the legendary Arledge, I kept my gaze steady, my voice calm. We discussed his vision of my job, which was standard issue: We'll give you plenty of work. We need more firepower on the street.

My turn. I said something like this: I can handle the work. But please don't hire me if you're going to big foot or allow producers to call my shots. I do the story my way. If you'll promise that, I'll come down from Boston. If you break your promise, I will walk, and not quietly.

Up to you, Mr. Arledge. I admire what you've done in the industry. Thinking back, I think I stole the last line from Robert Duvall's Tom Hagen character in *The Godfather*, when he told the corrupt movie producer Woltz that he admired his films very much.

The Hollywood guy wound up with a horse's head in his bed.

I didn't have to go that far with ABC. Arledge said the right things, and I took the job for two reasons: to keep Joe Spencer's legacy alive, and to get blankin' revenge on CBS. Which I did.

✪✪✪

From then on, your humble correspondent became a leading man. In 1988, tabloid television was raging. Shows like *A Current Affair* brought in big ratings. I got a call from two colleagues I had worked with at Channel 2 in New York. They were starting up a program called *Inside Edition*. At first I mocked them. Why would I leave ABC News, where I had appeared on *World News Tonight* more than one hundred times, for some dopey syndicated program that does stories about topless donut shops? The answer came back quickly: *Inside Edition* would double my salary and put a clause in my contract that said I could report on any story in the world that I wanted to cover.

That was extraordinary.

Word got around quickly. I was sitting in the makeup chair preparing to do an ABC News Brief when Peter Jennings walked in. "Are you blankin' crazy?" he asked me. "You're going tabloid?"

I explained to Peter the news coverage clause and the money aspect. Both he and I knew that I was never going to be a frontline anchor at ABC News. There were too many guys ahead of me named Forest and Stone, bluebloods whom ABC was much more comfortable with than some guy from Levittown.

Peter Jennings understood. He remains a major positive force in my life. In 2005, he died from lung cancer at the age of sixty-seven. I miss him to this day.

✪ ✪ ✪

Inside Edition was a blast. I signed on as the chief correspondent and substitute anchor for the primary host, British TV guy David Frost. Frost was world renowned for his interview with Richard Nixon and for hobnobbing with movie stars. However, there was one problem.

David Frost had about as much in common with American blue-collar viewers as Nelson Rockefeller. He had no idea how people lived in the colonies. Nor did he care. Also, David was very fond of long lunches complemented by extensive wine lists. So, when he showed up for taping, he was not a smooth operator, as Sade once sang.

David Frost was fired within weeks of the show's debut.

I took over. Things were grim. Ratings were terrible. But I knew the audience. They did not necessarily want salacious garbage, but they didn't want to be bored, either. *Inside Edition* put together a daily roster of interesting hard news stories as well as the Madonna stuff. I did the tabloid nonsense with a wink, and often made fun of it. I wasn't making fun of the audience. I was basically sending a message that we really don't take the latest Hollywood scandals seriously.

What we did take seriously was Donald Trump. He dominated tabloid coverage in New York City at the time. I interviewed him with regularity. That began my friendship with the president.

Inside Edition turned into a smash hit. I anchored it for six years, making parent company King World hundreds of millions of dollars. But I never liked those people, and they certainly were not fond of me. Why? Because I pretty much did what I wanted. What else is new? After two contract cycles, I decided to do something new. So, I went up to Cambridge, Massachusetts, to complete a master's degree at Harvard University's Kennedy School of Government. It was there that I designed *The O'Reilly Factor*.

✪ ✪ ✪

On October 7, 1996, the Fox News Channel went on the air. It was designed to give conservative/traditional Americans a point of view they did not receive from the other broadcast networks. In fact, the Right was completely shut out of the television news process.

Fox News was backed by the Murdoch family. Big money. And it was immediately attacked by people like Ted Turner, who owned CNN. Mr. Turner said something like, "We'll squash them like a bug." My rejoinder was, "There isn't enough Raid in the world."

The rest is history. Fox News still dominates the cable news ratings and often beats the network news. My program, *The O'Reilly Factor*, was number one for sixteen consecutive years. A dominant number one. That will never be duplicated.

I could write ten books about Fox News. Suffice it to say, I did my job. I was well paid, worked extremely hard, developed a very capable staff, and basically succeeded at a level I never thought possible.

This could only happen in America, as I've said many times. Capitalism rules here. If people like your program, you will make money. If you make money, you will become very famous and affluent. And that's what happened to me.

Along the way I had to endure smears, attacks, defamation, you name it. That is "life in the fast lane," to use a terrible cliché that the Eagles are responsible for. Looking back, it was worth it. But the constant attacks did a lot of damage, no question about it. These are not worth relitigating here because the theme of this book is what is most important.

✪ ✪ ✪

What is that theme? Here it is: Determined people can make it in America if they stay strong, honest, and engaged. You must perform. You don't have to sell your soul. The higher you want to fly in the marketplace, the more challenges you will face.

Finally, there is nothing wrong with settling down in a nice place with a good job and living a comfortable life. Most of my peers have done that. I'm the crazy one working for fifty years on the high wire. But that's what I wanted to do, and my success could only happen in the USA. Sorry, Portugal.

Today in America, millions want the government to help them through. Not me. I'm proudly independent and self-sufficient.

President Obama once told me on camera that the government helped me become a success, so I owed it. There's slight truth to that, and I pay enormous taxes in return for the opportunities I've received in the marketplace.

But, in reality, the government had little to do with my workplace failures and successes. I did the very heavy lift. I made the mistakes. That's what the founders gave all of us: a pathway of opportunity. But to negotiate the dollar world, you have to develop a clear vision and significant discipline.

It's all about will. With that, the way unfolds.

CHAPTER TEN

God Help Us

Pagans are on the march. Along with atheists, agnostics, cynics, and outright heathens. America is becoming a "godless" country.

That may seem to be an overstatement. So, let me back it up. According to the Pew Research people, only 40 percent of Americans ages eighteen to twenty-nine consider themselves "Christian." Incredibly, 44 percent of that age group say they do not believe in God at all.

This is a stunning statistic because the United States was founded on Judeo-Christian philosophy. As late as the year 2000, 80 percent of Americans identified as Christian. Now, that number is 60 percent. The minority religions have stayed pretty much the same: Jewish Americans comprise 2 percent of the population, Muslims 1 percent.

Around the world, a quarter of the global population are nonbelievers. There are 2.5 billion Christians on the planet, 2 billion followers of Islam, 1.2 billion Hindus.

The Muslim nations are pretty much stable as far as their belief system is concerned. But so-called Christian nations in Europe and North America are on a steep decline.

Why?

✪ ✪ ✪

To understand what is happening, we must analyze both the modern world and America's historical beginnings. Let's start back in the mid-seventeenth century.

I wrote a book called *Killing the Witches* that chronicles the arrival of the Puritans from Great Britain in December 1620. They were fanatical believers in Jesus Christ. They rejected the Church of England and all moderation in religion itself. These were brutal people, and their ideological excess led to twenty executions in Salem, Massachusetts. Innocent people were accused of being "witches"—that means agents of the devil. Without due process, nineteen were hanged.*

That was a harrowing beginning to the American legacy.

Evaluating this situation was a teenager in Boston named Benjamin Franklin. He actually visited one of the main witch-hunters, a man named Cotton Mather. Franklin was a genius, even at that young age, and understood perfectly what religious excess could do. So, years later, he brought that sensibility into the founding of the United States.

In the late eighteenth century, when the Constitution was being forged, there were two opposing camps. One, headed by Virginia Governor Patrick Henry, wanted the new country to be a theocracy—that is, to have government pay for Christan churches. The other group, led by Franklin, Thomas Jefferson, and James Madison, rejected that entirely. They did not want the new government to "impose" any religion on American citizens. That is the concept of separation between church and state.

Benjamin Franklin himself saw virtue as the core of religious faith. He questioned the divinity of Jesus and concluded that behavior ultimately defines a person's spiritual status.

Thomas Jefferson completely rejected organized religion. He was a

* The Salem witch trials were a series of hearings and prosecutions of people accused of witchcraft in colonial Massachusetts between February 1692 and May 1693. The hysteria began in Salem Village when young girls, including Betty Parris and Abigail Williams, suffered strange fits and accused local women of bewitching them. A special court was convened to hear the cases, allowing "spectral evidence"—testimony about dreams and visions—which made defense nearly impossible.

man who lived in his own mind. Despite that, he did respect the tenets of Jesus.

On January 18, 1824, Jefferson penned a letter to a minister friend. He is blunt:

> *Had Christianity never been sophisticated by the subtleties of Commentators, nor paraphrased into meanings totally foreign to it; it would be at this day the religion of the whole civilized world. But the metaphysical abstractions of Athanasius, and the maniac ravings of Calvin tinctured plentifully with the foggy dreams of Plato, have so loaded it with absurdities and incomprehensibilities as to drive into infidelity men who had not time, patience, or opportunity to strip it of its meretricious trappings and to see it in all its native simplicity and purity. . . .*
>
> *Not wishing to give offense to those who differ in opinion nor to be implicated in a theological controversy, I have to pray that this letter may not get into print*

And the letter did not. Until now.

✪ ✪ ✪

Thomas Jefferson's pal James Madison was not as militant as the King of Monticello. However, Madison did not embrace organized religion either. He thought that all beliefs were a matter of "conscience."

George Washington was more practical. He promoted "public virtue" because it led to better personal behavior. Washington demanded good citizenship and viewed God as a divine protector of America. He looked down on nonbelievers.

Later, Abraham Lincoln, who in his younger days was almost an atheist, turned to Christian themes to help him get through the Civil War. Lincoln's most dominant expression was that God *wanted* the United States to be one country, without the sin of slavery.

In September 1862, Lincoln wrote the following passage in his personal journal:

The will of God prevails . . . I am almost ready to say that this is probably true—that God wills this contest, and wills that it shall not end yet. By his mere great power, on the minds of the now contestants, He could have either saved or destroyed the Union without a human contest. Yet the contest began. And, having begun He could give the final victory to either side any day. Yet the contest proceeds.

Abraham Lincoln never joined a church. Most confident in the righteousness of the Union cause, he believed God would eventually grant victory to those suppressing the southern rebellion.

In the twentieth century, Franklin Delano Roosevelt governed as a secular Episcopalian. He did not often use God or the Bible to advance his political philosophy. Instead, he focused on social justice and service to the nation. However, during World War II, FDR clearly delineated Judeo-Christian ethics from the totalitarianism of Germany and Japan. In late December 1943, Roosevelt issued this proclamation:

Now that we know in our hearts that victory is certain, we can face the coming hard struggle ahead with confidence and certitude and let the spirit of Christmas pervade our thoughts bringing us comfort and a measure of happiness.

✪ ✪ ✪

For political reasons, almost every American president has embraced the Christian ethic. Not *one* has rejected it publicly. So, you can see that the United States is steeped in Judeo-Christian thought. In addition, all of the presidents honor the concept of Intelligent Design—that is, a benevolent creator who actively participates in the world.

As far as we know, there have been no atheists in the White House.

But that could soon change because the modern world is on a collision course with spirituality.

✪ ✪ ✪

American society is changing dramatically, veering away from religion into the science of artificial intelligence. For millions, the concept of God has become a cell phone in their hands. Individuals can now create their own worlds. They can establish personal rules of behavior, as long as they don't directly harm another person. There are few limits on artificial intelligence, which is the application of computer systems able to perform tasks normally requiring *human* intelligence. If a machine can do everything, why should the concept of "God" even exist?

In short, you don't have to think anymore or believe anything. You just have to switch on the computer.*

That has badly damaged the concept of Intelligent Design, which is the theory that says the universe did not arise by chance. It was designed by an all-powerful God. You either believe that or you don't.

So, today, the world is now facing a battle between Intelligent Design and artificial intelligence.

✪ ✪ ✪

I believe in God because I want to believe in God. It's as simple as that. Atheists reject the Deity because they don't want to believe. That equation defines the battle over religion in this world. Neither side has absolute proof of anything. Millions find comfort in the concept of a reward after death. However, millions of others do not want a religion telling them what they can or cannot do.

The reason I *want* to believe is because of what I wrote in my previous book, *Confronting Evil*. If there is no central creator, then heinous human beings get away with it. There is no judgment day. There is no reckoning. A person can do whatever he or she wants without fear of ultimate condemnation.

That is not justice. I am a justice seeker. I believe that civilization

* The rise of artificial intelligence (AI) represents a transformative technological revolution. Enabled by massive computing power, advanced networks, and vast data availability, AI has evolved from simple automation to advanced machine learning.

depends on the embracement of good and the rejection of evil and that there will be a final reckoning. I do embrace the Christian tenet of free will. You have to choose in this life between harmful and helpful acts. So, what's it gonna be? Good or bad?

✪ ✪ ✪

There are billions of people on the planet who could not care less about religion and God. They live solely for themselves. Or, like Thomas Jefferson, they create a vision of the world that excludes any kind of spiritual direction. I can't tell you how many people simply dismiss the idea that there may be a creator. And if *you* believe—you're a moron. We hear it all over the media, we see it in totalitarian countries like China and the former Soviet Union, we might even debate it with our own family members.

But read closely, because I am now going to tell you something extraordinary.

✪ ✪ ✪

Researching my book *Killing Jesus* was exceedingly difficult because written records from the time the Nazarene was preaching are few. However, with the help of the Israeli government, which opened its archives to us, and extensive examination of Roman records, we discovered something that is incredibly fascinating.

Here it is.

Jesus of Nazareth was a stonecutter. Some elderly Christians, after reading *Killing Jesus*, scolded me, saying, "No! Jesus was a carpenter!" Well, that is the dominant religious myth, but I would politely reply, "That would be fairly difficult, because there were few *trees* in Galilee." In the small village where Jesus lived, almost all the people resided in stone dwellings, and the Nazarene's father was a well-known builder.

Around his thirtieth birthday, Jesus began to preach in a one-hundred-square-mile area. At the time, there were scores of "Messiahs" roaming around Judea. It was actually an industry. Messiah Ed would roll into town; someone would give him dinner and a place to sleep. Then Ed would go on to the next town and gather up whatever the folks there would give him. The Jewish authorities and the Roman Emperor Pontius Pilate pretty much ignored those people. They were considered eccentrics and con men, but harmless.

That all changed with a man named John the Baptist. Kind of a flamboyant guy, the Baptist set up court along the banks of the Jordan River. He began preaching about the "Messiah" to come. John was a fanatical moralist. But then he stepped over the line. He began to criticize the Jewish "King" Herod for committing adultery. He did that constantly and loudly. It did not take long for Herod to throw the Baptist into prison. Eventually, John, a cousin of Jesus, was beheaded. That is a matter of record.

Coming up behind the Baptist was the Nazarene himself. In the beginning, he was almost alone. He had not yet enlisted his helpers, called the apostles. He simply traveled from hamlet to hamlet, speaking about God and what human beings had to do to earn His goodwill. It did not take long for Jesus to assemble a group of followers. They would go ahead of him to various towns, telling the poor citizens that Jesus would soon be arriving. At first, nobody really cared. But, slowly, crowds began assembling. They became larger and larger. Word got back to the Sanhedrin, the Jewish headquarters in Jerusalem. There, the temple authorities were not pleased. Jesus became a threat. So, they brought the situation to Pilate, who could not have cared less.

The Romans were in Palestine simply to collect taxes from poor people. They occupied the land but had little interest in it.*

Months passed, the crowds grew even larger. But why?

Most of the folks could not *hear* what Jesus was saying. He did not have a microphone. There were hundreds, sometimes thousands of people flocking to see him. And they could *see* him, as he stood on

* The Romans renamed the biblical region of Judea as Palestine in 63 BC after conquering the territory. The word originates from the Philistines, a seafaring people who lived near the Mediterranean coast.

a hilltop or in a boat on the Sea of Galilee. There, the Nazarene was visible. But as far as *hearing* what he was preaching, very few had that experience.

So, why did the huge crowds show up?

The answer to that question lies in paranoia. The Jewish authorities dispatched spies to follow Jesus wherever he went. They wanted to gather evidence against him to prosecute the Nazarene. Independently, Pontius Pilate did the same thing. He infiltrated Roman spies into the crowds assembling around Jesus. In both cases, the reports back said that most of the people who were clamoring to see the Nazarene did so because of the "works." That means the "miracles."

The Gospels are full of stories about Jesus healing terrible afflictions. Even raising people from the dead. But scripture is not history. It is impossible to verify that Jesus performed miracles.

However, the spies reporting back to the temple authorities and Pilate had no other explanation for the continuing crowds. So, while mocking the situation, the informers all came to the same conclusion: Something mysterious was happening in the ministry of Jesus.

And, if you think about it, there is no other rational explanation for crowds seeking out Jesus. These were people struggling to eat every day. There were no refrigerators. They had to work in order to survive. Every day. Yet, thousands abandoned their labor to seek out the Nazarene. Remember, they could not *hear* him. So, there had to be something else.

Healings, I believe, are the something else.

Had to be.

✪✪✪

This all culminated when Jesus arrived in Jerusalem riding on a small donkey. Hundreds of people met him in a frenzy of delight. That sealed his doom. The Jewish authorities understood the Jesus phenomenon had now eclipsed every other campaign of spirituality. They saw the Nazarene as a direct threat to their power. They passed that threat concept along to Pilate, who understood that any kind of "rebellion" would reflect poorly on him in Rome.

Thus, in short order, Jesus was condemned to death by crucifixion.*

✪ ✪ ✪

One more thing. How is it possible that a poor laborer has become the most famous person to ever exist in the world? Jesus lived more than two thousand years ago, but today billions still believe he is God. That legacy will be with humankind forever. But now, what was once accepted in America as a primary philosophy in government, Judeo-Christian ethics, is under siege.

The pagans, as I wrote, are on the rise.

✪ ✪ ✪

Why should you care? Well, there's one big reason: social order. Napoleon Bonaparte put it best: "Religion is what keeps the poor from murdering the rich."

Almost every study that we have accessed says the same thing. Religion and spirituality tamp down destructive behavior. In fact, the American Psychological Association examined fifty research studies, and all of them find that among churchgoing people, crime is dramatically lower than among those who do not believe.

Communities with a strong background in faith, like the Amish, Mormons, and Catholics, have the lowest levels of crime in the United States. The studies also show that increased commitment to prayer, church attendance, and traditional beliefs reduces antisocial behavior, especially among young people.

Based on those conclusions, even if you are a nonbeliever, the encouragement of religion and spirituality should be a major positive in any civilized society.

---

* The execution of Jesus did not help Pontius Pilate. Unrest in Palestine continued. Emperor Tiberius recalled him to Rome. He was then banished to the northern wilderness areas, where he died anonymously.

But in America, that is not the case. So, the question becomes: Why does the mass media in America disparage religion so much?

✪ ✪ ✪

According to a 2025 poll from the Pew Institute, two-thirds of American media reports about Christianity were negative that year—focusing on controversies, scandals, or "Christian nationalism." Other studies say that the majority of journalists are secular people who do not understand what traditional religion is all about. In addition, they often sneer at it. They diminish believers. They look for reasons to criticize a belief in God.

Comedian Bill Maher is the poster boy for this point of view. But there are many others who are not as honest as Maher. They do things in a sneaky way to send a message that religion is stupid. Bill Maher is up front about his atheism. I have no problem with that at all. Thomas Jefferson and James Madison would have no problem with it. All views about religion are protected in the United States unless there is a violent aspect attached to them.

Then there's Hollywood. Having dealt with those people for fifty years, I can tell you there is no more "godless" society on the face of this earth. Money and vanity rule.

A few years ago, I attended Mass at a church on Santa Monica Boulevard in Los Angeles. There were about eight people in the pews. It was an enormous building. Beautiful. Nobody there. In fact, the majority of attentive Catholics in LA are Hispanic. The dominant culture in the entertainment world is the pursuit of individual gratification.

That philosophy gets into the movies. Combined with television news, the message of secularism and anti-religion dominates far more than traditional concepts. No question about it. Hollywood often glorifies violence, substance abuse, infidelity, "alternative lifestyles," and gross materialism. This is what younger Americans in particular see on a daily basis. It is taking a toll.

✪ ✪ ✪

One more intense example.

In June 2023, a group called the Sisters of Perpetual Indulgence were honored by the Los Angeles Dodgers. This group is virulently anti-Catholic. Based in San Francisco, it has actually gone into Catholic churches and defiled the communion wafer. In my opinion, this is a hate group.*

The Dodgers are owned by a billionaire named Mark Walter, a finance guy out of Chicago. Walter is a progressive activist. He had to know that the Sisters of Perpetual Indulgence committed sacrilege against the Catholic Church. Apparently, Walter did not care one bit.

The incident led to demonstrations outside of Dodger Stadium and was an enormous embarrassment to Major League Baseball. Nevertheless, the "Sisters," who are men dressed up as nuns, received their award.

That would never have happened if these guys had attacked Islam. Just picture the backlash if the "Sisters" had invaded a mosque in Los Angeles. Not only would they be in grave danger of reprisals by fanatical Muslims, but the Dodgers would never have allowed the "Sisters" on their property. You know it, and I know it.

So, why is it acceptable for the most powerful Major League Baseball team in the country to mock the Catholic Church?

It is not acceptable. It is shameful. But the story quickly disappeared, aided by the *Los Angeles Times*, which was openly sympathetic to the Sisters of Perpetual Indulgence.

Another brick in the wall.

✪ ✪ ✪

Finally, public schools.

A 2018 study published by the University of Southern California finds the following: Since 1965, the number of religious courses offered

---

* Formed in San Francisco in 1979, the Sisters of Perpetual Indulgence face criticism primarily for their anti-Catholic sentiments, with detractors labeling them a "hate group" for using drag, religious garb, and satire—such as the "Hunky Jesus" contest—to mock Catholic beliefs and figures. Critics argue their performances are offensive and disrespectful to women and religious and sacred symbols.

in elementary through high schools has declined by *75 percent* in the United States. Today, classrooms only teach about the secular aspect of religions, like the clash between Muslims and non-Islamists. There is absolutely no religious explanation or instruction in the public school system.

Therefore, most Americans have no idea what Catholicism is, or Judaism, or Protestant beliefs. They don't know how they were formed. They don't understand what impact they have on society. Students never even think about it. That is a tremendous deficit for this country. It has to change.

There is no reason why public schools cannot teach religion in a historical way. Yes, the ACLU and other atheist groups would fight against that. But so what? History is history. Religion is involved. A phony argument about a separation of church and state could not possibly be upheld by an honest judiciary. Let's have the debate.

But there is no debate. The schools have banished religion. There is very little outcry, even among American clerics. Sadly, many of them, encompassing all religions, are cowards. They do not want to become involved in controversial subjects. So, they hide in their houses of worship. They are ashamed of the scandals that have enveloped the Catholic Church and others. This is a disastrous situation.

A few brave souls are confronting the anti-religion madness in America. Catholic Bishop Robert Barron's Word on Fire ministry fights the good fight on the internet. But the bishop is badly outnumbered. Unless more religious leaders begin confronting the diminishment of faith, America will be harmed forever.

✪ ✪ ✪

In May of 2025, I was invited to visit China, as we have written. That was quite an experience. I saw firsthand how an atheistic country operates. It's pretty simple. There is no value to the individual human life. The "state" rules. In fact, "crimes against the people" can get you vanquished into a Gulag for almost anything. No due process, no fairness, no morality. *You* don't matter. Only the "state" does. There is no such thing as "God."

This was the philosophy of Adolf Hitler, Joseph Stalin, Mao Zedong. Of almost every tyrant the world has ever seen. Human life has no value. You have no soul. There is no heaven or hell. There is no judgment on behavior. The "state" dictates your entire life. Any dissent can result in death.

Do you want to live that way? Does that sound good to you? Does that indicate a pathway to a worthwhile life? Subverting everything for the "good" of the "state"? Giving power-mad leaders complete control?

The rise of secularism will fuel totalitarianism. No doubt in my mind.

✪ ✪ ✪

The concept of Jesus is simple and succinct: All life is sacred. Human beings have a divine right to live in freedom, to make their own decisions. However, after death they will be held accountable for their actions in this world.

In the meantime, the United States of America is on the slide as far as spirituality is concerned. That has led to the rise of substance abuse, sadistic and violent crime, lying, cheating, and policies that are destructive to our children and to the elderly.

When there is no constraint, evil runs wild.

The Founding Fathers knew that. The tenets of Judeo-Christian philosophy in the Constitution are no accident. But we Americans better watch out. The decline of spirituality in this country is enormous.

And if it continues, all of us will be adversely affected.

CHAPTER ELEVEN

Never Too Much

Jeff Bezos has six houses. Wait, there might be *more* than that. But we know of six lavish mansions. So, if you want to visit Jeff, you've got to track him down. He could be in Beverly Hills, Washington, DC, New York City, Miami, or Maui, or on his vast Texas ranch. In total, the tech tycoon's real estate portfolio is valued at $700 million. I don't know if anyone is actually tracking Mr. Bezos, but it must be an exhausting job.

In fact, Jeff might not even be on land. He could be sailing around on his massive yacht called *Koru*—named after a South Pacific shell that, according to the Māori people of Polynesia, represents wealth and success. The four-hundred-foot vessel, built in 2021, cost $500 million and boasts eighteen bedrooms, twenty bathrooms, a ballroom, a movie theater, a helicopter pad, six dining rooms, and a marine bay featuring twelve Jet Skis. The boat burns six hundred gallons of diesel fuel per *hour*. No time for "climate change" when sailing the *Koru*.

Or, Jeff Bezos might be jetting to far-off destinations in his Gulfstream G700 or his fleet of other planes. For Jeff, there is no limit, including the sky.

The entrepreneur made his money honestly as far as we can tell.

He's worth about $250 billion as the founder and chief executive of Amazon, the world's largest e-commerce and cloud computing company.

In 1994, Bezos was living in San Francisco running a hedge fund. He succeeded. He then moved to Seattle with a $10,000 loan from family members.

There, he started Amazon.com as an online bookstore. Amazon quickly grew, selling all kind of merchandise that the company then delivered to the doors of customers. It was an almost-immediate success.

In 1997, Amazon went public and Bezos was on his way to becoming a billionaire. He was kind of a geeky guy. Very tech oriented, not so smooth in social situations. Over the years, however, Bezos changed. He acquired a flashy girlfriend, whom he eventually married in Venice, Italy.

That wedding is estimated to have cost about $70 million.*

Sorry I missed it.

Bezos also hired a private trainer and got into shape. Today, he zips around following the philosophy of Carly Simon: "You're where you should be all the time."†

In addition, the tech titan has purchased *The Washington Post* and, with an eye on paying less in taxes, become a citizen of Florida, one of the few states that does not impose a levy on personal income.

Bezos is the epitome of what Bernie Sanders calls an "oligarch." But, here's the dilemma. The Amazon founder earned his money the old-fashioned way. He worked hard, took chances, and had vision. It is *his* cash. So, under the US Constitution, he can spend it any way he wants, as long as he doesn't break the law.

---

* Jeff Bezos and Lauren Sánchez celebrated a lavish, three-day wedding in Venice, Italy, June 26–28, 2025, costing an estimated $70 million. The star-studded event featured a ceremony at the private San Giorgio Maggiore island, included exclusive parties at the historic Arsenal, and attracted top celebrities like Oprah, Tom Brady, and Kim Kardashian.

† The lyric comes from the 1972 Carly Simon song "You're So Vain."

In my opinion, that is *not* a good look. The average salary in America is about $67,000. Nearly forty million US citizens live below the poverty line—that is, they earn less than $31,000 a year. That's a lot of folks. I don't know what they think collectively about Bezos spending billions of dollars on himself. That would be an interesting study.

One diversion here. In Britain, 21 percent of the folks live below the poverty line. In France, it's 16 percent. In the US, 11 percent. The fact is that most people in the world struggle for their currency, including in the good old USA.

The average American under the age of forty has less than $5,000 in the bank. That figure rises to $15,000 for senior citizens. So, you can see that while most people live fairly well here, lavish spending is beyond the reach of 95 percent of the population. In fact, only 2 percent of Americans earn more than $500,000 a year.

Jeff Bezos is one of a thousand billionaires in the United States. There are 350 million American citizens. Obviously, Bezos and his fiscal pals are extremely rare. But that does not matter to the propagandists. People like Congresswoman Alexandria Ocasio-Cortez blame society's ills on the ultrawealthy. Many Americans actually believe that. Thus, the rise of socialism.

✪ ✪ ✪

You may have heard the name Warren Buffett. He's not quite as rich as Bezos, clocking in at $150 billion in total worth. Buffett is an investor. A conservative one. He is ninety-five years old, and his company, Berkshire Hathaway, is a financial titan. Total market value: $370 billion.

But Warren Buffett does not flash his wealth. In fact, he has given more than $200 billion to charity over his lifetime. He lives in a humble house in Omaha, Nebraska, that he bought in 1958: five bedrooms, two and a half bathrooms. He drives a twenty-year-old Cadillac. He pays fifteen dollars for a haircut.

Again, both Buffett and Jeff Bezos made their money legally. They can do what they want with their assets. But for me, Buffett's strategy is kinder. That's because throwing your wealth in the face of millions of working people is dubious, to say the least. I could not hang around with Jeff Bezos. It looks to me like he is a venal guy, and the wife seems to be quite happy with the lavish ride. I may be unfair here. I don't know these people. But they feed into the concept that the United States of America is full of greedy, self-absorbed folks who exploit our country for their own self-aggrandizement. As I mentioned, that feeds into the Socialist/Communist movement that wants to do away with individual achievement and have the government call the financial shots.

Bernie Sanders is a Communist. So is New York City Mayor Zohran Mamdani. In his inauguration address in January 2026, Mamdani suggested that self-reliance is stupid. "Collectivism" is what this country needs:

> Many of these people have been betrayed by the established order. But in our administration, their needs will be met. Their hopes and dreams and interests will be reflected transparently in government. They will shape our future.
>
> And if for too long these communities have existed as distinct from one another, we will draw this city closer together. We will replace the frigidity of rugged individualism with the warmth of collectivism. If our campaign demonstrated that the people of New York yearn for solidarity, then let this government foster it.

Again, that means Mamdani and his fellow Commies will tell all of *us* what we can and can't have. The far left is capitalizing on jealousy.

And Jeff Bezos is helping them.

✪ ✪ ✪

In 1987, a movie called *Wall Street* was a big hit. You remember Michael Douglas starring as a fictional character named Gordon Gekko. The famous line from the film is:

> Greed, for lack of a better word, is good. Greed is right, greed works. Greed clarifies, cuts through, and captures the essence of the evolutionary spirit.

To me, that is a complete distortion. Greed erodes kindness. It causes people to veer away from what is *really* important: Helping others. If you are a "give me everything" type of person, there's not a lot left over, at least emotionally, for anyone else.

There is a verse in the Bible that says, "It is easier for a camel to go through the eye of a needle than for a rich person to enter the kingdom of God."*

Interesting historical fact. The "eye of the needle" reference was to a very small gate leading into Jerusalem. A camel could not possibly pass through it. The message to the folks back then was, if you allow the pursuit of money to define you, bad things will happen. And in my opinion, that is true.

✪ ✪ ✪

One word: generosity. That is the antidote to greed. Now, I am going to tell you a tale of two foundations. The Clinton Charitable Group versus the O'Reilly Charitable Enterprise.

The Winifred and William O'Reilly Foundation is named after my parents, who had little money, but were generous people. They gave to the church, helped neighbors, and provided for their two children.

After hitting it big in the media, I understood I had an obligation to begin an organized pattern of helping other people financially. This is what is preached in Roman Catholicism and other religions. You are compelled to "give back."

Over the years, my foundation has donated millions of dollars to benefit disadvantaged children, provide educational scholarships, help severely wounded military people, and develop mentoring projects.

---

* Matthew 19:24 (English Standard Version).

COURTESY OF THE AUTHOR

Backstage with Bill Maher

JEFFREY R. STAAB/©CBS/COURTESY EVERETT COLLECTION

Friendly sparring with David Letterman

WILLIAM KIDD BY SIR JAMES THORNHILL. PUBLIC DOMAIN.

Captain William Kidd, a buccaneer

COURTESY THE FLORIDA INTERNATIONAL UNIVERSITY (FIU)

The Castaways Hotel and Wreck Bar on Miami Beach

Nancy Pelosi, tearing up President Trump's
State of the Union address

Rush Limbaugh receiving the Medal of Freedom
from the First Lady, Melania Trump

COURTESY EVERETT COLLECTION

COURTESY EVERETT COLLECTION

Ozzie and Harriet and *Leave It to Beaver* were the sitcoms that defined traditional family life in the 1950s.

COURTESY EVERETT COLLECTION

Doris Day, a class act on and offscreen

ZUMAPRESS.COM

Barbara Walters: a true professional

COURTESY OF THE AUTHOR

Bill O'Reilly during his 2025 trip
to Beijing, China

COURTESY OF THE AUTHOR, REPHOTOGRAPHED BY ROBERT JUDE PUGLISI

The O'Reilly family in Levittown, New York

COURTESY OF THE AUTHOR, REPHOTOGRAPHED BY ROBERT JUDE PUGLISI

The O'Reilly family

COURTESY OF THE AUTHOR, REPHOTOGRAPHED BY ROBERT JUDE PUGLISI

Bill O'Reilly at Marist College

COURTESY OF THE AUTHOR, REPHOTOGRAPHED BY ROBERT JUDE PUGLISI

Bill O'Reilly at Marist College

COURTESY OF THE AUTHOR, REPHOTOGRAPHED BY ROBERT JUDE PUGLISI

Bill O'Reilly teaches high school in Opa-locka, Florida

I take no money from the foundation. Many of my viewers and readers have offered to donate, but I do not accept because I don't want this to be a business. Every nickel comes from me. I take no expenses, other than tax filing.

My friends say I'm trying to buy my way into heaven. And that might be part of it. Certainly, I have deficits and must atone constantly. But, in seriousness, that's not my intention. I am happy to help other people. I don't need a yacht. I don't need ten homes. I don't need a Ferrari. In fact, when I walk into any store in the country, there is absolutely *nothing* I want to buy. I don't possess the material gene. I'm glad I don't have it.

Now, let's take a look at the Clinton Foundation.

This is a very difficult analysis because of tax-privacy shields. I cannot get copies of the Clinton books. But I have looked into the situation, and some things are very clear.

The organization is led by former President Bill Clinton and his daughter Chelsea, and the chief board member is Hillary Rodham Clinton. At this point, it looks like the Clinton Foundation has raised more than $2 billion. That money comes from a variety of sources, including foreign governments. Much of it was assembled while Hillary Clinton served as Secretary of State under Barack Obama.

The Clinton Foundation operates globally, donating money to causes related to healthcare, climate change, economic development, and various programs for children. The charity has donated tens of millions of dollars to Haiti. That money has been largely stolen. I've donated money to Haiti as well, funding a dental clinic there for the poor. However, my cash went directly to the nuns who run the operation. It was not given to any Haitian officials. That was no accident.*

Haiti is one of the most corrupt places on earth. Billions of dollars have poured into the country, which has a population of eleven

* The charity I'm referring to is the Haitian Health Foundation, an organization founded in 1982 whose mission is to improve the health and well-being of women, children, and families in Haiti through healthcare, education, and community development.

million. At this point, there is no functioning government, no infrastructure, and, tragically, most of the donations have disappeared. I actually told President Clinton this would happen at a conversation we had while watching a game at Yankee Stadium years ago. I also told the rock singer Bono, who has funneled a lot of money to Haiti, that he, too, was being conned. Same thing with actor Sean Penn. On my visits to Haiti, it was clear: Corruption was off the chart.

Now that doesn't mean the Clinton Foundation did anything wrong. But if you ask people for donations, there is an obligation to try exceedingly hard to make sure the money is used in a responsible, humanitarian way.

In 2015, the latest data I have, it was revealed that Bill, Hillary, and Chelsea Clinton were paid almost $27 million in speaking fees tied to the Clinton charity. Again, I have not done an audit, but it looks like the three of them were able to keep that money for themselves. I cannot prove that.

In addition, from 2003 to 2012, the Clintons spent $50 million on travel associated with their foundation. They flew around the world on private jets raising money. But along the way, they could do any leisure activities they wanted. That is dubious, to say the least. Charitable money funding unsupervised worldwide travel doesn't seem noble. Again, it would be unfair to accuse the Clintons of using their charity for personal benefit. But the data raises troubling questions.

✪ ✪ ✪

Working Americans are the most generous people in the world. In fact, 75 percent of us donate money to at least one charitable cause a year. Second place goes to Canada, where 50 percent of the population gives to charity. So, you can see we are far and away the most benevolent society on earth when it comes to helping others.

Annually, US citizens give away approximately $600 billion. That is an amazing figure when you consider that most Americans have to struggle financially because of the high cost of housing as well as other essentials of life.

We should all be proud that American tradition is steeped in helping the less fortunate. It is a historical fact that the US has spent trillions of taxpayer dollars trying to better this world. Billions of foreign nationals owe *us* their freedom.

That is very important to remember, especially when you hear "hate America" rhetoric, which applies to our next story.

✪ ✪ ✪

During the Iraq and Afghanistan wars, thousands of American military people were coming home with devastating injuries. Many lost arms and legs, were blinded, totally lost control of their functions. It was absolutely brutal.

In my position as the lead television anchor in the country, I decided to do something about it. The federal government takes care of wounded vets, but not to any great extent. For example, these disabled military folks were not able to purchase high-tech help because it is so expensive. A company in Minnesota developed what was called a Trackchair. This is an amazing machine. Disabled people can use it to go pretty much anywhere: to the beach, to hunt in the woods, to have mobility when they otherwise could not move around.

A charity called the Independence Fund out of North Carolina approached me with a request. Let's publicize these Trackchairs, which cost about $18,000 each, and raise enough money to buy them for the severely wounded.

It took me about ten seconds to agree. Again, not trying to be noble, but who wouldn't say yes?

And so, we embarked on a great adventure. My idea was to have all five living presidents at the time, Jimmy Carter, Bill Clinton, both Bushes, and Barack Obama, sign a dozen pictures of them all together at the opening of George W. Bush's library in Texas.

As I mentioned in chapter 3, President Carter was a dissenter. But we threatened to embarrass him, and he finally signed.

After a few weeks, we auctioned off the pictures, but not before duplicating them and selling each for twenty-five dollars. Ready? We raised more than $30 million to purchase the Trackchairs. Every vet and some police officers who needed the high-tech assistance received it. At this point the Independence Fund has awarded more than three thousand Trackchairs thanks to the donations of individual Americans.

That kind of largesse is what America desperately needs to continue. The regular folks banding together for a common cause, helping those who need help. Who *deserve* help.

The Trackchair program was the high point of my media career.

✪ ✪ ✪

In the 1980s, the duo Hall and Oates released "Possession Obsession." The tune issued a direct message—as John Oates sang:

> *"You know there's something you need . . .*
> *To fill the space inside of yourself, With money, love or power . . ."*

The Hall and Oates hit raised a simple question: Who exactly needs to spend billions of dollars on themselves? You may have a "right" to do that, but is it the *right* thing to do?

The answer is no. Generosity should be foremost in the minds of affluent people. Not personal gratification.

Right now, the United States government owes close to $40 trillion in debt, which is mostly held by China. Yet the Democratic Party and the left wing in America want to spend more money, which is putting the entire country in fiscal jeopardy. Much of the spending is directed toward helping poor Americans. That is noble. But, unfortunately, as exposed by Elon Musk and the Department of Government Efficiency (that's DOGE), billions of dollars are wasted by the federal and state governments every year. The politicians are simply too lazy to watch the money. This is not charity. This is fraud.

The truth is simple: It is easy to con many American voters into supporting projects that are described as charitable. But as we've seen in Haiti and other countries, it's not enough to give. You have to be responsible to the donors. And that is not happening, as we saw in the Minnesota daycare con.*

This has got to stop.

On the personal front, it's on us. Those who give money to help other people. We have to investigate, calculate, and write checks to enterprises that really help the folks. It's not that hard.

Every charity I donate to must answer all my questions about where the money is going. If they don't, the donations stop. There is a discipline here.

✪ ✪ ✪

A few years back, the marching band for Talladega University, a mostly Black school in Alabama, won the national championship competition and was invited to participate in the Macy's Thanksgiving Day Parade. But the college could not afford to send the band to New York City.

I heard about it; I called the school. They explained the kids were brokenhearted. I wrote the check. I donated the money directly to the university with the mandate that they use it to send the students to participate in the parade. The administration complied.

The Winifred and William O'Reilly Foundation covered the expenses. Then I wrote a few other checks for scholarships to Talladega. I also gave a million dollars to Marist College, my alma mater, to help students with financial aid. As a working-class guy from Levittown, Marist did me a tremendous amount of good when I attended in the late 1960s. The school was designed to help working-class and poor kids rise up. So, I was happy to give the college the money, and I named the scholarship after my favorite professor, Doctor Peter O'Keefe.

---

* In December 2025, independent journalists posted a viral video alleging that a number of Minnesota childcare centers receiving public subsidies and private donations were empty or not providing services at all. That video prompted heavy public attention. In response, Tim Walz, Minnesota governor and former vice presidential candidate, suspended his campaign for reelection. The total scheme is valued at $9 billion in wasted funds and fraud.

Unfortunately, the school changed administrators and became "woke." They began denying due process procedures, used skin color to make decisions, and generally supported far-left progressive thought. I was appalled. So, I asked for my money back. The university refused. But I don't regret the donation. It helped a ton of disadvantaged students. I *do* very much regret the change in outlook at Marist.

One final story.

Cardinal Timothy Dolan of New York invited me for breakfast one day. That is never a good sign for an affluent Catholic. You know what's coming. The cardinal, a charming guy, asked me to help him buy a series of rowhouses in Brooklyn. He said he needed the real estate to shelter the very poor. I gave him another million bucks.

I'm not telling you all this so that you will think better of me. I made the decisions based upon what I thought was the "right thing to do." After I gave the church the million for the Brooklyn buy, I never heard anything about it. There was no follow-up at all. To this day, I have no idea what happened. That's kind of my fault. I could have made some noise. But I decided to let it go.

Again, I'm glad I gave Cardinal Dolan the money. As long as I'm here on this planet, if I can help, I'm going to help. And you might consider doing the same thing. You're not always going to be rewarded, things will go south, but intent is everything.

✪✪✪

Finally, as mentioned, I have trouble being around the "fat cats." That's on me. My father struggled in the marketplace, and, at times, so have I. So-called nepo babies drive me crazy. These offspring of the wealthy parade around like they're something special. Not all of them, but enough to get on my annoyance chart. I often direct scorn toward nepo babies.

Once again, I am generalizing. But I do it to make a vivid point. There is far too much excess on display in America. However, I know a number of wealthy people, like Ken Langone, founder of Home

Depot, MacKenzie Scott, ex-wife of the aforementioned Jeff Bezos, and hundreds of others, who are donating billions to help their fellow human beings. In my mind, these people will be able to negotiate their way through the "needle's eye."

I hope that for myself as well.

CHAPTER TWELVE

Mythology in America

Jack Nicholson was adamant that Tom Cruise could not "handle the truth." That classic scene from the movie *A Few Good Men* has now become a national reality. Many will not accept what is happening right before our eyes. We don't want to. It makes us uncomfortable. The biblical instruction "The truth will set you free" is not held in high regard any longer.

This is a major problem for America. Here is the best example I can provide: the disastrous four-year presidency of Joe Biden. My analysis is not partisan or party-centric. It is absolutely true. I hope you can handle it.

✪✪✪

President Biden was inaugurated on January 20, 2021. He defeated Donald Trump by an electoral count of 306 to 232 and won the popular vote by seven million ballots. Almost immediately there were charges of fraud. Many Trump supporters believed that scenario because they *wanted* to believe it. As a journalist, I was open-minded to the possibility that criminal activity may have taken place. I stated that repeatedly. I also said I was waiting for solid information about where the fraud occurred and how it was perpetrated. I knew it would take time to assemble that kind of information. So, I counseled patience on the part of people who did not believe Joe Biden won the election legitimately. I told them to wait until facts were provided that would demonstrate massive voting fraud.

We are still waiting.

President Trump believes the election was "stolen" from him. This is not a phony posture. He fervently thinks that widespread criminality put Joe Biden into the Oval Office. As recently as December 2025, Mr. Trump told me that he had assembled evidence to prove his case.

I was respectful, saying, "I hope you will give me what you have first, Mr. President."

Again, I am waiting.

✪✪✪

President Biden strode into office and immediately issued Executive Orders that allowed as many as fifteen million foreign nationals to cross the southern border without supervision. Those orders are the most harmful in our nation's history, in my opinion. The border chaos has cost the US approximately $1 trillion to this point. That figure grows by $200 billion each year. Foreign criminals have wreaked havoc in many areas of the country, like California and New York. All of those things are true. Very few of them were reported by the corporate media. No acknowledgment at all by the Democratic Party about Biden's folly.

Kamala Harris lost the 2024 election to Donald Trump because she went on television and said she would not change *one* policy implemented by Joe Biden. That was it for the vice president. Any fair-minded person in America must know how pernicious the open-border situation was. The fact that Harris apparently doesn't believe that doomed her presidential ambitions.

Despite the border collapse, Joe Biden was 100 percent backed by his party. The media often lied about the situation, creating a myth that Mr. Biden was an effective president when he was not. In fact, Joe Biden visited the southern border just *twice* in four years, spending a total of six hours surveying the calamity. Six hours! That is simply incomprehensible.

With a disaster unfolding in our country, Mr. Biden could not be bothered to even look at it.

✪ ✪ ✪

Competency is the largest myth surrounding the Biden presidency, but there are scores more. Perhaps the most dangerous, to me and you, is the failure to monitor the president's mental and physical condition.

The leaders of the Democratic Party, and some of Biden's own cabinet members, simply did not tell the truth about the boss—which was an amazing display of deceit.

Chuck Schumer: "Joe's great, it's all right-wing propaganda!"
Elizabeth Warren: "He's as sharp as ever."
Alejandro Mayorkas: "I can't keep up with him!"

Mayorkas, of course, was the head of Homeland Security who presided over the disastrous border policy. After Kamala lost the election, old Alejandro disappeared. In fact, we can't find any sign that he even has a job. The word around Georgetown is that he plays a lot of handball.

With his résumé, that is understandable.

Even worse was Joe Biden's White House physician, Kevin O'Connor. In July 2025, he was called before the House Oversight Committee to explain his positive evaluations of the president's medical situation. Incredibly, O'Connor invoked the Fifth Amendment. He refused to answer any questions on the grounds he might *incriminate himself*. Are you kidding me? The nation was grossly misled about a Chief Executive's mental acuity and physical condition and his own doctor lawyers up?

We later learned, shortly after Biden left office, that he had been diagnosed with stage IV advanced prostate cancer that had metastasized to his bones. The fact that no one in the country knew that is something every American should be concerned about.

Why? Because it's dangerous to the nation.

✪ ✪ ✪

If you study Joe Biden's career, you know the entire history is one big myth. This is a man who associated gladly with segregationists like Senators Robert Byrd from West Virginia and Strom Thurmond of South Carolina. They were buddies. He loved them. They loved him. What the deuce is that about? Years later, when Biden was running for president, he's supposed to be the reincarnation of Martin Luther King Jr.? This is a myth accepted by his party and tens of millions of Americans who voted for him.

Then there's "working-class" Joe. The guy from Scranton. The hard-scrabble life that he was born into rapidly disappeared once he was elected to the US Senate at the age of twenty-nine. In my opinion, the evidence is overwhelming that, as vice president, he enriched himself and his family by making a series of foreign "deals" allowing his son and brother access to corrupt people in Ukraine, China, and beyond. This is the story of Hunter Biden.

Altogether, the Biden family amassed millions of dollars because of Joe Biden's elected positions.

In addition, Biden himself has amassed a real estate portfolio valued at more than $7 million and now lives a life of luxury. To be fair, most presidents capitalize on their profile. Gerald Ford, for example, had very little money coming out of Michigan. Before he died, he had acquired a fortune, including properties in Palm Springs, California, and Vail, Colorado. So, Joe Biden is not unique in this category.

But the way Mr. Biden was portrayed, both in and out of office, is absolutely a myth. There isn't anything true about his narrative. As a young senator, he opposed the desegregation of public schools. In November 1993, Biden voted for extremely stringent crime enforcement. He wanted to throw people off welfare. Maybe Joe saw the liberal light in his senior years. I guess that's possible. But his own party and the corrupt media whitewashed his history. They did not tell the American public what was *really* happening inside the White House or what Biden had embraced in his past.

✪ ✪ ✪

Here is the truth. Joe Biden, on any given day, was mentally incapacitated. It fell to a combination of Barack Obama and the actor George Clooney to finally lift the curtain and expose the myth of the Biden administration.

You may remember that in June 2024, Clooney hosted a major Hollywood fundraiser for President Biden's reelection campaign. Speakers included Julia Roberts, Barbra Streisand, Jimmy Kimmel, Barack Obama, and Biden himself. In total, the event generated $28 million for the Democrat.

But the Los Angeles appearance did not go as planned. Toward the end of the evening, a visibly confused Biden seemingly froze in place. Video went viral on social media showing Barack Obama delicately grabbing his former vice president's arm and leading him off the stage.

Anyone with an elderly parent or grandparent could immediately understand what was happening.

George Clooney himself was silent about the incident for three weeks.

However, after Biden's disastrous debate performance against Donald Trump on June 27, 2024, George decided to go public. On July 10, the actor penned an op-ed for *The New York Times* titled, "I Love Joe Biden, But We Need a New Nominee."

> I love Joe Biden. As a senator. As a vice president and as president. I consider him a friend, and I believe in him. . . .
>
> But the one battle he cannot win is the fight against time. None of us can. It's devastating to say it, but the Joe Biden I was with three weeks ago at the fund-raiser was not the Joe "big F-ing deal" Biden of 2010. He wasn't even the Joe Biden of 2020. He was the same man we all witnessed at the debate. . . .

Our party leaders need to stop telling us that 51 million people didn't see what we just saw. We're all so terrified by the prospect of a second Trump term that we've opted to ignore every warning sign.

It is inconceivable to me that Clooney would write that letter without direct approval from his friend Barack Obama. That missive sealed Biden's fate; Joe had to go. But he didn't want to. Let me amend that. His wife, Jill, did not want him to leave the White House. Nevertheless, extraordinary pressure grew, and eleven days later, he resigned from the campaign. On his way out the door, Biden handed Kamala Harris the Democratic Party nomination. She had not won any primaries or earned a single vote.

✪ ✪ ✪

My favorite Biden story is when he vehemently claimed his uncle "Bosie" was eaten by cannibals. The man's real name was Ambrose Finnegan. He flew single-engine planes during World War II in the Pacific theater. Unfortunately, Mr. Finnegan was forced to ditch his aircraft on May 14, 1944. President Biden said the incident took place over New Guinea, which has a long history of cannibalism dating back thousands of years.

But in reality, "Bosie" hit the ocean. His body was never recovered. Sharks *can* be cannibals. But in this case, the Pentagon clarified the entire situation:

> 2ND LT. AMBROSE J FINNEGAN: Unaccounted For. For unknown reasons, his plane was forced to ditch in the ocean. The engine failed at low altitude, and the aircraft's nose hit the water hard. Three men failed to emerge from the sinking wreck and were lost in the crash.

So, unless the "cannibals" of New Guinea had first-rate scuba gear, it might have been hard for them to consume the hapless Ambrose. No matter. The pro-Democratic press ate up Biden's story.

As Jimmy Durante once said, "I have a million of 'em."

✪✪✪

Mythologizing presidents is not new. What *is* new is the media now gleefully participating if the candidate fits their ideology. But throughout history, some major whoppers have found their way into the folklore.

George Washington is one of the greatest American heroes of all time; we all know that. A brilliant general and a president who did his very best to get the new republic up and running. But the mythology around Washington is incredible. The man, apparently, never made a mistake, was always in a good mood, and was dashing, perspicacious, and kind to every animal he ever met.

The truth, however, is a little bit different. This is not to say Washington was not a first-rate hero. He was. But if you read my book *Confronting the Presidents*, you will find out that George's mom did not like him! And it all had to do with money.

Mary Ball Washington was widowed but remained on the vast Virgina estate of her deceased husband, Augustine. Mary could not afford to maintain the plantation. So, she wanted money from her son George, who didn't have much cash on hand. His wife, Martha Washington, controlled the funds while the general was out defeating the redcoats. This did not please Mary Ball, who began writing letters to Virginia newspapers calling her son "cheap" and "mean."

Not good.

General Washington was very agitated by this. On February 15, 1787, he wrote to his mother:

> *My sincere, and pressing advice to you is, to break up housekeeping, hire out all the rest of your servants except a man and a maid and live with one of your Children. This would relieve you entirely from the cares of this world, and leave your mind at ease to reflect, undisturbedly on that which aught to come.*

Upon receipt of this letter, Washington's mother responded, "Fine, I'll come live with you and Martha in Mount Vernon."

George quickly wrote back:

> *My House is at your service . . .* but *I am sure and candour requires me to say it will never answer your purposes, in any shape whatsoever—for in truth it may be compared to a well resorted tavern, as scarcely any strangers who are going from north to south, or from south to north do not spend a day or two at it—This would, were you to be an inhabitant of it, oblige you to do one of 3 things, 1st to be always dressing to appear in company, 2d to come into in a dishabille or 3d to be as it were a prisoner in your own chamber.*

The breach between George Washington and his mom never healed. In fact, the nation's first president did not even attend her funeral.

✪ ✪ ✪

Then there's Abraham Lincoln. While practicing law in Illinois, Lincoln represented a Kentucky slave owner—a man named Robert Matson. Five of Matson's slaves were traveling with him in Lincoln's home state when they absconded. Illinois was free soil. The chaos wound up in court. Lincoln put forth that owners of "property," which slaves were considered at the time, could take their "cargo" anywhere in the country without local interference.

Lincoln lost. The court ruled that slavery was a "contravention of the Illinois Constitution." The Black family was declared free.

Now, you have never heard that story in any classroom or discussion about Abraham Lincoln. At least I don't think you have. The mythology surrounding Abe, like George Washington, paints him as an absolute saint.

Which he turned out to be. President Lincoln lost his life because he was so adamant about ending slavery in the United States. The heinous racist John Wilkes Booth was motivated to kill Lincoln at Ford's Theatre in Washington, DC, because the president supported freedom for Black people. If you read my book *Killing Lincoln*, you will see that the man's entire body broke down as he tried to banish slavery and win the Civil War. He went through a horrendous ordeal and, in my opinion, is the best president the nation has ever had.

The moral of this story is simple: people change. Redemption is possible. But there is a subtext. Myths surrounding famous Americans, like Abraham Lincoln and George Washington, become truth.

But that's not true at all, is it?

✪ ✪ ✪

My favorite bit of mythology surrounds Teddy Roosevelt, who very much disliked being called Teddy. It reminded him of his sickly childhood. So, you had to call him Theodore, or Colonel, or Mr. President. Not Teddy. Anyway, Roosevelt was an extraordinary man who had very common problems. His first wife, Alice, died after childbirth. His second wife, Edith, was a good woman but could not control the six rambunctious Roosevelt children. Especially the eldest, teenager Alice Roosevelt, named after her deceased mother.

Alice was what they call a juvenile delinquent. They didn't have that term back then, but trust me, she fits the description. To the horror of her father, she pronounced herself to be a "pagan," saying Christianity was "sheer voodoo." As Theodore Roosevelt was a traditional Protestant, that did not sit well with him.

Then there was Alice's social life. Apparently, she was very fond of accompanying unmarried young men through the streets of Washington, DC, where they partied hardy. On more than one occasion, she had to be corralled by the local authorities, who returned her to the White House. Alice did not like that very much. So, she began sneaking boys *into* the "people's house." In addition, she enjoyed smoking cigarettes. When her parents banned that practice, Alice snuck up to the roof of the White House to inhale. I don't think she chewed tobacco, but I wouldn't put it past her.

Anyway, President Theodore Roosevelt has a famous quote about his rebellious daughter:

"I can either run the country or I can control Alice, but I cannot possibly do both!"

Final Alice story.

In 1909, when the Roosevelt family was moving out of the White House, she buried a voodoo doll of the new First Lady, Nelly Taft, in the front yard. As the Tafts moved in, they discovered the frightening figurine and banished Alice from the premises forever.

What they didn't know was that Alice may have also left a live snake, which she had named Emily Spinach, inside the White House.

And you think you have problems with your kids?

✪ ✪ ✪

So, you can see that accurate reporting about American presidents has always been a challenge for the political parties as well as the media, which is now at a level of corruption never before seen.

Obviously, covering up presidential deficits is wrong—as all dishonesty is. But in today's world, the stakes are so high that we *must* know to whom we are giving power.

Mythologizing harms everyone.

✪ ✪ ✪

It would be a lot easier to deal with the myth problem in America if the citizenry were better educated. But it isn't. According to the National Assessment of Educational Progress (NAEP), only 13 percent of eighth graders are proficient in American history. As Sam Cooke once sang, "Don't know much about history." Sadly, that has come true. The reason the urchins are clueless is because history, geography, and civics are no longer emphasized in our schools. Here's some backup for that claim.

Only 18 percent of students can identify slavery as the central cause of the Civil War. Only 7 percent can name the first four presidents of the United States. Only 22 percent know what the Bill of Rights is.

With an ignorant population emerging in the United States, it will be far easier to mythologize *everything*. And we are seeing that on social media. Many younger Americans, especially, believe what they read on these stupid internet sites. There are no standards of accuracy. If you have a podcast, you can say anything. If you have a website, you can publish anything. Who's going to stop you? Even if you defame someone, you're up against "freedom of expression." You can sue, but it will cost you tens of thousands of dollars.

All totalitarian governments want to keep their populations ill-informed. The Third Reich, the Soviet Union, Red China, Vietnam: All banished truthful education. Propaganda was the rule of the realm.

Here in the United States, we don't have that situation. What we do have is a gross dereliction of duty. The school boards simply don't care if students know anything about their country. If they did, we would not have these horrendous test scores.

This has to change, because if it doesn't, we are going to get people in power who make Joe Biden look like a Mensa member. Mythology will dominate, not facts, not reality. The population can be easily manipulated if frames of reference are scant.

As a historian, I find this heartbreaking. I drilled into my kids the essence of their country. I have a personal library that is stunning. We don't debate things until we look them up. No emotion. All conversations in my house are fact based.

That's the way it should be in every American home. But it's not. And I am sounding the alarm.

CHAPTER THIRTEEN

A Matter of Respect

The unintended consequences of disrespectful behavior are staggering for America. Most conflict stems from a lack of courtesy—both on personal and policy matters. The two political parties now *loathe* each other because of boorish conduct on both sides. The media is a hateful mess that tries to destroy people it doesn't like. Relationships fracture at an alarming rate because civility disappears when opinions differ. Even families are falling apart over a lack of respect.

This is hurting the United States in dramatic ways.

The question now becomes: How do we change this trend?

But who am I to even address this? Many feel I am an absolute Visigoth. And at times, I might have leaned in that direction.

But onward we go.

✪ ✪ ✪

On March 28, 2017, I woke up early to appear on the *Fox and Friends* broadcast. I was promoting something; I can't even remember what it was. But before we got to that, I was asked a question about California Congresswoman Maxine Waters and her extreme left-wing views. The program played a clip of her attacking President Trump.

It wasn't anything unusual from Ms. Waters, who is an ardent liberal. So, I decided to make a joke of it. I said something like this: It was hard for me to pay attention to what she was saying because her hair so closely resembles that of singer James Brown.

Which was true. The Godfather of Soul and Maxine Waters had similar coiffures—at least at the time. However, my "analysis" could be interpreted as disrespectful. I didn't mean it that way. I was just having a few chuckles at Waters's expense.

Then all hell broke loose.

Almost immediately, the left-wing media accused me of being "racist," as did Congresswoman Waters herself. I couldn't quite figure that out. What does a hair resemblance have to do with skin color? But that was the narrative. Even *The New York Times* ran with it.

A few hours later, I was in my office when Fox executive Bill Shine, a good guy, strolled in looking earnest. I knew what was coming. Everybody in the building understood I meant no malice toward Maxine Waters and that my comments were just another way for the liberal media to bash Fox News. I *should* have known that myself. And therein lies the problem.

My awareness of possible disrespect was not what it should have been. I make no excuses. So, I apologized for an immature comment, which it was. At that point, Waters was seventy-eight years old. Why is O'Reilly mocking an elderly woman who is having a bad wig day? Why was that happening? I had no rationale.

The incident quickly diminished. The next day I was attacked for something else. That was the game plan for the far left. Just hammer O'Reilly ceaselessly and maybe we can get rid of him. Right out of the Saul Alinsky playbook.*

Since the Waters incident, I have done some thinking about how to present material without being boorish. It's not that hard. However, in the age of "woke," if you mock someone, especially a minority person,

* Saul Alinsky (1909–1972) was a fanatical progressive activist from Chicago. In 1971, he published a book called *Rules for Radicals*. In it, he outlines a tactic called "Keep the Pressure On" where nonstop personal attacks and public accusations are used to discredit and distract members of the "opposition."

you will be accused of dastardly behavior. There's no question about it. So, forget about satirical references to anyone outside of White men. Those guys, you can crush all day long.

✪ ✪ ✪

There are many ways to be disrespectful. You can be verbally inappropriate. You can ignore people. You can be deceitful. Gossip is always disrespectful. Always.

Unfortunately, alongside baseball, hearsay is a national pastime in the US. We routinely run down other folks without due process or any sensitivity whatsoever. This weakens our collective society. Casual malice is no longer considered a personality defect.

Okay, the lecture is over. Here are some examples of disrespect.

✪ ✪ ✪

I have had twenty number one *New York Times* bestsellers. In every case, there is an extensive marketing campaign to bring awareness of the book to the public. I'm sure you've seen me on programs touting my work. In most cases, the shows that invite me on have been respectful. In most cases.

One of my favorite interviews was with David Letterman, who is an ardent liberal. I was promoting my autobiography, *A Bold Fresh Piece of Humanity*. There I am on the cover looking angelic at my first communion. Dave pointed that out, then called me a "thug." The audience reacted, as of course Letterman knew they would. Then, I turned to Dave and asked a very simple question: "Can you back that up?"

Dave could not. Point to O'Reilly.

Letterman knew he was being disrespectful, and down the road, he actually said that I was one of his favorite guests because I didn't take any guff from him. I actually like David Letterman. He put me on *sixteen* times. Each was very entertaining.

✪ ✪ ✪

Today, things are different. On the network programs, there is a passive disrespect that is obvious if you think about it. I'm going to pick on CBS News anchor Jane Pauley to explain how that works.

Ms. Pauley began her network career on the *Today* show in 1976. She was very successful. Viewers perceived her as a nice person with traditional values. She had a good, long run on NBC.

Presently, she anchors the *CBS Sunday Morning* program. That is one of the few shows that actually has an effect on book sales. People who wake up early to watch are interested in a variety of topics. So, authors like myself want to talk with Jane.

Strangely, I have never met her. She is one of the few broadcasters I don't know. She's never said anything bad about me, as far as I can tell. She's married to left-wing cartoonist Garry Trudeau, but so what? Therefore, I figured I would approach Ms. Pauley directly to see if she was interested in talking about *Confronting Evil*. I have a lot of friends at CBS. One of them provided me with her direct email. I wrote a very polite note, saying there was no urgency, but I would like to meet her and, perhaps, talk about the book on her program. My thumb hit the button, and the message zipped over to Jane.

She never replied.

That is disrespectful. When you are a professional in a small business like the national media, the rules of the road are you treat other professionals responsibly. I routinely run into people with whom I disagree vehemently. We always manage to have a nice conversation about the business or their kids or whatever. It's easy. I literally get hundreds of emails and texts from other media people every year. I answer every single one of them in a polite way. Why? Because that is *respectful*, and there is no need to be *disrespectful*. If Maxine Waters emails me, I will, again, apologize for the hair stuff. And then ask if I can be of service.

I let it be known to my CBS acquaintances what Ms. Pauley did. They said if they see her in the hallway they might pass along my disenchantment—in a very nice way, of course.

But here's what really happened. Jane Pauley's program, throughout the entire year of 2025, did not interview one non-liberal author. Not *one*. Every person who wrote a book appearing on the *CBS Sunday Morning* show was a progressive. Pauley is directly responsible for that. She is the anchorperson. Obviously, that's the way Jane wants her program to be—exclusionary. Plus, I'm sure she thinks I'm a barbarian. Come to think of it, that puts me in a much stronger position to write a book like *Confronting Evil*.

✪ ✪ ✪

Next up is Anderson Cooper. I know him a little bit. We shared an agent at one time. I did the same thing with Cooper that I did with Jane Pauley. I wrote him a very nice email saying that his ratings on CNN would probably spike if I appeared on the program because many viewers would be curious. Since Anderson reaches about half a million people a night, a ratings boost might be a good thing for him. Now, I didn't say his ratings were terrible—maybe ten years ago I would have, but I didn't do it this time. I explained this could be a very interesting segment that could benefit both of us.

Anderson Cooper never replied.

Same thing. We investigated and could not find any examples of Anderson booking non-liberal authors on his program.

In addition, Anderson Cooper has a reputation around the media of not being a great guy. That might sound disrespectful. I may be a hypocrite for writing it. I can't prove Cooper's questionable demeanor without revealing my sources, and I'm not going to do that. But if you're reading this, Anderson, you might think about upping the respect quotient a bit.

And then there was the late Rush Limbaugh.

✪ ✪ ✪

In my opinion, the conservative commentator is the most successful radio broadcaster of all time. Paul Harvey is second. For some reason, Mr. Limbaugh was not a big fan of mine. In fact, he nicknamed me "Ted Baxter"—the pompous newsman on *The Mary Tyler Moore*

Show, played by Ted Knight. I liked Knight's performance, so I wasn't insulted. However, I was a bit surprised that Limbaugh was going out of his way to diminish my career. I thought it was a bit disrespectful. And it was. But unlike Jane Pauley and Anderson Cooper, there was a reason.

In May 2002, I launched *The Radio Factor*. The show competed directly with Rush Limbaugh's program. We never expected to beat him in the ratings, but we did take some of his audience. Especially in Los Angeles, where, in some months, we beat Rush in the twenty-five-to-fifty-four demographic, which is coveted by advertisers.

In addition, Rush Limbaugh never really made it on national television. And I did. I was also becoming very popular among people who liked him, although our styles were vastly different. So, "El Rushbo" was not a big fan of mine and let the whole world know it.

Disrespectful? Certainly. Was I angry? No. I understand the intense competition in the media industry.

A couple of years after Limbaugh branded me "Baxter," I actually ran into him at a Fourth of July party in Garrison, New York. He was by himself and, because of his hearing loss, wasn't engaged in a lot of conversation. I walked over to him. The partygoers stopped everything and stared. With a smile, I shook his hand, told him I thought he was a legend, and asked him how he was feeling. In short, I showed the man respect.

From then on, I didn't hear a lot of the "Ted Baxter" stuff, and a few years later, his brother, David, helped me out a bit. So, my decision not to confront a disrespectful situation turned very positive. Keep that in mind.*

✪✪✪

* Rush Limbaugh (1951–2021) was an American radio personality, author, and television host who transformed talk radio and became a defining voice of modern American conservatism. In February 2020, shortly after receiving the Presidential Medal of Freedom from President Donald Trump, Limbaugh announced he had been diagnosed with lung cancer. He continued to host his show through his treatments. He passed away on February 17, 2021, at age seventy.

Political disrespect in this country has been rising since the Vietnam War. But after the 9/11 terror attack, the country came together under President Bush the Younger. The vitriol between liberals and conservatives lessened. We were all in this together. That ceasefire ended after the Iraq War went south. Then, the political disrespect began to surge in America.

It got completely out of hand during Barack Obama's first presidential campaign. You may remember Mr. Obama saying in April 2008 that many Republican voters "get bitter, they cling to guns or religion or antipathy toward people who aren't like them." That assertion did not help the country. It was also disrespectful because it generalized millions of Americans in a negative way. The anti-Obama forces ran wild with the candidate's statement.

Payback came on September 9, 2009. President Obama was delivering a speech before a joint session of Congress. In the middle of the address, South Carolina Congressman Joe Wilson yelled out, "You lie!" Mr. Obama did not lose his cool, calmly stating, "That's not true." But Mr. Wilson was totally disrespectful to the office of the presidency.*

On the other side of the aisle, the fanatically left-wing Nancy Pelosi committed a gross act of disrespect as Speaker of the House. On February 4, 2020, she was seated directly behind President Trump during his State of the Union address. The camera constantly caught Pelosi vamping; she made a series of ridiculous faces. It was abundantly clear she had absolutely no respect for the commander in chief standing before her.

Then, when Donald Trump finished his address, Pelosi tore it up in front of the cameras. The incident was seen on television by thirty-seven million Americans. That shocked even people who supported the Speaker of the House. She did not care whatsoever, telling CNN,

---

* Joe Wilson remains a member of the House of Representatives from South Carolina's Second District.

> I tore up a manifesto of mistruths. It was necessary to get the attention of the American people to say, "This is not true. And this is how it affects you." And I don't need any lessons from anyone, especially the president of the United States, about dignity.

Dignity, Madame Speaker? I don't think you showed any dignity, respect, decorum, or class by destroying a State of the Union address. I believe most Americans feel the same way. There is no excuse for what you did. You fostered political disrespect and harmed your country. That is the truth. Own it.

✪ ✪ ✪

The seriousness of the respect issue can be seen in violent crime. Most of the murders in the nation's inner cities are committed by young men or juveniles. When they are caught, inevitably, they tell police they were "disrespected" by another individual. The gang code says that is a capital crime. Death or severe injury must follow any disrespect. This is the credo of the streets. Young criminals, of all colors, will hurt you if they perceive you are downgrading them. The culture is so volatile that the mere *perception* of insult can get human beings killed.*

On the political front, we now have social media that has nearly destroyed the concept of respect. This is all about money. If you are a reasonable person, it is far more difficult to get attention online than if you attack others in a personal, vicious way.

This practice began on talk radio, and it continues unabated. People tune in for nasty stuff. You know who they are. I don't have to name them.

Occasionally, early in my career, I fit into that category. At least somewhat. But I can't remember ever attacking people personally. My style was to win the debate using fact and logic. But sometimes, things went awry.

---

* According to data from the FBI and the Bureau of Justice Statistics, Black men between the ages of eighteen and forty-nine are responsible for 59 percent of homicides in America, despite making up just 7 percent of the total US population.

Two famous incidents. The first was Congressman Barney Frank, who came on *The O'Reilly Factor* in October 2008 to talk about the faltering economy. For months, the nation's entire banking system teetered on the brink of collapse because of unpaid mortgages.

Frank was part of the Fannie Mae and Freddie Mac federal mortgage program—he oversaw it. So, he knew people were getting home loans who could not qualify for them.*

Unfortunately, Barney Frank lied about that. Well, I crushed him. I called him out; I called him names. It was bloody. You can look it up if you want to see it, but in the end, I was disrespectful to Congressman Frank. I should have handled it differently. Although, it did benefit me as I received loud cheers from partisans who did not like Barney.

The reason I unloaded on the congressman was because he was disrespectful to my audience. He did not tell the truth. If you mislead someone, you are not acting in a respectful way. Same thing if you steal from someone, same thing if you cheat. It's all about positive or negative behavior. My job, to this day, is to point both out.

Second example is Geraldo Rivera. Now, here it's a little bit different. Geraldo is very pro-immigrant. On April 5, 2007, he arrived at *The Factor* to talk about criminal illegal aliens. He actually wound up defending them, at least in my opinion. And, again, like with Barney Frank, things got a little heated.

The coverage of our on-air spat went global. Wrote Howard Kurtz in *The Washington Post* two days later:

> It felt as if you had wandered into a barroom brawl, and the only question was when someone would get smashed with a broken beer bottle. . . .

---

* Fannie Mae (Federal National Mortgage Association) was created during the Great Depression to help poor Americans secure home mortgages. Freddie Mac (Federal Home Loan Mortgage Corporation) was established in 1970 to increase lending to those with low credit scores and other financial difficulties. Both were used in the early 2000s to secure mortgages for Americans who would not typically qualify. Those agencies contributed greatly to the banking crisis under George W. Bush.

> It was Geraldo Rivera vs. Bill O'Reilly, a trash-talking, vein-popping, finger-thrusting shout-fest. . . .
>
> The rising decibel level Thursday night on Fox News Channel's "The O'Reilly Factor"—an arena not renowned for delicate discussion—was an instant YouTube classic as the two Fox fighters went at it on the subject of illegal immigration.

Accurate reporting by Kurtz.

Again, you can look it up if you want to see it. Here, I wouldn't do *anything* differently. I thought Geraldo's position was absolutely outrageous. And, in addition to that, would get people killed.

Subsequently, that's exactly what happened after President Biden opened the border and millions of foreign criminals poured into the country. A number of Americans died. Violently.

To this day, Geraldo and I remain friends. Barney Frank retired from politics in 2013 and passed away in May 2026. I wish I handled that interview a bit differently. I think that is the respectful thing to do. And there is no reason not to do it. Right? *

✪ ✪ ✪

Finally, self-respect. This is another enormous problem in the United States. Alcoholism and drug addiction are the primary indicators that a person is simply self-destructive. You cannot respect yourself and then, at the same time, do harm to your mind or body. If you don't appreciate yourself, then nothing really matters, including other people. This self-loathing business is on the rise. I am not a psychiatrist, but I've been around. I have seen a huge deterioration in personal behavior. This is extremely damaging to America. Did you know that almost 40 percent of adults have tattoos? I never got it. It's not that the tattoos themselves are disrespectful, that would be ridiculous to claim.

---

* Barney Frank retired from the House of Representatives in January 2013. He died at his home in Ogunquit, Maine, on May 19, 2026, from heart failure. He was eighty-six years old.

Some people like self-expression and want to have a panther on their neck. Okay. We live in a free society. But marking yourself up can hurt you. Unless you're playing for the Phoenix Suns. Why? Because many employers, particularly in the white-collar world, do not want men or women with sleeves of tattoos up and down their legs, arms, face, neck, whatever. That sends a message.

Many people disagree with me. They say tattoos have nothing to do with self-respect. It is true, you have a perfect right to look like Post Malone. But think about it. If you want to maximize your potential on this earth, you must have as many options as possible. Showing up for a job interview looking like a Hells Angel is not going to advance your cause in most places. Americans need to think about self-respect. If you can achieve that, life will be much easier.*

When I raise this issue with young people, I get the "what about" stuff. What about this person or that person? They have a tattoo and *they're* successful. There is no answer to that. But here's what I say in general to younger Americans: Everything you do should be done for a reason. There are only two valid postures on this earth. The first is to help other people. Your tattoo does not do that. The second is to help yourself. Here, the tattoo may bring you some kind of comfort. I'll accept that.

But be very, very convinced before you drastically change your appearance. I believe we were all put here for a reason. We were born, as Lady Gaga sings, "*this way*." I don't need some guy named Freddy with a drill putting a shamrock on my back. That does not seem to be part of *nature's plan*.

✪ ✪ ✪

Throughout our country's history, we have had many famous people treat respect as a major issue. By far, the league leader is President Andrew Jackson; if you dishonored him or his family, he would challenge

* Based on 2023–2025 research, approximately 39 percent of American adults have at least one tattoo, with about 22 percent of all US adults having multiple tattoos. That figure rises to 40 percent for Americans under the age of forty-five.

you to a duel. Real guns and bullets. Old Hickory, as he was called, would shoot you dead without hesitation. As Charles Dickinson found out in 1806.

Dickinson, a Nashville attorney, accused Jackson of reneging on a horse bet. Not only that, he called him a "coward and equivocator." My God, an equivocator?! Then Dickinson crossed the line. He labeled Rachel Jackson, Andrew's young wife, a "prostitute."

A duel quickly followed. Charles Dickinson was shot dead, but before he fell, he fired a bullet into Jackon's chest. For the rest of his life, Andrew had the bullet inside his body. When Andrew Jackson became president in March 1829, he was not as physically capable as he might have been. That bullet became a daily reminder of Jackson's battle for respect.

And it is a battle. Some people will scorn you. It's tough to walk away from that. But many times it is absolutely necessary.

The cliché is "don't let the bastards get you down." But a more important sentiment might be "don't be a bastard." Stow the disrespect.

✪✪✪

Let's end our respect journey with the Native American warrior Tecumseh, a man of honor.*

He was a pithy guy who summed up his philosophy this way: "Show respect for all people but grovel to none."

Wish he were around today.

* Tecumseh (1768–1813) was a Shawnee leader, orator, and war chief who built a massive, multitribal confederacy to resist US expansion in the Old Northwest. A gifted visionary, he sought to unite tribes from Canada to the Gulf of Mexico, aligning with the British in the War of 1812 before his death at the Battle of the Thames in present-day Ontario.

CHAPTER FOURTEEN

It's a Family Affair

My teenage friends in Levittown, Long Island, called my parents Ozzie and Harriet. If you don't remember that sitcom, which debuted on ABC in 1952, it was basically a white bread, gentle look at the American family. Ozzie apparently had no job, but enough money to support his wife, Harriet, and their two sons, David and Ricky. Ozzie never raised his voice, unlike my father, and usually appeared in cardigan sweaters. My dad had plenty of those. Harriet served milk and cookies to everyone, apparently around the clock. So did my mother.*

That program was a phenomenal success and defined families in White America. There was never conflict of any importance, and life was sweet. After the show became a hit, other White sitcoms emerged, like *Leave It to Beaver*. That was basically Ozzie and Harriet somewhere in the Midwest. Same tone, but the producers added a subversive element with the character Eddie Haskell. He was a troublemaker. The "Beaver" and his brother, Wally, towed the family line.

They rolled their eyes at Eddie, the agitator across the street. June

---

* *The Adventures of Ozzie and Harriet* (1952–1966) was a pioneering, long-running sitcom starring the real-life Nelson family—Ozzie, Harriet, and sons David and Ricky—representing the quintessential 1950s American nuclear family.

Cleaver, the mom, wore a dress on every episode. No sweatpants for her. Ward, the father, actually ate supper with his family wearing a TIE! Way beyond the pale. So much so that my father actually *mocked* Ward Cleaver. Old Dad was definitely *not* wearing a tie to eat boiled hot dogs and fish sticks.

Those early television sitcoms defined the traditional family in the USA. It wasn't until 1974 that Black Americans had their own series, called *Good Times*. Jimmie "J. J." Walker was the lead—his big line was "DY-NO-MITE!" Walker portrayed a very funny kid who dealt with a variety of challenges.

So, an entire generation grew up with an idyllic view of the family that was, of course, fictional. In reality, maintaining a disciplined household is very hard work. Conflicts emerge all the time, temptations abound. The family unit can often devolve into battle stations. Obviously, this is very bad. It must be confronted.

✪ ✪ ✪

The first rule of family life: Don't have kids if you can't make them your top priority. That is very difficult for many adults to do. They put themselves and *their* needs before the children. Those parents rarely admit it, but the epidemic of selfishness is obvious. Again, do not have children unless you are entirely devoted to their welfare—unless you would *die* for them.

The second vital part of American family life is this: The government cannot help you. There is no parenting legislation or intervention from the federal and state apparatus. It's your family. You can pretty much do what you want outside of abusing and neglecting the tykes.

This places an enormous burden on many parents who have no blankin' clue how to raise their children. You see it everywhere. Kids totally out of control, living in very unhappy situations, many going to therapy on a weekly basis.

Good parenting takes skill. You must be smart and disciplined. But, most of all, you have to be motivated.

This takes time away from *your* pursuits, especially if you have a demanding job. The wealthy often farm out parental responsibilities to nannies or caregivers. This almost always ends in disaster. The *parents* have to mold the children. No one else is going to do that.

✪ ✪ ✪

After World War II, millions of American GIs returned home to start families. At the same time, modern technology was drastically altering how we lived. Television was the game-changer. In my Levittown house, we had a little black-and-white TV with four channels. This provided a much-needed diversion. Kids could stare at *The Mickey Mouse Club* in the afternoon and not annoy the parents. At least for a few minutes, in my case.

Things were fairly smooth in US culture from 1946 until 1960. Yes, there were problems on the civil rights front, and American society was not an equal playing field. However, the traditional family, which began to form before World War II, was acceptable to almost everyone. The stats are amazing.

Consider this: In 1960, the "average" American household consisted of two parents, three children, one household pet. In 2025, the profile was one parent, one child. The divorce rate is now 50 percent, compared to 14 percent in 1960.

Despite all the psychobabble gibberish, divorce *always* hurts children. Any kind of traumatic change deeply affects kids who depend on security and consistency. I know the idiotic child psychology industry disputes that, but they're full of it. The best situation for a child is stability, affection, and gentle discipline.

In 1960, the average age that a man married was twenty-two. Twenty for women.

In 2025, it's thirty-one years old for men, twenty-nine for women.

So, you would think that the more mature adults are when they have kids, the better the situation. But no. That's because our society has drastically changed for the worse. The "do your own thing" philosophy that emerged in the 1960s has wreaked havoc on the family. Your "own thing" is not going to help your offspring. It is undeniable that America's move to the Left in the 1970s has deeply affected the family unit. Earlier in the book, we cited the horrendous crime statistics coming out of homes where the father is absent. There are no two sides to that debate. If you interview incarcerated Americans, you will almost always hear they were abused, disrupted, or ignored as children.

✪ ✪ ✪

Now let's look at American society in general. A sociology study put forth a definition of the liberal philosophy toward the American family. I'm not picking on liberalism here, but I do want to show you the vast difference between how the Left and how traditional Americans see the family environment:

> The liberal definition of family emphasizes function and chosen bonds over traditional structures, viewing family as any group providing love, support, and care, including non-nuclear setups, same-sex couples, multi-generational households, and even close friends, focusing on the commitment and nurturing roles rather than just blood, marriage, or legal ties. It values inclusivity, individual choice in forming relationships, and the evolving nature of family to reflect diverse realities, recognizing that family can be defined by shared lives and emotional connections.

To me, that is as destructive an outlook as you could have when raising children. Interestingly, it is the exact opposite of the Asian view of the family. In countries like Japan and South Korea, traditional households are the standard. And, of course, the children coming out of that structure are far more equipped to handle life's challenges. All you have to do is look at Asian American academic test scores and the proof is right before your eyes. One caveat. Just because the kids are smart doesn't make them good people. But I've spent some time in

Asia, and I can tell you that it's a far more disciplined society than we have in America.

Traditional family philosophy in the US values long-standing beliefs like religion, patriotism, and personal discipline. From that comes an emphasis on hard work, loyalty, and adherence to the truth. I was raised in a traditional home. Two Irish American parents, a nice sister, and me, a huge problem.

But the family unit stuck together even though my house was not suitable for "Beaver" Cleaver or Ricky Nelson. There was volatility on the part of my overworked father. Mom was the stabilizer. And upon both of their deaths, they were treated with the utmost respect and kindness by my sister and me.

Now, this is not to say that a "blended family" is bad. Many times people *have* to divorce. There is no choice, and heroic efforts are made to comfort the children. Anyone demeaning a household after it splits apart is doing a terrible thing. But, in my opinion, traditional family values should be *emphasized* in every school, in every church, and out of the mouths of every politician. Of course, that is not happening.

In fact, in many cases it's the opposite. Listen to former First Lady Hillary Clinton, who has reared an admirable daughter, Chelsea.

Ms. Clinton believes it "takes a village" to raise a child:

> We need to understand that there is no formula for how women should lead their lives. That is why we must respect the choices that each woman makes for herself and her family. Every woman deserves the chance to realize her God-given potential.

Well, with all due respect, that's just blather. American women can pursue their potential in many different ways without handing the kids over to a so-called village. In my mind, that's about as irresponsible a belief as you can hold. This utter nonsense that your feminism, or, for men, machismo, is a factor in your family decision-making is crazy. America must get away from this.

✪ ✪ ✪

In 1984, NBC premiered a sitcom called *The Cosby Show*. Comedian Bill Cosby was the lead, raising five children with his very kind wife. That was an amazing sociological factor. Cosby, who has a degree from Temple University, used his comedic skill to provide a good example, particularly for minority viewers. The show continues to air today despite Bill Cosby's criminal personal behavior, which has destroyed him and his legacy.*

The Cosby Show is an example of how positive family depictions are desperately needed. Picture this: You are a kid living in a squalid apartment in a run-down neighborhood. Fractured families all over the place. You witness horrible adult behavior: drug abuse, profanity, physical violence, crime. Skin color does not matter; this happens all over the United States. How can children exposed to barbaric conditions be saved? It's almost impossible.

Why? As stated, the government cannot force parents to be responsible. Also, the entitlement giveaways that America has embraced can help a little bit, but only if the entitlement money is spent responsibly. That is not happening. There is no follow-up to the money flow, no supervision. Adults are not even drug tested before they receive direct payments from the government. This is a gross dereliction of our national responsibility. Which is to PROTECT THE CHILDREN.

✪ ✪ ✪

Okay, the lecture is over. I hope you think about what I have written, especially the concept of "doing your own thing" when you're a par-

* Bill Cosby, once famously known as "America's Dad," has seen his reputation and career destroyed following allegations of sexual assault from over sixty women, with recent legal developments in 2026 resulting in significant civil liability. In 2018, Cosby was convicted of aggravated indecent assault and sentenced to three to ten years in state prison. However, on June 30, 2021, the Pennsylvania Supreme Court vacated his conviction and released him, ruling that his due process rights were violated because a previous prosecutor had promised not to charge him. Cosby has continued to maintain his innocence.

ent. I think selfish moms and dads are awful people. They actually flee when they see me in my neighborhood. They fear I will confront them. On a few occasions I have. Probably out of line, but I felt it had to be done. In my presence, no one will abuse a child. If every American adopted that rule, and didn't look away, we'd be a much better country.

✪✪✪

So, let's get back to Ozzie and Harriet living at 11 Page Lane in Levittown, New York. My parents tried their hardest. They were good Americans. They weren't drunks, they didn't spew profanities, they didn't use racial invective, they attended church on Sunday, they tried to give my sister and me the best upbringing they could.

Why can't we all be like that?

It doesn't take a "village." It takes will. Individuals have to put their children first and be honest with the urchins. Everyone in my neighborhood thought I would wind up in prison. When I was working at Channel 2 in New York City and went back to visit my parents on Long Island, neighbors would ask, "Why aren't you in jail?"

The question was valid. I was a mischievous kid. I paid the price for that. My father was on me all the time. It wasn't always positive. He took a lot of his frustration out on his son. But I always knew that my dad and mom cared for me, so my sister and I toughed it out. We had no choice. The cliché we embraced was, "It is what it is." My parents were not going to change, and that led to one of the biggest confrontations of my life.

When I was seventeen years old, my father was still giving me a hard time about dumb stuff. He worked twelve hours a day, and he was tired and cranky when he came home. For example, if I didn't walk with my shoulders back, I got a sarcastic remark. If I did something dumb, not unusual, that became a controversy. Well, finally, I had enough of it.

I can't remember what lit the fuse, but it was stupid. My father began yelling about something insignificant, at least that's how I saw it.

I tried to walk away, but he gave me the usual, "Don't you walk away from me!" So, I turned and stared at him eye to eye. My dad was six foot three. But I was six foot four and stronger than he was. So, I said these words: "You are never going to raise your voice to me, to my sister, or to my mother again."

William James O'Reilly Sr. was stunned. He knew this was a rite of passage. After about ten seconds, he said this: "Well, I guess you're on your own."

My reply: "Fine with me."

✪ ✪ ✪

I look upon that moment as a net positive. I drew the line with my father. My mother actually cried because our voices were so loud. I had to do it. However, I never carried animus toward my dad, ever. I took the time to understand him. He was raised in a volatile family headed by a New York City beat cop, my grandfather. Not a lot of "interactions" in the house. John O'Reilly Sr. put down the rules; they were obeyed.

My cousin Eddie didn't make it through the tough upbringing. He died very young from alcoholism. He inherited the same situation I did. To be clear, I'm not glorifying traditional upbringings that fail to constrain volatile behavior. That is unacceptable. Parents must control themselves. If they can be nice, like Ozzie and Harriet, that's a very big plus. Let's see more cookies and cardigans.

✪ ✪ ✪

Everyone in my Levittown neighborhood was raised in a similar way. It was bedlam on the streets. Scores of kids roaming around playing stickball, touch football, keep-away, and generally having a great time without parents participating. These are great memories. My friends all had nicknames: "the Bear," "the Bug," "Tortillo" (because he looked like a Mexican), "Bunky," on and on and on. Nobody was called by their real name. I still have friends who I have known for seventy years. They all have one thing in common: They value tradition. No one had any money. Child psychologists today would be horrified at what went on in my Levittown neighborhood. Ask Billy Joel, he was there. There were very few civilities. The "Beaver" would have been scorned and mocked.

Sadly, the United States has lost vision in family matters. We have become polarized. Liberals think this way; conservatives think that way. Schools are abdicating all kinds of social responsibilities because teachers are afraid. As I wrote earlier, when I taught high school, I got involved. This was not greeted enthusiastically by the administrators even back in 1971. Too bad. I did my job.

In January 2026, I became ill. Thousands of people all over the world sent emails and texts of concern. One of those was incredible.

A student I taught fifty-five years ago, who became a doctor, emailed me this: "Bill, you have all the good thoughts and prayers from your former students. None of us ever forgot how you cared about us and pushed us to do our best. We are always here for you."

I'm not going to identify the former student, but I am so proud of her, and this is what I mean when I say that teachers, next to parents, are most vital to this nation.

✪ ✪ ✪

A couple of more things regarding the family arena.

America is not a "village." We are a nation of separate beliefs, strong emotions, and enormous weaknesses on the personal level. With kids, it's a one-on-one situation. In my opinion, child psychology is an industry that often does far more harm than good. I want all parents in this country to sacrifice for their children. To do their best. To raise them as decent human beings. That is not easy.

Therefore, if you're not "in it to win it," don't have the kids. If you marry a miscreant, you're going to damage innocent children as well as yourself. You have to think about all this stuff because it's the most important part of your life. And, of course, the most vital part of your children's lives.

✪ ✪ ✪

One final thing. I am addressing this paragraph to every American child. You also have an obligation. "Honor your father and your mother." Fifth Commandment. No excuses. Even if your parents weren't the best, you must help and respect them if you can. That is a primary responsibility in your life.

Don't evade it.

CHAPTER FIFTEEN

The Destroyers

Hard work and determination did it. By the year 2002, *The O'Reilly Factor* was dominating the cable TV ratings. The Fox News Channel had been on the air for six years, and my program was the most talked-about presentation in the country. We cost NBC and CNN billions of advertising dollars in the long run.

I didn't think much about that. My primary focus was dethroning CNN's Larry King as the highest-rated cable program. That happened in late 2002. Along the way, I passed Chris Matthews at MSNBC, and we diminished him as well. *The O'Reilly Factor* was successful because we presented the news in a very flamboyant way—it was almost impossible to be bored when watching *The Factor*. We had robust debates. We had on-air controversies. We had people like Dennis Miller as regular contributors. The formula changed the television news industry forever.

Earlier, I wrote about Ted Koppel and how dismissive he was of the whole situation. But Mr. Koppel was an outlier. Everybody in the television news industry knew there was a new sheriff in town. Sorry to use that horrendous cliché.

Sometime in the year 2000, I was puttering around my house on Long Island when my agent called. At that point I had been represented by Carole Cooper for about twenty-five years. Truthfully, I was an annoying client because I didn't take any guff from my so-called superiors. Poor Carole had to deal with *that* on a routine basis. Yes, she made a good dollar doing it, but Carole's agency had plenty of big-time talent. They didn't need me.

Until.

Carole asked me if I would take a call from the CEO of General Electric, a man named Jack Welch. Of course I would. Mr. Welch was perhaps the most powerful executive in the United States at the time. He ruled General Electric, which owned NBC, for twenty years. They called him "Neutron Jack." Tough guy. Irish Catholic, Boston-area upbringing. If Jack Welch wants to talk to you, why not?

Apparently, I was doing so much damage to NBC's bottom line that Welch wanted to hire me. It was a great conversation. He said, "You can do whatever you want over here. A primetime show on NBC. MSNBC. News Specials. You name it, O'Reilly. Sound good?"

For most of the human race it would have sounded good, but I had worked at CBS and ABC News. I knew the ferocity of the network corporate culture. Jack Welch was trying to hire me for purely economic reasons. He wanted to damage the Fox News Channel. No problem, that's what executives do. But I was on the ascent at FNC, and I worked for a guy I trusted, Roger Ailes. So, while many people would have jumped at Welch's offer, I did not.

However, I was *very* respectful. I said I would talk it over with my family and my agent and we would get back to him in the next few days. I think Jack was a little surprised. He wasn't used to having "TV talent" hesitate. General Electric was waving huge money in front of my face. But what Jack did not know is that I have *never* worked for money. I don't particularly care about legal tender. I understand the security and power it brings, but, as stated, I don't need a Lamborghini. Or a $500 watch. Or any of that stuff. You can take the boy out of Levittown, but you can't take Levittown out of the boy. Another cliché. I don't know what's wrong with me.

I ended up turning down Jack Welch, who was very nice about it.

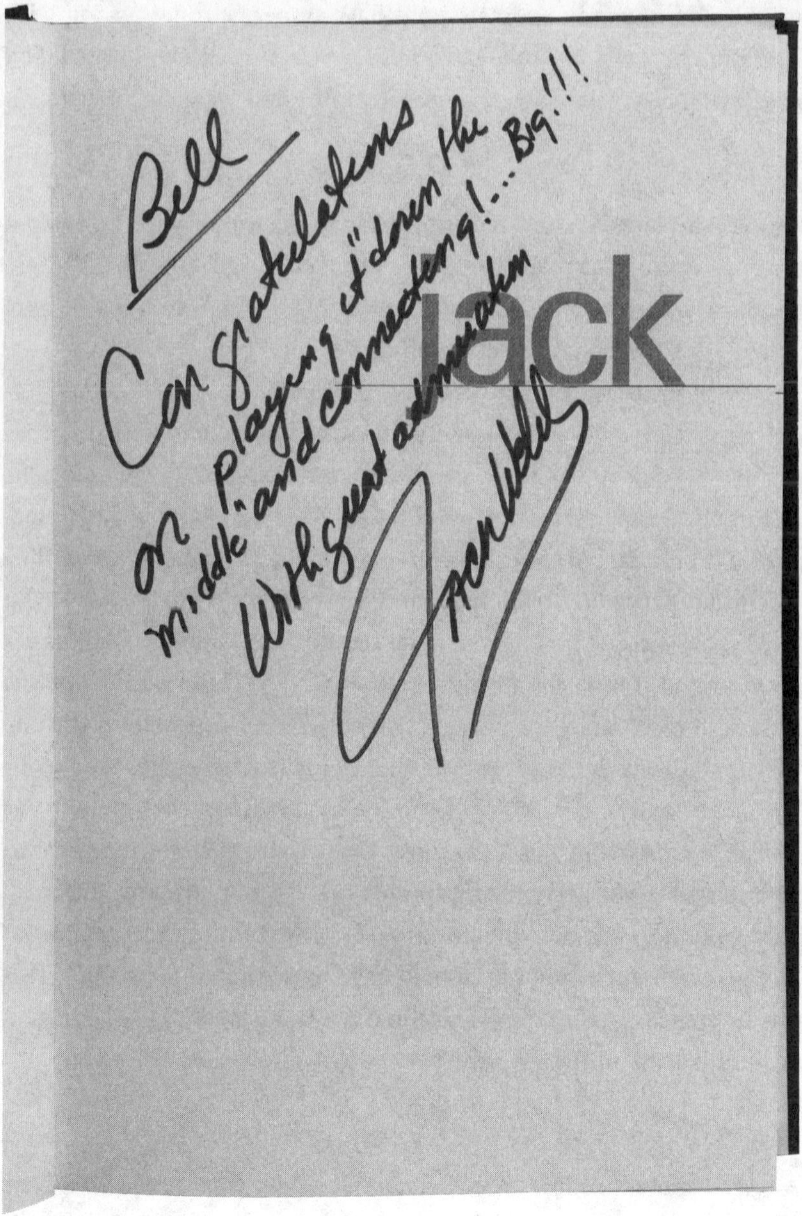
Bill
Congratulations
on playing it "down the
middle" and connecting!... Big!!!
With great admiration
Jack Welch
Jack

I thought that would be it. I did tell my boss, Roger Ailes, about the interaction, as loyalty demands. But I didn't leverage the NBC offer against Fox as many people would have done. Nothing wrong with that. But that's not my style until new contracts are being forged. Fox was paying me a fair wage, and I did my job. I don't shake people down.

✪ ✪ ✪

I'm telling you that story because it has to do with a horrendous period of my life. Jack Welch retired from General Electric in 2001. He had increased the company's value from $12 billion to $400 billion. The guy was an amazing businessman.

Replacing Welch as CEO of General Electric was a man named Jeffrey Immelt. He was a disaster. On his watch, the company's financial performance dropped 30 percent by some measures.

But the worst thing Immelt did was to allow some broadcasters at MSNBC to launch a series of personal attacks against people they didn't like. Smears. Vitriol. Invective. Every single night.

MSNBC had turned from a news organization into a far-left channel trying to compete with the conservative Fox News network. Fine. You want to go after the progressive audience, no problem. But the way that the talent behaved at MSNBC was despicable. And your humble correspondent was right in the crosshairs.

The result of that was something I never anticipated. I had crazed people on my property trying to hurt me. Threats through the mail, on the phone, even horrible things said to my young children. I had to hire armed security guys to actually live in my house for a time. This was unprecedented in the television news industry.

And Jeffrey Immelt was the person who allowed it.

✪ ✪ ✪

About a year into these vicious attacks, I was invited to watch a New England Patriots game at Foxborough by the team owner, Robert Kraft. I showed up to see the Pats play the Dolphins. Kraft, a billionaire, has a luxury box on the fifty-yard line. Food and spirits are unlimited. It's a fun experience. The box seats about thirty guests. One of them was Jeffrey Immelt.

High noon.

While most civilized people would have avoided a confrontation, I do not fit into that category. Certainly, I was aware that punching Immelt out, which I would have done in some alley, would be inappropriate. Robert Kraft would have been embarrassed beyond the pale. So, I had to use another strategy.

Immelt was aware of my presence but stayed on the other side of the box. At halftime everybody rises for libations and food. That was my chance. Slowly, I strolled over to Immelt, who was there with some lackey. I looked him in the eye and said I would like to talk in private for a moment. The man was about six foot. Nothing distinctive about him. His sidekick was inconsequential. I didn't wait for Immelt to answer. I just launched.

It went something like this: "Are you aware that you are allowing people on MSNBC to put my family in danger? Do you know what kind of pressure that puts on little children when their father is attacked on national television every single night? Do you understand how *wrong* that is?"

Immelt actually said this: "I don't even know about what's happening there. Can you explain it to me?"

"Yeah, I can." Then I proceeded to run down the unbelievable defamation and hatred that MSNBC was directing toward me—and by extension my family.

Immelt said something like, "I'll look into it" or some other inane remark. I stared right through that guy. He'll never forget it. I *did* want to punch his lights out. I admit it. But that would have made me worse than Immelt.

✪ ✪ ✪

Karma got him. Old Jeff was eventually fired, humiliated, accused of bad management. Immelt disappeared from the public arena in October 2017.

Good. Folks who pay their employees to destroy other human beings are not worthy of holding responsible positions. We have a lot of those people in the United States of America. They must be exposed and vilified. It is righteous to do that.

✪ ✪ ✪

Unfortunately, legions of destroyers prosper to this day. They exist primarily in the ideological and business communities. Both the liberal and conservative worlds embrace this garbage. Let's run it down.

✪ ✪ ✪

GEORGE SOROS

He is perhaps the most famous destroyer in America today. A far-left guy, ninety-five years old, he lives north of New York City. Soros established the Open Society Foundations, which has an annual budget $1.2 billion, much of it from his personal fortune. In fact, the OSF operates in more than 120 countries. But it is in the US that Soros does the most damage.

I've been pounding the guy for almost thirty years. He made his vast fortune through questionable financial dealings. In 1992, Soros earned the moniker "the man who broke the Bank of England" by betting against the British pound. As the currency plummeted on September 16, known as "Black Wednesday," Soros netted about $1 billion in profit.

He did not face any legal consequences for his "investment." In fact, many in the financial community lauded Soros, claiming his wager was legal, market-driven speculation, not a criminal act.

Meanwhile, the United Kingdom sank into recession and unemployment jumped to 11 percent.*

* In 2002, a French court convicted George Soros of felony insider trading related to investments he made in the early 1990s. Soros was fined roughly 2.2 million euros ($2.3 million), a ruling he appealed through French courts and the European Court of Human Rights, ultimately failing to overturn the conviction.

✪ ✪ ✪

Today, George Soros has handed management of the Open Society Foundations to his son Alex. But the money continues to flow. The Soros boys gave Joe Biden $28 million. Hillary Clinton $25 million. Barack Obama $3 million. Senator Chuck Schumer and the Democrats $16 million.

Now, there's nothing wrong with that. The Supreme Court has ruled individual Americans and foundations *can* give unlimited money to political action committees, also known as PACs. It's not a crime, and if George Soros wants to be a Democrat, fine with me. But promoting a political party is *not* really what the billionaire wants to do.

No. He's out to radically change American society. He wants open borders. Leniency toward violent criminals. He supports libertine policies toward social order. Simply put, the guy despises traditional America and wants to destroy it. That is my opinion, based on three decades of research.

Here's the backup. Soros has financed the campaigns of Manhattan District Attorney Alvin Bragg, Los Angeles DA George Gascón, Philadelphia DA Larry Krasner, and Chicago DA Kim Foxx. These people, along with dozens of others that Soros funded, have instituted policies where criminals are not charged—they simply walk. For example, you can punch someone in the face in New York City. Even if you're arrested, which is a long shot, you will not likely be held on bail. Your case could very well be dropped. Meanwhile, the victim has a broken nose, jaw, or whatever. Thousands of dollars in medical bills. Then, the miscreant goes on to cause more damage. Thank you, George Soros.

Again, in my opinion, Soros is perhaps the most effective destroyer in America today. But it's all legal. And the Soros boys are not going to stop.

One further thing. I often get letters asking why George Soros does what he does. I don't know. He's never really explained himself or the political philosophy that motivates him. All you can find is blather about "democracy, open societies, and human rights."

✪ ✪ ✪

MOVEON

This radical organization is tax exempt, if you can believe it. A 501(c)(4) nonprofit. It was founded in 1998 to protect President Bill Clinton from impeachment. Its budget today is around $60 million.

MoveOn uses much of that money to harm people it doesn't like: me, Sean Hannity, George W. Bush, Donald Trump, Ted Cruz, on and on. This is a vicious outfit that lies, deceives, and uses its millions to attack individuals.

Here is the mission statement from their website:

> MoveOn members are a force for social justice and political progress. We come from all 50 states and all walks of life. Together, we are at once large and nimble, targeting our resources purposefully, yet pivoting quickly as we identify new opportunities for change and mobilize to seize them. Our rapid-response organizing and campaigning, communications interventions, digital innovation, rigorous data science and testing, and culture of grassroots participation have repeatedly combined to produce real-world impact, changing outcomes and making our country better.
>
> MoveOn is more than our name. It is our challenge to America: to move forward boldly and fearlessly, upholding and enacting the values that will make our country work for all of us.
>
> We are the many, and we are powerful. Every day, together, we fight to win.

MoveOn is behind the movement against US Immigration and Customs Enforcement, or ICE. It despises Israel. It promotes social disorder.

It also continues to raise an enormous amount of money to do its dirty work.

✪✪✪

AVAAZ

Chances are you have never heard of this shadowy group. The term *Avaaz* means "voice" in some Middle Eastern languages. It was launched in the year 2007 to promote far-left causes worldwide. The organization claims it has more than seventy million members, but that's bull. What it *does* have is a lot of money donated by foolish people.

When I left Fox News in April 2017, Avaaz was the primary group attacking me. They hired protesters to stand outside the FNC headquarters in Manhattan holding professionally made signs that defamed me. They fed hatred, vitriol, and an amazing array of irresponsible claims to news outlets around the world.

Like the Soros crew, this is a vicious enterprise. It needs to be exposed.

✪✪✪

NEW VENTURE FUND

Same thing with the New Venture Fund. This group has a $900 million annual budget. That's a lot of jack. And it specializes in "dark money." According to the Oxford Dictionary, the definition of "dark money" is: Funds raised for the purpose of influencing elections by nonprofit organizations that are not required to disclose the identities of their donors.

The goal of NVF is "social justice." That's code for the abolishment of prisons, instituting socialism, and, in general, attacking traditional belief systems.

✪✪✪

NEVILLE ROY SINGHAM

In January 2026, on *No Spin News*, we reported on a man named Neville Roy Singham. Singham is an American multimillionaire businessman, a Socialist activist, and the founder of the IT consulting firm *Thoughtworks*. Based in Shanghai, China, he is behind the financing of a global network of nonprofits, media outlets, and activist groups that promote talking points aligned with the Chinese Communist Party.

Investigations suggest Singham's network acts in coordination with Chinese state propaganda efforts to influence public opinion, with groups sharing office space with a Chinese media company dedicated to "telling China's story."

A 2023 *New York Times* investigation reported that Singham financed organizations like the People's Forum, the ANSWER Coalition, and Breakthrough News. These groups are active in organizing far-left, anti-US, and anti-Israel protests in America, such as the Shut It Down for Palestine campaign.

The billionaire, born in Connecticut to Sri Lankan parents, is currently funding many outfits that encourage violent protests against ICE.

So far, no legal action has been taken against Singham in the United States, which is very unusual. This is a dangerous man, and he continues to operate with few limitations because he is a US citizen.

✪ ✪ ✪

THE NEO-NAZIS

Now let's take a look at the far right, where there are plenty of destroyers. The difference here is money. Extremist loons like the "neo-Nazis" don't have a lot of cash; approximately $3 million a year is spent on hating other people, according to the FBI.

The bureau says there are about 110 neo-Nazi groups operating among all fifty states. The largest are the Blood Tribe, Patriot Front, and the National Socialist Movement. But they're almost invisible. It's not like they have headquarters where you can go in and have a chat.

These are furtive people who sporadically emerge to spread hatred against Black and Jewish people as well as other minorities.

According to a 2017 poll from Reuters, about twenty million Americans passively support the neo-Nazi ideology—that is, 5 percent of the population. Obviously, just one Nazi supporter is too many.

✪ ✪ ✪

THE KU KLUX KLAN

By 1871, President Ulysses S. Grant had seen enough. Elected to lead the nation after the Civil War, the Union general was appalled by racial violence sweeping the South.

A paramilitary organization, founded by Confederate leader Nathan Bedford Forrest, was growing at an alarming rate. The Ku Klux Klan opened chapters from Virginia to Texas. Membership soared into the millions. The terror network used violent tactics, like firebombing and lynching, to stop minorities from voting.

To stem the bloodshed, President Grant dispatched the army to directly confront the Klan. He suspended the constitutional right of habeas corpus, allowing US citizens to be detained *without* due process.

Nine counties in South Carolina were placed under martial law, thousands were arrested, an unknown number executed. Grant basically told the army to do what it had to do.

But in 1883, the federal government's war on the KKK was terminated by the Supreme Court. In a unanimous decision, the justices ruled that Washington, DC, could *not* interfere with local and state elections. That ruling prevented many Black residents from voting and gave the Klan and other racists a huge club.*

Hello, "Jim Crow."

---

* *United States v. Harris* (1883) was a landmark Supreme Court case that severely limited federal power to prosecute private acts of racial violence, including those by the Ku Klux Klan. The court held that Grant's Ku Klux Klan Act of 1871 was unconstitutional because the Fourteenth Amendment only authorized federal action against state violations, not individual crimes. It was part of a series of cases that systematically dismantled Reconstruction-era policies to protect African Americans.

✪✪✪

Under federal pressure, the Klan went underground but did not disappear. It continued to terrorize Blacks, Catholics, Jews, immigrants, and so-called race mixers, as well as Communists, but it wasn't a "mass movement."

Then, in the early twentieth century, the KKK rose again. With ferocity. Its resurgence was fueled by the 1915 film *The Birth of a Nation*. The silent movie, depicting hooded Klansmen defending White Southerners from freed slaves, became a national sensation. At the request of President Woodrow Wilson, *The Birth of a Nation* was the first motion picture screened at the White House.*

After World War I, many White, native-born Protestants felt threatened by rapid industrialization, urbanization, and the influx of immigrants from southern and eastern Europe.

The so-called invisible empire of the Klan fed off that. Hatred was on the march.

In 1924, the KKK had a significant influence at the Democratic National Convention at New York City's Madison Square Garden. Many southern delegates were secret members of the organization. Klan marches were held on Long Island. A cross-burning ceremony took place in Orange County, about seventy miles north of Manhattan.

A *New York Times* article published in 1927 listed the names of agitators arrested at a pro-Klan march in Jamaica, Queens. One of them lived at 175–24 Devonshire Road. That was the childhood home of Frederick Trump, President Trump's father.

While researching my book *The United States of Trump*, I asked the president about the incident. He said that his father had no involvement with the KKK and that it was unfair that *The New York Times* singled him out.

---

* *The Birth of a Nation* was screened at the White House on March 21, 1915, because President Woodrow Wilson—a southerner with segregationist views—agreed to a private request from his friend and former classmate, Thomas Dixon, who wrote the book on which the film was based.

At this point, it is impossible to verify the accusation against Frederick Trump. But that has not stopped many in the press from smearing the family.

✪ ✪ ✪

It wasn't until the mid-1960s that President Lyndon Johnson unleashed FBI Director J. Edgar Hoover to finally marginalize the Klan. Thousands of agents were dispatched to the South. By 1990, the vicious outfit was largely eradicated.*

Today, the KKK is mostly a nonfactor in the US. Membership is estimated at about five thousand, down from eight *million* in 1925. But racism, in other forms, continues to vex American society. So let me make one thing "crystal clear," as Jack Nicholson and Tom Cruise once said in *A Few Good Men*. If you hate a person because of their skin color, religion, or ethnicity, you are a destroyer.

And you should be confronted.

✪ ✪ ✪

THE PROUD BOYS

This idiot group came into prominence after the election of 2016. The Proud Boys don't have a central headquarters. They exist on social media. The founder is a man named Gavin McInnes. The flamboyant co-creator of the alternative media outlet VICE gained national attention on Twitter and remains popular on YouTube. McInnes claims the Proud Boys promote "pro-western fraternity." That, of course, is complete BS. What the Proud Boys are in business to do is marginalize liberals, gays, and minorities.

The radical Black Lives Matter movement actually helped the

* J. Edgar Hoover dismantled the Ku Klux Klan in the 1960s primarily through counterintelligence programs designed to disrupt, discredit, and infiltrate the terror organization. By 1968, the campaign had significantly reduced the Klan's membership and power through a combination of heavy surveillance, psychological warfare, and exposing their extremist activities to the general public.

Proud Boys recruit. The more insanity that BLM people put forth, the more attention the Proud Boys received. It all came to a head when President Trump lost the election of 2020.

The Proud Boys played a central role in the attack on the US Capitol that occurred on January 6, 2021. Members of the group acted as "shock troops," breaching the complex and overrunning security. Several Proud Boy leaders, including Enrique Tarrio, were convicted of conspiracy and sentenced to long prison terms in 2023.

They were all pardoned by President Trump on January 20, 2025—the first day of his second term.

Today, the Proud Boys membership is most likely less than one thousand. The group has no credibility, and no purpose, other than to destroy the fabric of American society.

✪ ✪ ✪

Because I have been in the culture war business for more than thirty years, I can tell you that I despise people who try to destroy this country and damage fellow citizens. I can proudly say I have *never* done that. I will bring every fact I can to negate the influence of people and groups I feel are harmful to America. But I don't want to kill them, hurt their families, or even put them out of business. George Soros has a legion of attorneys to make sure he doesn't break any laws. Good. I don't care whether Soros or his son continue their destructive Open Society Foundations. If they break the law, get 'em. If they don't, expose them. But you can't justify destruction by wreaking more destruction.

That's how the Nazi Party gained power in Germany in the 1930s. The people there were suffering because of the Great Depression. Hitler and his cutthroats blamed certain groups, like Jews and Communists. The Germans bought in; the horrifying destruction began.

That was evil. All decent people should reject violent tactics. But they should also stand up against the destroyers themselves. Some of them are paid millions by media corporations. These are vile people. Cable TV as well as social media is now their swamp—they live there, happily in the bile.

The Constitution allows it. But the destroyers are perhaps the most dangerous element in the country today. No other country on earth can destroy us without being destroyed in turn.

But evil Americans have gravely damaged this country by dividing us, encouraging rebellion, sanctioning violence, and generally attacking the traditional tenets of the United States.

Stand against them.

CHAPTER SIXTEEN

The Buccaneers

Conformity in America is a good thing if you are a conventional person. Doing what is expected is not going to bring you a lot of grief. Especially if you work for a corporation or live in a traditional environment. Hell-raising is only for a very small segment of the population. However, some of those people have contributed mightily to the nation's welfare.

I call flamboyant people "buccaneers," playing off the ocean pirates of the seventeenth century. Back then, there were no rules. If these plunderers were chasing, you'd better be fast. Most of the time there was no mercy. They would take everything you had, then throw you overboard. Sounds a lot like Hollywood, correct?

My two favorite buccaneers are Jean Lafitte and William Kidd. Lafitte was an interesting character. He hung around Louisiana preying on Spanish ships. Brutal guy. But effective. In fact, the British offered Jean Lafitte an enormous amount of money to help them attack New Orleans during the War of 1812. Lafitte smiled and asked to think about it.

Then, the buccaneer hightailed it over to General Andrew Jackson, who was defending New Orleans for the young United States. He and Jackson came to an arrangement.

They would defeat the British force together. And they did.*

For his efforts, President James Madison granted Jean Lafitte a full pardon for the terrible things he had done throughout his life, and there were many. The buccaneer accepted the pardon, then went right back to pillaging. Quite a guy.

Fun fact: Nobody knows where Jean Lafitte is buried or how he died. This was one crazy dude.

✪ ✪ ✪

Then there was Captain William Kidd, who roamed around the Atlantic in the middle of the seventeenth century doing whatever he wanted. Kidd was what they called a privateer. His official job was to hunt down pirates and French ships on behalf of the British government. But Kidd was really self-employed. He began looting every ship he could find from Nova Scotia to Jamaica. He didn't care what flag the vessel sailed under. The Brits did not get their cut.

Legend states that Captain Kidd buried his vast amount of treasure on Gardiners Island in the Long Island Sound. I live just a few miles away. Nobody is allowed on Gardiners Island. It is privately owned. Occasionally I look over and think I should get a couple of guys with shovels because most of Kidd's booty has never been found.

Eventually, British authorities had had enough of this guy. He was lured to Boston under the false pretense of a full pardon and then arrested. Kidd was then taken to London's Execution Dock. A noose was placed around his neck, and the platform beneath his feet opened. But the rope snapped, and Kidd survived. Not for long. Almost immediately, the English guards scooped him up and hanged him again.

To serve as a warning to other pirates, Captain Kidd's corpse was dipped in tar, bound in chains, and left to rot over the River Thames—a

* Andrew Jackson and the pirate Jean Lafitte formed a temporary alliance during the War of 1812. Though Jackson initially despised Lafitte, he accepted his aid in defending New Orleans, utilizing their weapons and local knowledge. Lafitte and his men provided expert gunnery skills, flint, and cannonballs. After the victory, Jackson publicly thanked Lafitte's crew, whom he branded "America's Favorite Hellish Bandits."

process called gibbeting. His skeleton remained on public display for three years.*

✪ ✪ ✪

So, buccaneering does not sound like a safe path. It is full of chicanery and risk-taking. But if you step back and look at American history, many of the great accomplishments were initiated by very flamboyant people. The most vivid example of this, in my opinion, is President Donald Trump.

We'll get to him in a minute. But first, I want to tell you that my father, William J. O'Reilly Sr., was not even *close* to being a buccaneer. He toed the line. And he regretted it. On his deathbed, he looked at me, his only son, and said, "My biggest mistake was not fulfilling my potential."

I looked at him and said, "I'll do it, Dad."

Whereupon he said his last words: "And you're an extension of me."

✪ ✪ ✪

It is true that I am a buccaneer. I have taken an enormous amount of risk in my life. And I did that because I saw what happened to my father. He was afraid. He was a man of immense talent but did not use it to advance his own cause. That reality caused me to ditch convention and form my own point of view, as well as an aggressive game plan.

✪ ✪ ✪

Now to Donald J. Trump.

I've known the man for thirty-five years. He has not changed at all. He's the "same guy he used to be," as Steve Winwood once sang. Now, for many of you, that is a very bad thing. President Trump understands

---

* Captain William Kidd (1654–1701) was a Scottish-born privateer turned notorious pirate, often considered one of history's most dangerous mariners. Originally commissioned to hunt pirates and enemy French ships, Kidd was betrayed by political backers and hanged in London in 1701 after being convicted of piracy and murder. It is believed he buried as much as 40,000 British pounds on Gardiners Island, the modern equivalent of $200 million. The full treasure has never been found.

your posture. But he doesn't like it. In fact, if you go after him, expect vengeance. It will come.

However, there's zero question that no one has governed like Mr. Trump. His swashbuckling style put him into the White House in the first place—much to the annoyance of his many detractors.

You may remember, Mr. Trump embraced his inner buccaneer during his first debate. It was August 3, 2015. There were ten wannabe Republican presidents on the stage in Cleveland, Ohio. The exposition was unfolding.

But it wasn't much of a debate. It was a massacre. The buccaneer Trump began personally attacking Jeb Bush, Ted Cruz, Marco Rubio, John Kasich, and all the others. He gave demeaning nicknames: "Lying Ted," "Boring Jeb," "Little Marco."

I was watching the spectacle in New York City with members of my staff. Remember that scene in the Mel Brooks film about a fictional musical, *The Producers,* when the dance number "Springtime for Hitler" was rolled out? Brooks cut to the audience. Everyone was frozen, their mouths agape. That was the reaction to Donald Trump's first debate performance. We were stunned. This had never happened before.

✪ ✪ ✪

Donald Trump calculated that many folks were fed up with establishment politicians. So, he decided to blow up the process. That gained him the loyalty of millions of Americans. However, millions of others have come to loathe the president.

But there is no question that he has changed history. In my book *Confronting the Presidents*, we run down the personality traits of all the men who have inhabited the White House. Nobody is even close to Trump. Most politicians are very cautious. They are unemotional. They are calculating. Obviously, President Trump does not fit into that category. However, he is a man of impulse—a nonconventional provocateur.

At any given time, Mr. Trump can say anything, and I mean that literally. It doesn't matter if it's true or if it's appropriate. If the man wants to say something, he's going to say it. He will absolutely board the political vessel and throw everybody overboard.

Again, this might not be a good thing for the country. You must decide that. But Donald Trump was elected twice to the presidency. So, his buccaneer style has enormous appeal. In 2024, seventy-seven million Americans voted for him.

✪ ✪ ✪

I got to know Donald Trump because I covered him in New York City. He was always running around doing something flamboyant. He loved being on TV and was available. I chronicle all that in my book *The United States of Trump*. But I noticed a couple of things about him that impressed me. Behind the scenes, he was very kind to almost everybody. His staff in the Trump Tower was extremely loyal to him. His children love him. And he has been very kind to my son when he didn't have to be.

President Trump will go down in history as a Chief Executive who lacked discipline but had vision. At this point, I can't tell you how his second administration is going to work out. I can tell you the man loves his country, works nonstop, and has done some very good things, in my opinion.

But that lack of discipline, which is a trait for most buccaneers, could eventually hurt his legacy.

✪ ✪ ✪

Now let's take a look at the lighter side of buccaneerism.

I grew up in Levittown, New York, close to where Billy Joel lived. I know him because, during the very hot summers, teenagers would gather at the so-called village green. Occasionally, Joel and his crew would float over from the Hicksville section of Levittown. Billy wore a leather jacket in August. Once I asked him, "Aren't you a little warm in that thing?"

He blew cigarette smoke in my face.

Back then, all of us sang a cappella to pass the time. Joel was phenomenal. I knew he was going to be a big thing, even at the age of fourteen. Eventually, he formed a band called The Hassles, playing clubs on Long Island. They even had a Top 100 hit called "Every Step I Take."

Billy Joel's story is well known. But what you might consider is that the man is a buccaneer. He broke every convention. The guy is a musical genius. He amassed a $90 million fortune before he was forty years old. Billy did not pay attention to the money. He was busy running around being a pop star, doing what he wanted to do. So, his manager and brother-in-law, Frank Weber, mismanaged or stole much of his wealth.

After a high-profile lawsuit, Weber settled out of court, filed for bankruptcy, and disappeared from the music business.*

But setbacks do not stop buccaneers. Joel built up a fortune once again using his incredible talent and showmanship to succeed as few other musicians have. Remember, Billy Joel didn't have the greatest preparation. His father left the family; his mother didn't have much money. He made it without any help. The buccaneer did it on his own.

Over the years, I've stayed in touch with Bill, as he likes to be called now. When I asked him why, he said, "I'm seventy-six. Why are people still calling me Billy?" I answered, "Because they spend $500 seeing you at Madison Square Garden and that's the name they see on the marquee."

He looked at me and would have blown smoke in my face, but he gave up that habit a long time ago. Billy Joel has contributed tremendously to the culture of this country. A bold guy makes it big. A very good thing.

✪ ✪ ✪

* After being fired by Billy Joel in 1989 following an audit that revealed massive embezzlement, Frank Weber faced a $90 million lawsuit from Joel but ultimately settled out of court, disappearing from the mainstream music industry while allegedly keeping a portion of the funds. It has been reported that Weber may have moved to Japan, where he was previously known, and continues to work in music at a lower level.

Another buccaneer is the actor Jack Nicholson. I got to know him later in life when I was anchoring *The O'Reilly Factor*. Every few months my crew went out to Los Angeles, where I would attend Lakers games.

As you may know, Jack Nicholson is an enormous Lakers fan, mesmerized when the Laker Girls run out on the floor during time-outs. Anyway, my seats were close to Nicholson's, and we started trading barbs. It was all good natured, but he clearly watched *The O'Reilly Factor* and was interested in politics.

Like Billy Joel, Nicholson had a chaotic upbringing. He lived in New Jersey in a dysfunctional family. He didn't even know who his mother was until he was thirty-seven years old. But the guy has enormous talent. He moved to Los Angeles, got lucky with a movie called *Easy Rider*, and became a huge star.

At the same time, Nicholson was kind of crazy, hanging out with Marlon Brando and other Hollywood celebrities who did whatever they wanted to do. The reason I'm putting Nicholson in this book is to show you that, again, like Joel, he made it completely on his own. He was a buccaneer blessed with talent, and he hit it big. That is one of America's strengths—there are more possibilities in this country than anywhere else.

Over the years, Nicholson and I have had a lot of conversations about America. He's a liberal man, but he doesn't like phonies. He wants the country to be respected and can see through politicians who are simply selfish. We trade questions. I ask him about his showbiz associations, he asks me about political people. We both answer honestly.

The most illuminating conversation we ever had was about the movie *The Shining*. The director, Stanely Kubrick, was certifiable. A methodical guy, he would have Nicholson and his co-star, Shelley Duvall, do scores of takes, hours in front of the camera. That apparently broke Duvall. Word is she had a breakdown and never recovered professionally from the experience.*

---

* *The Shining* (1980), directed by Stanley Kubrick, is a landmark psychological horror film known for its intense production and meticulous detail. The movie is based on the book by Stephen King. Kubrick was a perfectionist who often demanded

Nicholson has great stories about Warren Beatty, Brando, all the big-time movie stars of the 1970s and 1980s. He is an incredible weaver of cinematic history. His friends call him "the Colonel" after his character in the film *A Few Good Men*. Another tremendous performance that actually stole the movie from the topliner, Tom Cruise.

After all these years, we still need Jack on that wall.

He was also extremely nice to my son.

✪✪✪

How about this name? Clint Eastwood. Basically a working-class guy, Clint was a big *Factor* fan. I only learned that when I was visiting the Monterey, California, area, where he lives. I was riding down Route 1 when I pulled into a pharmacy. At the time, Eastwood owned a restaurant in Carmel called the Hog's Breath Inn. He had also run for mayor of that town because he was mad the city council banned ice cream.

After getting out of my car, I ran into Clint almost literally. He was standing on the sidewalk. I introduced myself, and he said, "I just listened to *The Radio Factor*!" That was a syndicated program I was doing at the time. He went on to ask me a whole bunch of questions. It was one of the most surreal experiences of my life. I was hoping that he would say, "Do you feel lucky, punk?" But Eastwood was very polite.

We stayed in touch. I've had a few dinners with Mr. Eastwood at the Sardine Factory in Monterey. They were very similar to my conversations with Jack Nicholson. I ask him about showbiz. He asks me about politics. So, I got the lowdown about *Dirty Harry*, spaghetti Westerns, and how the man went from digging pools to being the biggest star in the world.

---

excessive shoots and schedules. The scene where Wendy (Shelley Duvall) swings a baseball bat at Jack (Jack Nicholson) holds a record for 127 takes.

He, in turn, would ask me about the Iraq War, 9/11, John McCain, Mitt Romney, Donald Trump, and Barack Obama.*

I admire Clint Eastwood for the same reason I admire Billy Joel and Jack Nicholson. These guys are all buccaneers. I hate to be repetitive, but they had no help in achieving enormous success. They did it on sheer personality, talent, and perseverance. All of these men have brought entertainment value to millions of people, a tremendous achievement in itself.

Perhaps the best perk from being in the media all these years is that I got to meet the buccaneers.

✪ ✪ ✪

And then there was Old Hollywood. I don't know why, but vintage actors generally love me. I corresponded with Doris Day, Kirk Douglas, Charlton Heston, Jonathan Winters, and Ernest Borgnine. It was fascinating. I was at a Hollywood soiree one time and a whole bunch of actors like Tab Hunter and George Hamilton engaged me in conversation. Thinking back, Hollywood at one time was conservative.

Remember, Ronald Reagan was the president of the Screen Actors Guild; he was generally very well liked in Los Angeles.

That, of course, has changed drastically.

Here's an example. A few years ago, I was sitting in a restaurant when the comedian Chelsea Handler walked in. I had never met her. But she locked in on me almost immediately and walked over. Her first words were these: "You're not allowed to be in Los Angeles."

She wasn't smiling.

Whereupon your six-foot-four buccaneer rose from his seat and towered over the now-somewhat-shaky Chelsea. I said, "Nice to meet you, Ms. Handler. Thanks for all the laughs."

---

* At the 2012 Republican National Convention, Clint Eastwood delivered an improvised twelve-minute speech on August 30, 2012, to endorse Mitt Romney, largely featuring a one-sided conversation with an empty chair representing President Barack Obama. The unscripted performance criticized Obama's economic record.

COURTESY OF THE AUTHOR, REPHOTOGRAPHED BY ROBERT JUDE PUGLISI

Bill O'Reilly and actor Jack Nicholson

COURTESY OF THE AUTHOR, REPHOTOGRAPHED BY ROBERT JUDE PUGLISI

Bill O'Reilly and comedian Jay Leno

COURTESY OF THE AUTHOR, REPHOTOGRAPHED BY ROBERT JUDE PUGLISI

Bill O'Reilly and Donald J. Trump

COURTESY OF THE AUTHOR, REPHOTOGRAPHED BY ROBERT JUDE PUGLISI

Bill O'Reilly and Jon Stewart on *The Daily Show*

COURTESY BARACK OBAMA PRESIDENTIAL LIBRARY

Bill O'Reilly interviews President Barack Obama in the White House

COURTESY OF THE AUTHOR, REPHOTOGRAPHED BY ROBERT JUDE PUGLISI

Bill O'Reilly and Hillary Rodham Clinton

COURTESY OF THE AUTHOR, REPHOTOGRAPHED BY ROBERT JUDE PUGLISI

Bill O'Reilly interviews President Donald J. Trump

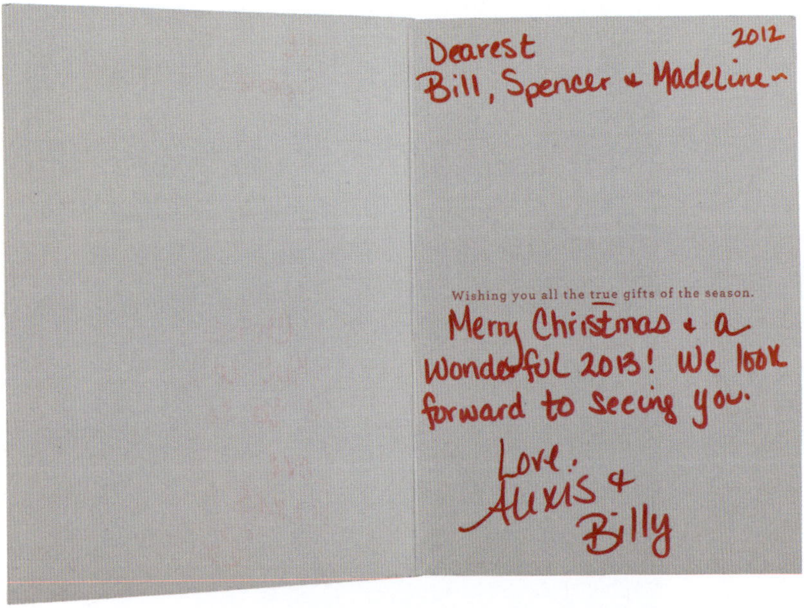

Dearest 2012
Bill, Spencer & Madeline—

Wishing you all the true gifts of the season.

Merry Christmas & a wonderful 2013! We look forward to seeing you.

Love,
Alexis &
Billy

COURTESY OF THE AUTHOR, REPHOTOGRAPHED BY ROBERT JUDE PUGLISI

A Christmas card from musician Billy Joel to the O'Reilly family

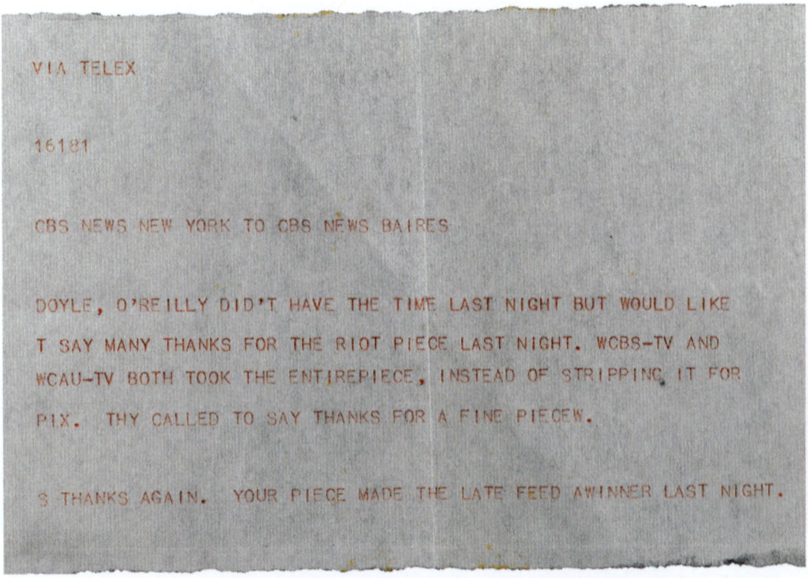

VIA TELEX

16181

CBS NEWS NEW YORK TO CBS NEWS BAIRES

DOYLE, O'REILLY DID'T HAVE THE TIME LAST NIGHT BUT WOULD LIKE
T SAY MANY THANKS FOR THE RIOT PIECE LAST NIGHT. WCBS-TV AND
WCAU-TV BOTH TOOK THE ENTIREPIECE, INSTEAD OF STRIPPING IT FOR
PIX. THY CALLED TO SAY THANKS FOR A FINE PIECEW.

S THANKS AGAIN. YOUR PIECE MADE THE LATE FEED AWINNER LAST NIGHT.

COURTESY OF THE AUTHOR, REPHOTOGRAPHED BY ROBERT JUDE PUGLISI

The CBS memo sent to Buenos Aires during
Bill O'Reilly's Falklands War coverage

COURTESY OF THE AUTHOR, REPHOTOGRAPHED BY ROBERT JUDE PUGLISI

Bill O'Reilly and journalist Mike Wallace

COURTESY OF THE AUTHOR, REPHOTOGRAPHED BY ROBERT JUDE PUGLISI

Bill O'Reilly's name card from the Beijing Club during his 2025 trip to China

COURTESY OF THE AUTHOR, REPHOTOGRAPHED BY ROBERT JUDE PUGLISI

Actor Clint Eastwood, Bill O'Reilly, and his son Spencer

COURTESY OF THE AUTHOR, REPHOTOGRAPHED BY ROBERT JUDE PUGLISI

William James O'Reilly Sr. and his wife,
Winifred Angela O'Reilly

COURTESY OF THE AUTHOR, REPHOTOGRAPHED BY ROBERT JUDE PUGLISI

Bill O'Reilly reporting from the Berlin Wall

COURTESY OF THE AUTHOR, REPHOTOGRAPHED BY ROBERT JUDE PUGLISI

The photograph signed by five US presidents: Barack Obama, George W. Bush, Bill Clinton, George H. W. Bush, and Jimmy Carter

COURTESY OF THE AUTHOR, REPHOTOGRAPHED BY ROBERT JUDE PUGLISI

Bill O'Reilly and US service members in Kabul, Afghanistan

COURTESY OF THE AUTHOR, REPHOTOGRAPHED BY ROBERT JUDE PUGLISI

Bill O'Reilly at the Al-Faw Palace in Baghdad, Iraq

I gave her a wink and sat down. The normally loquacious Chelsea Handler said nothing.

✪ ✪ ✪

There are exceptions to the Young Hollywood rule. Jack Black was very respectful when I ran into him. Not so much Denzel Washington, who is one of my favorite actors. I complimented him on a number of his performances. I think he grunted twice. I was not going to be co-starring in *The Equalizer 4* any time soon. Hold that thought. Maybe if Denzel waxed me like he does with all the other villains, I might have a shot.

The younger Hollywood people, in my opinion, are not nearly as accomplished as the older stars who generally came up the hard way. I don't see many buccaneers in Hollywood today. A lot of these people are nepo babies. Others just play the liberal political game to get parts. The talent is there, but the attitude is far different than it used to be.

Final Hollywood story.

For some reason I was invited to a dinner party at an agent's house in the Hollywood Hills. I didn't want to go. I'm not good at small talk, and I was busy. However, the man was very persuasive and respectful, so I attended.

At the party were Elon Musk, Bill Maher, a whole bunch of Hollywood producers, and Kate Hudson, whom I was lucky enough to be seated next to. I know Ms. Hudson's stepfather, Kurt Russell, who's kind of a conservative man and a very smart actor as well.

Anyway, the wine guy was coming around, and I told him, "No, thank you." Whereupon Kate looked at me and commented that it was a very good, expensive wine. I replied, "I don't drink at all." Kate looked very perplexed. After ten seconds, she said, "Oh, I know. Weed, right?" I looked at her and said, "No, when I mow the lawn, I just throw all the clippings away."

Dumb remark, but it was clear that Kate Hudson had no blankin' idea who I was. That amused me greatly. I did have a very nice conversation with her about her career, which has been an excellent one.

Bill Maher and I have a long history. We'll never be buddies. He's a big weed guy, so maybe that's where Kate got the thought. But we're cordial. There's no reason not to be.

Elon Musk was very interesting that night. Most of the crowd didn't really understand who he was because Musk had not yet hit it big with Tesla. I had no idea about the man's background, but I watched him. I knew the name. I think he and I had something in common. We were both there to observe the dinner party, rather than participate in it.

Anyway, Elon Musk is a huge buccaneer, as everybody knows. But on that night, he kind of sat it out.

✪ ✪ ✪

One of the major influences on American culture was the late-night talk show guy David Letterman. Talk about a buccaneer. Unlike Jay Leno, Johnny Carson, and Jimmy Fallon, Letterman is *not* currying favor. I think he'd admit that. On his program, he wasn't trying to coach you into a touchy-feely place. Amazingly witty, Letterman appeared on more than six thousand late-night episodes. That is a record, even surpassing Johnny Carson.

I, your humble correspondent, appeared with Dave *sixteen* times. Two buccaneers going at each other.

✪ ✪ ✪

It was January 4, 2006. The Iraq War was raging. I had scorched an anti-war activist named Cindy Sheehan on *The Factor*. Ms. Sheehan had lost her son Casey in the conflict, which was obviously terrible. But, in her grief, she was comparing American soldiers in Iraq, who had deposed the heinous Saddam Hussein, to Muslim terrorists. In the summer of 2005, Sheehan spoke with NPR. During the exchange, she blamed the dictator's brutal regime on President George W. Bush, accusing him of committing genocide.

> We propped him up and sold him weapons for years! We propped him up in his war against Iran, and I have to wonder for the rest of my life if my son was killed by a weapon that America sold to Saddam. Another thing is Saddam was a bad man. But that's not why the president told us that we were invading Iraq. He told us it was because Iraq had weapons of mass destruction and that Iraq had something to do with 9/11, and both of those were lies. . . . And now the mission is to kill more people because so many people have already been killed.

That statement was the backdrop to me walking out onto Letterman's stage in New York City. You should know that Dave never speaks to his guests before the program, as Jay Leno and most of the others do. Also, his studio is about fourteen degrees below zero—Letterman likes it cold.

Didn't matter to me.

Anyway, I sat down after polite applause from the audience, and Letterman began:

LETTERMAN: I'm very concerned about people like yourself who don't have nothing but endless sympathy for a woman like Cindy Sheehan, honest to Christ.

O'REILLY: No, I'm sorry. No way a terrorist who blows up women and children is going to be called a freedom fighter on my program.

(APPLAUSE)

LETTERMAN: I'm not smart enough to debate you point to point on this, but I have the feeling—I have the feeling about . . . I have the feeling about sixty percent of what you say is crap, but I don't know that for a fact.

O'REILLY: Sixty?

LETTERMAN: Did I say sixty percent? Sixty percent, that's just—I'm just spitballing here now.

O'REILLY: Listen, I respect your opinion. You should respect mine.

LETTERMAN: Well, I—I—yes, okay.

(APPLAUSE)

O'REILLY: Our analysis is based on the best evidence we can get.

LETTERMAN: Yes, but I think there's something—this fair and balanced, I'm not sure that it's—I don't think that you represent an objective viewpoint.

O'REILLY: But you have to give me an example if you're going to make those statements.

LETTERMAN: Well, I don't watch your show, so that would be impossible.

(LAUGHTER)

O'REILLY: Then why would you come to that conclusion if you don't watch the program?

LETTERMAN: Because of things that I have read, things that I know.

O'REILLY: Oh, come on, you're going to take things that you've read? You know what they say about you? Come on.

(LAUGHTER)

O'REILLY: Look, watch it for a half an hour. You'll get addicted. You'll be a *Factor* fan. We'll send you a hat!

(APPLAUSE)

That was a clear victory for me. And, while other big-time entertainers might have been angry, Letterman was impressed. I stood up to him. It was fascinating television. That's why he invited me back again and again.

✪ ✪ ✪

It was March 31, 2009, and I was promoting my autobiography, *A Bold Fresh Piece of Humanity*. Once again, I sat across from David Letterman.

LETTERMAN: This book is a crazy bestseller. How many weeks has it been on the bestseller list?

O'REILLY: Six months on the bestseller list.

LETTERMAN: See, here's what breaks my heart about this . . .
(HOLDS COVER OF THE BOOK)
LETTERMAN: In my mind, I think of you as a goon. But then when you look at this picture, look at how sweet and adorable that kid is. It breaks my heart because I have a sweet and adorable kid like that, and I think, "Oh great, what if he too becomes a goon?!"
(LAUGHTER)
LETTERMAN: You know?
O'REILLY: Do you want me to respond to any of this?
LETTERMAN: No.
(LAUGHTER)

✪ ✪ ✪

To this day, I believe that David Letterman was the best late-night host in history. Better than Johnny Carson. Why? Because Letterman had a sense of outrage and didn't hide it. That led to some very good discussions. It wasn't just a joke-fest or trying to play coy with the audience.

David Letterman is a buccaneer. Once again, he had no help in his career. He began as a weatherman in Indiana, rose to prominence, and influenced the culture.

You don't have to like buccaneers, but you should know that they almost always shake things up. To me, that is a good thing.

✪ ✪ ✪

Not all of my talk show appearances were under control. I appeared on *The View* nine times. Back then it was run by Barbara Walters, who, as I mentioned earlier, I knew pretty well.

Barbara was a buccaneer because she broke through the "men's club." Her father was a show business guy, so she did have connections, but she went up against the male-dominated news industry and succeeded on a level never seen before. Barbara was a liberal woman, but not an ideologue. She was genuinely interested in hearing all sides of a story. She wasn't dismissive, as *The View* hosts are today.

My most dramatic appearance on *The View* took place October 14, 2010. The subject was building a mosque near Ground Zero in Manhattan. On 9/11, the World Trade Center towers were destroyed by jihadists. That wound had not healed nine years later. It was still raw. The fact that an imam wanted to build a mosque at the site where three thousand Americans were slaughtered offended me greatly.

And so, the conversation began.

O'REILLY: Let me break this to you, seventy percent of Americans don't want that mosque down there.

JOY BEHAR: I wanna see that poll!

O'REILLY: I'll show you that poll in a minute!

WHOOPI GOLDBERG: Why is that? Why aren't we saying—

O'REILLY: Because it's inappropriate!

GOLDBERG: Why is it inappropriate?

O'REILLY: Because Muslims killed us on 9/11!

GOLDBERG: No! Oh my God! That is such bullshit!

O'REILLY: Muslims didn't kill us on 9/11?! Is that what you're saying?

GOLDBERG: Extremists did that!

O'REILLY: And what religion were they in?!

BEHAR: I don't want to sit here anymore. I really don't.

(GOLDBERG AND BEHAR WALK OFF TO CROWD APPLAUSE)

BARBARA WALTERS to AUDIENCE: You have just seen what should NOT happen. We should be able to have discussions without washing our hands, screaming, and walking off stage. I love my colleagues, but that should not have happened.

✪ ✪ ✪

The fact is, I was happy Ms. Goldberg and Ms. Behar had walked off the set because I knew everyone in the country would see what happened in the replays. And they would understand my position. You do not disrespect the dead, even if you have a positive intention. The imam could have built a mosque at a variety of other places in lower Manhattan. As stated, an Islamic presence at the site of Ground Zero was and remains inappropriate.

You would not build an American cultural center in Hiroshima, Japan.

I did appear on *The View* a few more times before they lost their collective minds. Buccaneers do not fear boarding ships, no matter the threat. So, if I got an invitation, I took it. Then, Disney decided to go far left, all the time, on *The View*.

Instead of robust debate, it became a constant diatribe against conservatives, and, in particular, Donald Trump. The audience changed. It used to be people from all persuasions. Now it is home to hardcore progressives.

I really don't understand why Disney allowed that program to spin out of control. In the year 2025, *The View* booked no conservative guest on the program—not one. The closest was Arnold Schwarzenegger, who was talking about how his muscles are sagging . . . or something.

If Jean Lafitte were still alive, I would pay him to sack *The View*.

✪ ✪ ✪

If you analyze the media, there are very few buccaneers in that industry. Most of the on-air talent plays it safe. They are scared. They don't want to make "mistakes." Their paycheck is everything. You see it every day. Television news is not a business for risk-takers. However, there are a couple of exceptions.

As mentioned earlier, I've gotten to know Stephen A. Smith pretty well. I developed a concept called the Three Americans, which includes Chris Cuomo, Smith, and myself. We do specials on NewsNation. In October 2025, we did a two-hour event at the Kennedy Center in Washington, DC. That was before Donald Trump demanded his name be put on the building. It was amazingly successful. An estimated twenty-four million people watched it on linear TV or social media.

No regular television news program comes close to that kind of an audience.

One aside. On November 7, 2025, when I did Bill Maher's program on HBO, he gave me some jazz about "not being on TV." I expected Maher would do that. So, I coolly looked at him and said, "Hey, Bill, maybe you missed it, but I hosted a special on NewsNation that got twenty-four million views. I don't think all of your shows on HBO add up to *that*."*

Advantage O'Reilly.

Anyway, Stephen A. Smith is a very interesting guy. Once again, and I hate to be repetitive, he had no advantages. Born in the Bronx, raised in Queens, father in and out, he rose up to be the highest-paid sportscaster in history. Why? Because he's a buccaneer. He's liable to say anything at any time. He has no fear. He goes on ESPN, speaks his mind, and is willing to take the flack. Most of the commentators are sitting there telling you what you already know. They play it safe. Not Stephen A.

In my private conversations with him, it's clear he's a smart guy. I suspect he may have some political ambitions in the future. But to do that, he would have to walk away from an enormous amount of money. Obviously a very tough decision.

But watch this guy down the road.

Cuomo, Smith, and I get along very well, and you would not think that would be the case. Chris is a dedicated Democrat. His father, Governor Mario Cuomo, was a brilliant liberal thinker. But Cuomo's not a Kool-Aid guy. However, there are times when I have to rough him up in true buccaneer fashion. He mostly gives it right back, which is a good thing. Robust debate is a positive for the USA.

While Cuomo is a doctrinaire Democrat, Stephen A. is unpredictable. And I like that. He's also very respectful. He understands exactly what

---

* Highlights from the special earned more than twenty-four million views across NewsNation's digital platforms, including the NewsNation website and YouTube. Clips were viewed more than eighteen million times on TikTok.

I'm doing on television because he does some of it himself. Two bucs in a pod.

✪ ✪ ✪

I've saved the best buccaneer for last. The man is Mike Wallace. When I was a kid watching a black-and-white TV with my father in Levittown, Mr. Wallace hosted a show called *Night Beat*. He was obnoxious. I loved it. So did my dad. Wallace would lean in and deliver all kinds of questions that nobody on television would ask back in the 1950s. He became a force in my mind.

At that time, I had no journalistic or television ambitions at all. But I watched Mike Wallace every chance I got. He was tough. He was a buccaneer. He had no fear. He made mistakes, but the guy was unbelievably genuine.

When he interviewed Ayatollah Khomeini in November 1979, Wallace said that Egyptian leader Anwar Sadat had called the cleric a "lunatic." The camera came in close, allowing the audience to see a very hateful look on the Ayatollah's face.

In October 1981, Anwar Sadat was assassinated in Cairo.

I got to know Mike Wallace because of the success of *The O'Reilly Factor*. He and *60 Minutes* boss Don Hewitt watched the show a lot; they liked the confrontational interviews because that's what they did. So, they decided to interview me on *60 Minutes*. The date was February 22, 2007. I knew Wallace was going to give me a hard time. He could not come off with a cupcake interview and keep his fierce reputation.

So, I decided to hijack the interview from the very beginning. Here's what I said in the show open.

O'REILLY: You know, you're responsible for this O'Reilly deal. I always tell everybody, you got a problem with me, you call Mike Wallace. He's responsible for the O'Reilly deal.

WALLACE: What are you talking about? Are you serious about this?

O'REILLY: I'm always serious. When I was growing up, I had no interest in the news. But my father liked you. I thought, "That guy is

> pretty interesting." Because he's giving people a hard time.... Then I got older. There were three guys I liked to watch. You, Howard Cosell, and Tom Snyder. You were the three. So, you're responsible! Howard's dead. But you're still here! So, you're responsible! That's why I tell people, "You got a problem with O'Reilly, talk to Wallace."

I vividly remember sitting in my living room with two cameras, lights all over the place, about three feet away from Mike Wallace, thinking to myself, "Are you kidding me? I'm being interviewed by this guy?" But I had to bring my A game because Mike was not in the tank for anyone.

He was a true buccaneer.

✪✪✪

Shortly before his death, I took Mike Wallace and his wife Mary to dinner. We talked about the decline of journalism and how money was dominating television news. We made fun of a lot of people we both knew and had a terrific time. When we were walking out, he stumbled a bit. Mike was clearly feeling the effects of age. I took his elbow, raised him up gently, and said, "Hey, don't worry about it, I do that all the time. At least when you do it, everybody pays attention. When I do it, people want to kick me."

Mike Wallace died from natural causes on April 7, 2012, at the age of ninety-three. He was the best TV journalist I have ever seen and perhaps the best modern-day media buccaneer in the world.

To this day, I miss him very much.

So, let's all raise a glass to the buccaneers. They make life more interesting; they break through tired convention.

America needs more of them.

CHAPTER SEVENTEEN

The Deceivers

We take from each other and give nothing at all.
—James Ingram, "Yah Mo B There"*

One of the most damaging things currently on display in the United States of America is the rise of deception as well as the fall of moral inhibitors. It used to be that every kid in the country knew the Ten Commandments, even if their families were not religious. Now, try going to a mall and asking the urchins to name *three* commandments. Most will not be able to do that. Sadly, collective "morality" in America is in steep decline. Here's some backup.

- According to data from the National Institutes of Health, 70 percent of all divorces are caused by "lies and deception."

- Around 40 percent of clinical depression in the US is linked to "lies and a sense of betrayal from friends and family."

---

* "Yah Mo B There" is an R&B single released by James Ingram in 1983. The song, written and produced by Quincy Jones, is a stylized version of "Yahweh Be There," intended to convey that God will always be present to guide and support his people throughout life's struggles.

- A full 64 percent of Americans believe lying can be justified in certain situations. That's up from 42 percent in 2006.

- In addition, 70 percent of job applicants in America admit to lying on their résumés.

- Finally, 86 percent of us say we lie to our parents.

All of this indicates a dishonest society. And we're not the only ones. All over the world, the traditional tenets of honesty and loyalty are disappearing.

✪ ✪ ✪

There is a reason that Judas Iscariot is featured prominently in the New Testament. If you don't know who Judas is, you might listen up. One of the twelve apostles, Iscariot is the biggest traitor in the annals of history. He turned Jesus of Nazareth over to authorities he knew would eventually kill him. Judas did that for money.*

The night before the betrayal, Jesus actually addressed Iscariot at the Last Supper. He said to his apostles that one of them would betray him. The quote is this: "It would have been better for that man if he had not been born."

According to the scripture, Judas himself was unfazed even though he was branded "Son of Perdition."†

Most people in America describe themselves as "Christian," but very few attend weekly religious services. That, of course, is up to you. Just because you go to church doesn't mean you are a good person.

But clearly, scripture is warning people about deception and

* According to the Gospel of Matthew (26:15), Judas Iscariot was paid thirty pieces of silver to betray Jesus. Biblically, thirty pieces of silver was the legal compensation for the death of a slave (Exodus 21:32), indicating it was a disrespectful amount intended to demonstrate how the religious leaders viewed Jesus. Overcome with guilt, Judas returned the thirty pieces of silver to the chief priests before hanging himself.

† Perdition is a state of eternal damnation, spiritual ruin, or hell, often referring to the final punishment of the wicked. It signifies total destruction of the soul.

betrayal. It is very difficult to come back from that. Yet millions of Americans don't believe this is a problem.

It is.

Any society that accepts untrustworthy behavior is enabling weakness. If you can't trust people, your life will be extremely difficult. And that is where we find ourselves today in America.

✪ ✪ ✪

More statistics. According to data from Harvard University's Department of Sociology as well as the University of Michigan, the average American lies about twice a day.

There's also a big gender difference here. The study suggests men lie about six times per day, while women lie three times. Of course, some people never lie, which brings the average down. But you can see that honesty, the basis of all human interaction, is under siege.

So, my question is: Who's doing anything about it?

The answer is difficult to ascertain. We all know that politicians exaggerate, embellish, obscure, and deceive to get what they want. In business, you've got to watch everything. People will steal from you. In court, perjury is now an epidemic. Even though most jurisdictions do not even prosecute lying under oath, about ten thousand Americans are convicted of perjury each year.

Ask any attorney. They will roll their eyes as far as telling "the truth, the whole truth, and nothing but the truth."

That rarely happens despite your right hand being placed on a Bible.

✪ ✪ ✪

The only person I know in my life who was never betrayed was my mother. Winifred Angela O'Reilly. That's because she lived a narrow and focused life. She was raised in a traditional manner in Teaneck, New Jersey, earned a college degree from Boston University, and married my father shortly after World War II. My parents stayed together until my dad died.

My mother never remarried or even dated. She was loyal to my father.

Ann had a simple life. Her biggest complication was me—and trying to keep her son out of trouble. Otherwise, she lived in an orderly manner where there were few opportunities for deception. My father provided protection for the family.

Everyone else I know has gotten hosed by other people, and I have interacted with thousands of human beings. In my life, I have seen it all. Here's the kicker: There's very little remorse these days when one human being hurts another. There's excuse making, rationalizations, whataboutism, and outright apathy. Sometimes a "sorry" will be uttered almost as an afterthought.

Perhaps the most amazing deception I have ever seen was the Bernie Madoff case. The guy lived about a mile from me in eastern Long Island. I never met him. He had a nice oceanfront house, limousines taking him everywhere, private jets, you name it.

How did he get all these things? Well, it's estimated that Madoff stole $65 billion. He did that by running a Ponzi scheme: taking money from friends, telling those people he was investing it, and then paying them dividends from other funds he acquired through deception. Madoff's victims include Yeshiva University to the tune of $140 million, Holocaust survivor Eli Wiesel for $30 million, director Steven Spielberg, actor Kevin Bacon, and TV guy Larry King. In total, Madoff fleeced about forty-two thousand people across 127 countries over a period of three decades.

On June 29, 2009, Bernie Madoff was finally sentenced to 150 years in prison for the incredible damage he did all over the world. The criminal served twelve years before he died behind bars at the age of eighty-two.*

His son Mark hanged himself two years after his father was arrested. His other son, Andrew, died of cancer at forty-eight, blaming

---

* Bernie Madoff died on April 14, 2021, at the Federal Medical Center in Butner, North Carolina. He died of natural causes, having suffered from end-stage renal disease and other chronic medical conditions.

the disease on the stress his father caused him. Madoff's wife, Ruth, disappeared from public life. She currently resides in a $4 million home in southern Connecticut. She does not deserve to live there.

Madoff's brother, Peter, served a ten-year prison sentence for helping in the massive fraud. His sister, Sondra, was killed in a murder-suicide with her husband in February 2022.

So, you can see that the scripture quote "It would have been better for that man if he had not been born" plays out perfectly in the Bernie Madoff case.

✪ ✪ ✪

Individual dishonesty, however, pales beside the deception coming from powerful people. Elected officials can impose taxes, interest rates, laws, and regulations, even regarding where you live (zoning). And it is in the political precincts where a massive deception is underway.

It all has to do with the attack on capitalism. The far left in America has decided that the US should be a Socialist/Communist country. This, of course, goes against the Constitution, which allows freedom of expression. Under that banner you are able to accumulate wealth and prosperity without interference—if you do it legally.

The Democratic Socialists of America, a growing organization, completely reject economic freedom. Its website states:

> We want to collectively own the key economic drivers that dominate our lives, such as energy production and transportation. We want the multiracial working class united in solidarity instead of divided by fear. We want to win "radical" reforms like single-payer Medicare for All, defunding the police/refunding communities, the Green New Deal, and more as a transition to a freer, more just life.

But seizure of private assets and property is not "just." It is theft. The Constitution gives Congress the right to tax, but not to force people to hand over their stuff. That is what the Socialists want.

✪ ✪ ✪

The big daddy of the Socialist/Communist movement in America is Senator Bernie Sanders of Vermont. The eighty-four-year-old has acquired fame and fortune by pushing radical left economic views.

In 1988, Sanders, then mayor of Burlington, Vermont, traveled on the taxpayer dime to the Soviet Union. Apparently, he was on his honeymoon but told Vermonters he was visiting Burlington's sister city, Yaroslavl. That trip set up a lifetime of Sanders living off the American taxpayer.

The next year, Bernie shows up in Cuba. Again, on the taxpayer dime.*

Here's what Sanders said:

> I did not see a hungry child. I did not see any homeless people. Cuba today not only has free health care but very high-quality health care. . . . It's unfair to simply say everything is bad. When Fidel Castro came into office, you know what he did? He had a massive literacy program. Is that a bad thing?

Under Fidel Castro, you needed healthcare because if you stepped out of line, you got the hell beat out of you. Sanders conveniently overlooks the unbelievable repression that Castro brought to the island nation. In fact, today it is estimated that 89 percent of the Cuban people live in poverty.

What say you, Bernie Sanders?

✪ ✪ ✪

Then there's Bernie's symbolic daughter, Congresswoman Alexandria Ocasio-Cortez. She's even more radical than he is. Raised in comfort-

---

* Bernie Sanders traveled to Cuba in March 1989 for an eight-day visit, primarily to meet with dictator Fidel Castro and study the impact of the Cuban Revolution. At the time, Sanders was the outgoing mayor of Burlington, Vermont, and was interested in exploring the Socialist-oriented policies of left-leaning governments, particularly in healthcare, housing, and education.

able surroundings, Ocasio-Cortez now rails against the evil of profit. She describes it this way:

> Capitalism, at its core, involves the absolute pursuit of profit at all human, environmental, and social costs. This is not a redeemable system for the prosperity and peace of the vast majority of people. . . . No one ever makes a billion dollars. You TAKE a billion dollars.

Ocasio-Cortez, just thirty-six years old, has a bright future in politics. In 2028, she may run against Senator Chuck Schumer for the New York seat. She could very well win.

✪ ✪ ✪

Then there's Mayor Zohran Mamdani, who now runs the largest city in the country, New York.

This guy doesn't even try to fake it, as Sanders and Ocasio-Cortez do. He's right out of the Karl Marx playbook. Here we go:

> Then there are also other issues that we firmly believe in, whether it's BDS [Boycott, Divestment, and Sanctions of Israel], right, or whether it's the end goal of *seizing the means of production*.

That's communism. The government controls the private marketplace. Mamdani got this gibberish directly from Bernie Sanders, who, in 1988, said this: "What being a socialist means is human beings can own the *means of production*."

Incredibly, the corporate media, consisting of perhaps the most greedy companies on the face of the earth, have embraced Sanders and Ocasio-Cortez. They are not shunned. They are applauded by *The New York Times*, *The Washington Post*, CNN, and others. They almost have a cult following. It is absolutely incredible to watch this.

While many Americans dismiss these radical leftists, I do not. They are deceivers at the highest level. They want to seize private property and constrain individual freedom.

This is a dire threat to the country, and many younger Americans are embracing the Socialist/Communist platform. Of course, they are foolish to do that. Jealousy is in play, as is a lack of historical knowledge. Communism threatens personal freedom, as we have seen time and again.

Nevertheless, the radical left has some momentum in the United States.

✪✪✪

So, what can we do about "the deceivers"?

Well, my philosophy is to call them out. But I have paid a heavy price for doing that. There are a number of groups in America that try to obliterate their political opposition. This is not about dissent, it's about destruction. Over the years on television, I have pinpointed those groups as I have done in this book. I learned one very interesting lesson: Most of the deceivers do not care that they are disloyal to the country. They embrace it. They justify it.

In America, we have the First Amendment, which allows citizens to say deceitful things as long as they are not criminal. You can lie your butt off, but unless you directly threaten somebody, nothing will happen to you. That is, unless the court of public opinion turns against you.

That's what the "Me Too" movement was all about. They tried to "cancel" people they didn't like. No due process, little fact-finding, all headlines were convictions.

Despicable.

I'm sorry to paint such a dark picture, but I believe irresponsible personal behavior as well as political extremism have weakened America dramatically. I have a basis of comparison because I am the son of parents who were labeled the "Greatest Generation." For those of you not versed in history, that group of Americans suffered through the Great Depression of the 1930s, then fought the most destructive war of all time against the Nazis and the Japanese.

Deception was rare for the Greatest Generation.

Now, it is not.

And therein lies something that must change. But the government cannot force people to be honest in their personal dealings. If you lie to your spouse, no agency is going to come to your house. With America's public schools abdicating responsibility to teach good and evil to students, this looks like a problem that will never be formally overcome in this country.

Therefore, good Americans must lead by example and confront the bad guys themselves. That takes courage. The deceivers *will* strike back. They don't have any rules. So, many decent folks are frightened. I wrote about this extensively in my last book, *Confronting Evil*. To me, there is no doubt that evil is on the rise in America.

✪ ✪ ✪

One way I cope with the situation is to surround myself with honest people. I have succeeded in doing that even though I've been disappointed on some occasions by treacherous behavior among those I trusted. The Nazarene saw the same thing happen to him. There really is no protection from deceit.

It is simply a part of life.

But you don't have to give in to it. If a person is untrustworthy, they get put on waivers by me. Gone. But because I am a Christian, if they show repentance, I give them another chance. I am a sinner, too, and want that consideration.

But I must tell you, it is very rare these days to see the betrayers admit what they've done.

If that could change, the United States would be a far stronger nation.

CHAPTER EIGHTEEN

The Bubble People

I'm a man without conviction,
I'm a man who doesn't know.
—Boy George

Some people are so uninformed it is almost tragic. I'm sure you know a few of them. I don't want to be condescending, but living in a free society should demand some kind of information gathering. If you don't care about individual freedom, you could very well lose it. As Benjamin Franklin famously said, we live in "a republic, if you can keep it."

The problem is distractions. Not all uninformed people are stupid. However, Americans can easily get lost in trivial pursuits. That takes away from any kind of awareness, both individual and collective. Then you add in the public school education system, which, as we've discussed, has largely abdicated its responsibility to train students in the complexities of their country and society. It's much easier to live in a place like China, where you are told exactly what to do—and you'd better do it. In the United States, you have many options that people in totalitarian societies do not have. My oft-delivered quote is: "The Constitution gives you the right to be a moron."

✪ ✪ ✪

A good example of a person who had no blankin' idea what was happening in his own country was a guy who once cut my hair. Brilliant barber, but every time I would sit in the chair, he would ask me very basic questions, like, "Who attacked us on 9/11?" Not wanting to be disrespectful, I patiently answered things that a seven-year-old should know, but this guy did not.

I shouldn't have been annoyed because the man was doing a satisfactory job, was a good dad, and, I think, a decent person. But me being me, I kind of developed an attitude. So, one day, I turned the tables.

I began this way: "Hector, do you ever read a newspaper?" He said he did not. Second query: "Do you watch any television news programs?" Hector smiled because he knew I was a TV anchor. He then answered, "My wife tells me about what you say."

"That's nice," I replied. "But why don't you sit there with her and check it out?" Hector was a little perplexed.

"I'm busy!" he finally said. That's valid. The man was trying to make a living. But then I pressed: "You know, if you spent twenty minutes a day gathering information, you would be up to speed."

The barber paused again. He didn't know what to say. So, I jumped in, as I often do: "How do you spend your leisure time?"

"Video games," he said.

"Ah! Now we're getting down to it. How many hours a day are you playing the games?" Hector didn't know how long he spent on the machine. Then I asked another follow-up: "Do you ever go online and seek *information*?"

Hector said he did not. He corresponded with friends, played his games, watched videos.

Hector is the classic bubble person.

Now, I'm not judging my former barber. But I can't hang around with people like that. What would we talk about? There's only so much you can get out of hair gel. And Hector was more than happy with his circumstances. He felt no need to increase his frame of reference or know what the deuce was going on in the world. I did ask Hector if he voted. He replied, "Sometimes." To me, that meant, "Not much."

Unfortunately, there are tens of millions of Hectors running around the United States, and there's another aspect to this bubble person phenomenon: ideology. There are countless Americans who simply will not read or explore views that differ from their own. According to political scientists, the bubble people situation is often described this way:

> The phenomenon where individuals, communities, or political actors exist within highly insulated social, geographic, or digital environments, interacting primarily with those who share their exact political views and consuming media that reinforces their pre-existing beliefs.

Polling data finds 48 percent of Democrats live in neighborhoods with little exposure to opposing points of view. The number for Republicans is 19 percent. The studies go on to say that these individuals "often surround themselves with like-minded people, creating insulated, homogeneous social and residential environments."

Hello, Hollywood! Hello, Manhattan!

So, there is a one-two combination happening here. Apathetic and sometimes lazy people who will not go out of their leisure zones to actually find out what's going on. And then there are the crazed ideologues who refuse to consider opposing points of view.

The merger of those groups is becoming an enormous problem in the United States.

✪✪✪

The key to America's future is good leadership. That means elected officials who are invested in solving complicated problems. But if voters don't know or care about what these politicians are putting out there, how can we elect the best and the brightest? The answer is: We can't.

A study of X (formerly Twitter) users by *Forbes* magazine finds that 84 percent of liberals and 78 percent of conservatives live in ideological bubbles—that means the Xers only want to see stuff they agree with. That has led to the rise of "people believe what they want to believe." That's dangerous. All you have to do is go to the Islamist world to understand that fanatical Muslims think it is fine to actually kill "infidels" who don't see religion the same way they do. This is called Wahhabism. It has led to millions of deaths all over the world.*

We don't have that kind of craziness in America, but we *do* have a rising far-left movement that does not believe in punishing violent criminals, supporting aggressive police protection, obeying immigration laws, or respecting private property. Twenty years ago, these people were on the lunatic fringe. Now, they control state legislatures in New York, California, Minnesota, Massachusetts, Illinois, Oregon, and Washington State.

That's frightening to me. In fact, a poll from Axios finds that 67 percent of Americans aged eighteen to twenty-four believe socialism is better than capitalism. Those people, of course, are absolutely ignorant. There has never been a successful Socialist country on earth. All of them have devolved into totalitarian regimes where individual rights are suppressed. If you can't own anything (private property) and the government has the right to seize your assets, you really don't have any rights. You are at the mercy of Mao, Stalin, Castro, and the rest.

And 67 percent of young Americans don't know that?

✪✪✪

It may be time for a new horror movie series called *Revenge of the Bubble People*. We can do four or five of them, kind of like *Halloween*. Here's the premise: Innocent civilians get infected by these ideological social media platforms, through some kind of osmosis coming from the machine. I can't explain it because I have no clue how that would

---

* Wahhabism is an ultraconservative movement within Islam, founded by Muhammad ibn Abd al-Wahhab in eighteenth-century Arabia. It promotes a strict, literalist interpretation of the Quran and rejects practices deemed idolatrous or innovative. The movement became the dominant religious doctrine in Saudi Arabia in the mid-twentieth century.

happen, but no matter. Horror audiences are very generous in accepting absurd situations.

Then all of these bubble people suddenly become zombies, running around biting regular folks, turning them into new bubble people. If you are a Hollywood mogul, please call me immediately as this is a "high concept."

I see monster box office here.

We have already written a letter to Senator Bernie Sanders to underwrite this project. He says he's a "Democratic Socialist," as we've pointed out. But Bernie has lots of money. Much of it gleaned from his wife's rather dubious college administration career in Vermont. You can look that up if you want the information. Of course, the bubble people *don't* want information, so they won't.

Anyway, *Revenge of the Bubble People* would be a killer on Netflix. So, we're going to try to get that project underway. Many CNN pundits will be cast.

✪ ✪ ✪

My mother and father could never have conceived of how our society has devolved with all these devices and political craziness. According to data from the National Institutes of Health, 57 percent of Americans are now addicted to their phones and computers. They check them more than five times an hour.

In addition, 24 percent of Americans suffer from *severe* addiction to their devices—watching them more than six hours per day. That *has* to alter your lifestyle and narrow your world. The devices are controlling you.

Finally, the average American punches up their phone 224 times every twenty-four hours.

That's insane.

✪ ✪ ✪

Craven politicians understand the mass technological addiction we are seeing in America. They know they can now manipulate many social media sites. They also understand there is no standard of behavior on these platforms. Most people will believe what they read without checking any further. That has led to the rise of destructive propaganda across the board.

There does not seem to be any antidote to this. The First Amendment allows social media companies to pretty much do what they want to do, unless they issue direct threats to individuals or defame them. In the defamation area, if you're a famous person, forget it. You have no rights at all. But most importantly, the result of this mass device addiction, and the collapse of public schooling, is that actual knowledge is disappearing from our society.

More backup. According to a study from the University of Pennsylvania, only 34 percent of Americans can identify the three branches of government, and 70 percent cannot name their state's two senators. In addition, 63 percent of millennials (people born between 1981 and 1996) do not know that six million Jews were killed in the Holocaust.

Here's the kicker: More than one-third of Americans don't feel they are informed enough to participate in the political process.

Thus, the aware voter is becoming rare, maybe even endangered. So, it will be far easier for bad people—destructive individuals, even criminals—to gain political power in the US.

Obviously, that is a dangerous situation that must be confronted, or else artificial intelligence will overwhelm this country, leading to political disasters. That is not a hard prediction to make. Remember, AI can be programmed and manipulated by human beings.

Get ready.

✪ ✪ ✪

Let me end with another personal story. Very few people want to engage me in a political discussion. That's understandable. I make my living gathering information and analyzing it. I've been to eighty-six countries. I've covered four wars. I know pretty much every powerful person in the United States. If you're shaky on your facts, or couldn't care less, O'Reilly is not the guy with whom you want to have a political conversation.

That limits my ability to find out people's motivations. I do know that the rise in substance abuse wipes out any kind of civic responsibility. I have fought hard against that. The legalization of marijuana is incredibly destructive to children and will lead to massive health problems down the road. Wait and see. In some schools, the kids are totally inebriated on cannabis "edibles." These products have no odor, so teachers and administrators have no clue as the students sit stoned right in front of them.

Once in a while, I will come across a group of younger people aware of who I am. There will be some back-and-forth about the state of the nation. My opening question to them is always the same: "Who is the vice president?"

I must tell you, the blank stares outnumber the answers of "J. D. Vance" by about five to one. You should do the same exercise if you're around some younger people. Be polite. Just tell them you're curious about their generation. "What do they think about the vice president?"

You will immediately know if the person has any idea who that is. The odds are he or she will *not* know. Or care.

But, if you ask them about excellent videos on TikTok, you'll be talking to them for hours.

So let me put it this way. TikTok, the clock of mass voter ignorance, is marching toward the midnight hour in the US.

It's getting very dark, very fast in the land of the free.

CHAPTER NINETEEN

Asides

Sometimes change is impossible. Improvement is not forthcoming. Help is *not* on the way.

Only one strategy: tough it out. But never simply accept bad situations or people. Hope that karma will kick in and apply a semblance of justice. But often it can look like the miscreants get away with it. That drives me crazy.

My life has been unpredictable. Only in America could I have become a television news icon as well as the best-selling nonfiction author in the world. Could not have achieved that in Finland. Would have been in the sauna far too much.*

It is imperative that we Americans keep opportunity vibrant and try to expand it in our country. First rule: A giant government colossus is not helpful in motivating individuals. The self-reliant cliché is "get out of my way." The cliché is true.

The growing far-left Socialist movement believes in taking assets from the successful, then giving the seizures to the less fortunate. That never works. Reasonable taxation is necessary to promote the public

---

* According to the United Nations, Finland has been ranked the "happiest nation on earth" for eight consecutive years. For example, 68 percent of the Finnish people believe taking a daily sauna is a major factor in living a "happy life."

good, but punishing achievement is destructive. That creates bitterness as well as corruption because the system cannot track where the redistribution of wealth actually goes. Thieves and grifters love big government, as we saw in the massive Minnesota fraud described earlier in this book.

The other side of the Socialist story is that it saps personal motivation. Human nature. Giving folks an unlimited supply of free stuff creates dependency and sloth. Why work hard when my economic destiny is assured? Chill. The check is in the mail.

It is no accident that the USA leads the world in achievement and has ever since World War II. Most Americans admire hard work and success. However, this creeping socialism thing is a danger to the nation. Creating a legion of slackers will damage our society. It already has.

It is vital we fight against it.

✪ ✪ ✪

In addition to an abundance of bread and butter, my success in the marketplace has led to an amazing array of experiences. I've visited all fifty states, every capital city, eighty-six countries. In addition, I've met thousands of people. Most of them good, but a minority bad. Yes, I am judgmental, and that is not going to please Saint Peter when the time comes. But forming strong opinions is in my DNA. Therefore, I've got some stories to tell.

Let's begin with an archenemy of mine, far-left comedian and former Senator Al Franken. Awful human being, in my opinion. Let me back it up.

In 2003, Franken released a book called *Lies and the Lying Liars Who Tell Them*. My picture was on the cover. The smear merchant opined that I was not raised in working-class Levittown but, rather, in a more affluent neighborhood.

Total lie, as we prove in this book with a picture of the deed to my parents' house.

Come to think of it, Al Franken did have the pedigree to write his

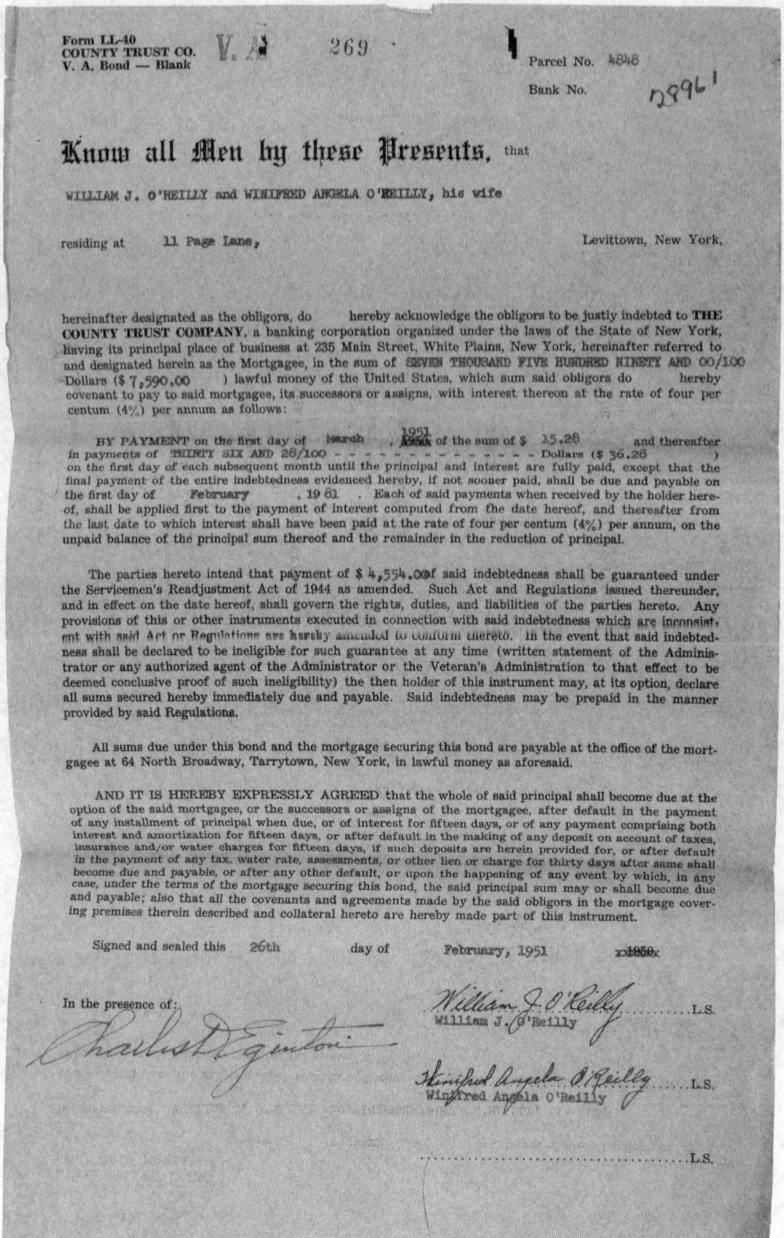

Form LL-40
COUNTY TRUST CO.
V. A. Bond — Blank

V. A. 269

Parcel No. 4848

Bank No. 28961

Know all Men by these Presents, that

WILLIAM J. O'REILLY and WINIFRED ANGELA O'REILLY, his wife

residing at 11 Page Lane, Levittown, New York,

hereinafter designated as the obligors, do hereby acknowledge the obligors to be justly indebted to **THE COUNTY TRUST COMPANY**, a banking corporation organized under the laws of the State of New York, having its principal place of business at 235 Main Street, White Plains, New York, hereinafter referred to and designated herein as the Mortgagee, in the sum of SEVEN THOUSAND FIVE HUNDRED NINETY AND 00/100 Dollars ($ 7,590.00) lawful money of the United States, which sum said obligors do hereby covenant to pay to said mortgagee, its successors or assigns, with interest thereon at the rate of four per centum (4%) per annum as follows:

BY PAYMENT on the first day of March, 1951 of the sum of $ 15.28 and thereafter in payments of THIRTY SIX AND 28/100 - - - - - - - - - - - - - - - Dollars ($ 36.28) on the first day of each subsequent month until the principal and interest are fully paid, except that the final payment of the entire indebtedness evidenced hereby, if not sooner paid, shall be due and payable on the first day of February, 1981. Each of said payments when received by the holder hereof, shall be applied first to the payment of interest computed from the date hereof, and thereafter from the last date to which interest shall have been paid at the rate of four per centum (4%) per annum, on the unpaid balance of the principal sum thereof and the remainder in the reduction of principal.

The parties hereto intend that payment of $ 4,554.00 of said indebtedness shall be guaranteed under the Servicemen's Readjustment Act of 1944 as amended. Such Act and Regulations issued thereunder, and in effect on the date hereof, shall govern the rights, duties, and liabilities of the parties hereto. Any provisions of this or other instruments executed in connection with said indebtedness which are inconsistent with said Act or Regulations are hereby amended to conform thereto. In the event that said indebtedness shall be declared to be ineligible for such guarantee at any time (written statement of the Administrator or any authorized agent of the Administrator or the Veteran's Administration to that effect to be deemed conclusive proof of such ineligibility) the then holder of this instrument may, at its option, declare all sums secured hereby immediately due and payable. Said indebtedness may be prepaid in the manner provided by said Regulations.

All sums due under this bond and the mortgage securing this bond are payable at the office of the mortgagee at 64 North Broadway, Tarrytown, New York, in lawful money as aforesaid.

AND IT IS HEREBY EXPRESSLY AGREED that the whole of said principal shall become due at the option of the said mortgagee, or the successors or assigns of the mortgagee, after default in the payment of any installment of principal when due, or of interest for fifteen days, or of any payment comprising both interest and amortization for fifteen days, or after default in the making of any deposit on account of taxes, insurance and/or water charges for fifteen days, if such deposits are herein provided for, or after default in the payment of any tax, water rate, assessments, or other lien or charge for thirty days after same shall become due and payable, or after any other default, or upon the happening of any event by which, in any case, under the terms of the mortgage securing this bond, the said principal sum may or shall become due and payable; also that all the covenants and agreements made by the said obligors in the mortgage covering premises therein described and collateral hereto are hereby made part of this instrument.

Signed and sealed this 26th day of February, 1951 ~~1950~~

In the presence of: Charles D. Eginton

William J. O'Reilly ........L.S.
William J. O'Reilly

Winifred Angela O'Reilly ........L.S.
Winifred Angela O'Reilly

....L.S.

book on "liars" since he is an expert. Even after his fraud was exposed, there was no apology from small Al.

Anyway, we sued Franken and his publisher but got nowhere because famous people in America (me) have no rights in civil court.

The lawsuit delighted Franken, and he sold far more books than he would have. Big mistake on my part as I actually helped the grifter. Hate making miscues like that.

For years, there was no justice for the radical weasel until the aforementioned karma brought him down. In the US, bad behavior often goes unpunished by our system. We can't change that because freedom of expression allows some brutally unfair things to happen.*

What we all *can* do is scorn the contemptible among us. But make sure your facts are correct and you respect due process. America is once again becoming a land of witch hunts because unproven allegations are now accepted as facts by millions of us. This we *can* change if enough Americans care.

Because I am a Christian, I am compelled to forgive trespasses. But not if there is no acknowledgment of wrongdoing. Then, a sense of bitterness takes the floor. I am not a revenge kind of guy, but I do believe in justice. Sometimes, however, the Deity will have to apply it as I stand powerless.

Which reminds me of a well-worn joke: What is the definition of Irish Alzheimer's?

You forget everything but the grudges. I confess that I remember the bad stuff more than the good things—a failing of mine, no question.

✪ ✪ ✪

* Franken resigned from the Senate in late 2017 under enormous pressure from fellow Democrats. In December 2006, the comedian posed in a salacious picture with radio broadcaster Leeann Tweeden during a USO tour of the Middle East. The problem was that Ms. Tweeden was asleep at the time. Today, Franken appears in small roles on streaming services like Netflix.

Now, we proceed to a fascinating encounter I had with one of the most famous women in the world: Michelle Obama.

Throughout my career, I have tried not to have preconceived notions about people. The strongest example of this is former First Lady Michelle Obama. It is absolutely a fact that many Americans, perhaps most, form impressions of famous individuals based on false data. They "hear things." However, this is not fair, and it needs to change.

As everybody knows, the media is no longer an honest industry. Of course, I am speaking generally, but the odds of you getting the truth about high-profile Americans from the press are very low. I believe Mrs. Obama is a prime example of that. Yes, she is a liberal woman, and that means that some conservatives dislike her based on politics. This is not unusual in our polarized country.

In December 2009, I was invited to the White House Christmas party and took my ten-year-old daughter with me. I felt it would be an excellent experience for her to see the Executive Mansion as well as experience some patriotic events.

As part of the event, the Obamas agreed to take pictures with the invitees. The evening unfolded this way: You enter the White House, there's a big buffet dinner, and you can wander around looking at the Christmas decorations. So far, excellent. My daughter and I were having a lot of fun when it was announced the Obamas were ready for picture taking. That involved standing on a line, waiting for the First Couple to see you. The actual interaction with the Obamas was short because there were so many people in attendance.

Unfortunately, my daughter became very nervous. I tried to divert her attention, but it was obvious to me she was overwhelmed by the experience. However, we soldiered on and finally got to the First Couple, who were standing in front of a portrait of George Washington.

At the time, I had been critical of President Obama, but not in a personal way. I actually admired him for gaining the Democratic nomination against Hillary Clinton, then going on to defeat the Republican John McCain. Barack Obama was a relatively unknown senator from Illinois, did not have a spectacular voting record, yet convinced the folks that he should lead the country. Any fair-minded person would admire his accomplishment.

The president himself was not a fan of Fox News because the network tilted conservative. But he was gracious enough to invite me, something Joe Biden never did. I was pleased to accept the invitation. I thought it was a classy thing for the president to do.

So, there we were, my ten-year-old and myself, staring at the most powerful couple in the world. Almost immediately, Michelle Obama recognized that my daughter was a bit frazzled—perhaps because the First Lady has two children of her own. She gently took Madeline aside and spoke with her for a good minute or so while the president and I commiserated about God knows what, I can't remember. Then the First Lady put my daughter right in the middle of the picture. Madeline had a genuine smile and seemed very relieved.

I never forgot that kindness. The First Lady did not have to do that. There were hundreds of people she had to deal with that evening. Yet, she took the time to comfort my young daughter.

Outstanding display of awareness and compassion.

Subsequently, I had a fairly good relationship with President Obama, but not very much interaction with Michelle. However, every time I was involved with the Obamas, as we have discussed earlier, they were very professional and, at times, generous to me.

But sometimes the ride got bumpy.

You may remember that on February 20, 2008, Michelle Obama ignited national headlines by saying this: "For the first time in my adult lifetime, I am really proud of my country." That comment, made in Milwaukee, referred to her husband's campaign and the growing support for it. It was a partisan political statement, not a slam at the US.

However, I did not like what she said because it seemed to be too flippant. Something like that can be taken a variety of different ways, which it was. But I understood what was happening.

Michelle Obama was raised on the South Side of Chicago to working-class parents. Her father, Fraser Robinson III, worked

in a water treatment plant. This was not a luxury situation for the Robinsons. You can imagine how tough it was for Michelle and her brother, Craig, to prosper in school, which they did. I mean, I had a tough time with two White working-class parents breaking out of a fairly downscale neighborhood. Michelle's journey was much more difficult than mine, primarily because of skin color.

To this day, she carries that weight.

Therefore, I was not going to classify the First Lady as a strident critic of the United States. People often say things the wrong way. Two weeks after the controversy, Michelle Obama told a Philadelphia newspaper the following:

> What I was clearly talking about was that I'm proud in how Americans are engaging in the political process. For the first time in my lifetime, I'm seeing people rolling up their sleeves in a way that I haven't seen and really trying to figure this out—and that's the source of pride that I was talking about.

Whatever her intentions were, all of the political stuff was overridden by Michelle Obama's kindness toward my daughter. Why? Because that's what life is all about. We Americans can differ on all sorts of things. When someone shows you a kindness, and they don't have to, that should be noted and put in an exalted position when evaluating that person. If more of us did that, the USA would be a better place.

✪ ✪ ✪

America would also be a better place if there were more people like Doris Day. Many of us have forgotten about the actress who dominated the movies for about ten years in the late 1950s and early 1960s. Ms. Day was an extraordinary talent: beautiful, funny, extremely appealing on the screen. She was the top box office actress for a number of years, starring in romantic comedies like *Pillow Talk* and *Calamity Jane*. But it was offscreen where Doris made significant contributions to this country.

One of her frequent co-stars was an actor named Rock Hudson. He was a leading-man heartthrob in the 1950s who blended very well with the effervescent Day. They appeared in three films together and remained close friends offstage.

Very few people knew it at the time, but Rock Hudson was gay. The movie studios kept that quiet. However, some showbiz folks were aware of his flamboyant lifestyle. In the early 1980s, Hudson acquired AIDS, which was a death sentence back then. He disappeared from public view; there were rumors but nothing concrete.

In 1985, Rock Hudson went on Doris Day's television program, shocking the public with his gaunt appearance. The story about his malady broke worldwide. Doris Day stood behind Rock Hudson and helped him to the very end, when many in Hollywood turned their backs on the ailing actor. On October 2, 1985, Rock Hudson died, leading to this statement by Ms. Day:

> Dear God, what can I say? This is when our faith is really tested. It's so terrible, I can't believe it. All those years of working with him I

saw him as big, healthy and indestructible. I am saddened by this and all I can do is uplift my thinking. Life is eternal. I hope we will meet again.

Hudson's body was cremated. A private, invitation-only memorial was held in his Beverly Hills backyard. Those in attendance included Ms. Day, Elizabeth Taylor, Carol Burnett, and Angie Dickinson. An eccentric guy to the end, Hudson's farewell also featured a mariachi band, margaritas, piñatas, and a conga line.

✪ ✪ ✪

About fifteen years later, Doris Day sent me a very nice letter even though I have never met her. She was extremely complimentary about my program, *The O'Reilly Factor*, explaining that she loved her county and wanted the best for it. At the time, Ms. Day was one of the most successful advocates for the protection of animals in this country. She lived in Carmel, California, and used her celebrity to raise funds for animal shelters, clinics, and adoption agencies.

Over the years, Doris Day and I corresponded on many topics. On December 28, 1998, she wrote me this note:

Dear Bill, watching you tonight was sheer joy! You are the best and I thank God that you are here for us. . . .

Hang in there Bill. Stay strong and we will win.

With admiration, gratitude, and love, Doris Day.

Yes, you are correct that I obviously have a fondness toward Doris Day. She lived an extremely generous life and did a lot of good for people and helpless animals, as well as loved her country.

What more can you ask for?

There are a number of other famous people who fit that category: Kirk Douglas, Jonathan Winters, Charlton Heston, Ernest Borgnine, the list goes on and on. All of them developed a relationship with me, your humble correspondent. That was perhaps the best perk I could have imagined in my job—interacting with talented, creative Americans who love their country.

We need more of them.

✪ ✪ ✪

Let's wrap up this chapter with something that many of us rarely think about—our legacies. Younger Americans, in particular, live in the moment. Or maybe the next twenty-four hours. It's all about: What am I gonna do? When am I gonna do it? Will it be fun? There's not a lot of vision going forward. I am speaking generally, of course.

Unfortunately, I was one of those dopey kids. I didn't think about what my actions and words would lead to in the future. I just spouted blather and did pretty much what I wanted to do within the confines of the law. That was dumb.

However, I do have an excuse. NOBODY ever told me that human beings are the sum of all their parts. That means that what you do is on the record and will define you to a great extent. Yes, we Catholics have confession and, if truly sorry, are forgiven our trespasses. But they still are on the record. Parents and teachers should at least mention this to the urchins. Again, what you do will be judged and can either help or hurt you. There is no statute of limitations.

✪ ✪ ✪

Here's an amazing story. You may know a guy named Bernie Goldberg. I use him often on *No Spin News*, and he contributed to *The O'Reilly Factor* as well. Bernie was a CBS News correspondent for more than twenty years, racking up dozens of Emmys and carving out a very distinguished career. In 2001, Bernie wrote a book called *BIAS*, which accused CBS News of not being fair in its presentations of what was happening in America. Bernie posited that CBS often tilted left. For that opinion, Dan Rather and others shunned him. Even though what he said was absolutely true. I worked for CBS, I know.

A few years ago, I got a call from Bernie asking if I knew a certain woman who lives in Miami. I did not recall the name. Remember, I have interacted with thousands of human beings.

In 1972, I was teaching high school, as we discussed earlier. I was paid very little and needed to make some extra money. So, I decided to apply for a weekend job at the Wreck Bar, a nightclub attached to the Castaways Hotel on Miami Beach. To steal a line from Barry Manilow, it was the "hottest spot north of Havana."*

One Saturday afternoon, I walked into the club to apply for a bartender job. It was a mobbed-up place. The guy in charge looked at me and said, "We have enough bartenders. We need some people on the floor."

That means he wanted a bouncer.

I stood six foot four, weighed about two hundred pounds, and was presentable. I actually wore a sports coat to apply for the job. Remember, this was in the early 1970s, when formal footwear was sandals. Anyway, the guy hired me at seven dollars an hour (off the books) to patrol the dance floor from about 9:00 p.m. to 2:00 a.m. Easy money for me.

The place was a madhouse. The featured band was called Tommy Strand and the Upper Hand. They were great. One problem: A few months after I started, some members of the band were arrested. At least that's what I heard, but could never confirm. A new band arrived.

My job was to signal the managers if I saw any trouble developing in the club. At the door were guys with guns. Back then, and even now, Miami is not a place where you take chances.

Thankfully, I didn't have many confrontations. A few guys got drunk, but the thugs at the door quickly ushered them out. My main task turned out to be escorting the "go-go girls" to their cars after the club closed.

Now, if you don't know what a go-go girl is, I feel sorry for you. Google the television program *Hullabaloo*. You will see some very attractive ladies with high white boots and short miniskirts dancing in

* The lyric comes from the 1978 Barry Manilow song "Copacabana (At the Copa)."

faux cages. The female rock group the Go-Go's was named after the dancing crew.

Anyway, most of these young women were constantly hit on by guys and needed protection in case things got out of control. Unfortunately, a lot of the men working inside the club were also soliciting these ladies. That was not good. Many of the dancers were single moms with little kids at home. Obviously, they did not have easy lives. I was smart enough to understand that and treated them with respect and humor. I wasn't thinking about my legacy going forward, it was just the right thing to do.

Back to Bernie Goldberg.

Incredibly, he ran into one of the Wreck Bar's former go-go girls, who recognized him as being part of my TV news presentations. Double incredibly, she remembered me walking her to the car and being a nice guy, a fact she related to Bernie. I was caught completely by surprise when Goldberg related this story to me. I couldn't imagine that more than fifty years had passed and this woman remembered her interactions with yours truly. Thankfully, they were all positive.

What a tremendous story, right? But it goes to show that whatever you do in this life is "on the record." Therefore, think about even the little stuff. Because a good American wants to be remembered as a positive force in this world. If we can all incorporate that kind of thought process, how much stronger would our country be?

The answer: a lot stronger.

Afterword

You made it. *Confronting America: What Has to Change*. Lots of stuff, although we remain the world's hope. There's no question about that.

So, here's a brief rundown of how O'Reilly and Hammer see improvement in our nation. Yes, you've read the book, but let's call this afterword a "handy guide."

- The United States *must* improve its educational system. We don't have to mimic some Asian nations, where they drive students crazy. But schools cannot continue to accept antisocial behavior. Let's teach the urchins lessons necessary for a successful life. That includes patriotism, personal responsibility, kindness, a search for knowledge. It's not that hard to do. Most American teachers understand that along with academics must come a sense of decency. That must be highlighted in the classroom.

- Define race in these terms: Skin color doesn't matter. The evil legacy of slavery is real, and barriers continue to exist. But in America, anyone can make it if you have the will and develop personal discipline. Role models should be cited. People like President Obama, Marco Rubio, Oprah Winfrey, the success list is endless in this country. That has to be emphasized.

- Sorry, but "hip-hop" culture is toxic, especially to unsupervised children. It has badly damaged the African American pathway to success. Miscreants have been glorified, and so has antisocial behavior. This isn't "music," this is a destructive diatribe, generally speaking. All Americans should be aware of how pernicious this industry is.

- Tell the truth about parenting. If dad or mom splits, the children suffer. That's not hard to understand. But is that the message in the media or academia? Generally not. Cowardice prevents a candid national discussion about irresponsible parents. That has to change.

- Patriotism is important. All loyal Americans have a duty to their country. Simply celebrating the Fourth of July is not going to cut it. The USA has freed billions of oppressed people all over the world, at great sacrifice. Individual Americans have accomplished that. Our role in being a force for good should be emphasized in every school.

- All of us have an obligation to help the nation. That's no longer in vogue. You may remember that President Kennedy said this: "Ask not what your country can do for you, but what you can do for your country." We must get back to that wise command.

- Enough with the drugs. No more excuses. It's not cool or positive in any way. Substance abusers destroy their families, their friends, their country, and, of course, themselves. You buy drugs, you empower the evil drug merchants. A sane society does not condone this behavior. Substance abusers may have a propensity toward illness, but they are not hopeless—it takes courage to get clean. Find it.

- Fake news must be condemned. Today, there is a dangerous one-two combination taking place in our country. First, a preponderance of misinformation. Second, social media platforms that spread propaganda for profit. For the republic to survive, people need reliable information, not stupid videos on TikTok. The corporate media has largely sold out for money. They routinely tell people what they want to hear, not what the truth indicates. The First Amendment protects them. But *not* from our scorn.

- The work ethic is on the decline. That's what socialism does. Statistics show half of US homes receive some kind of welfare. Free stuff. Food, shelter, childcare, healthcare, transportation. Give me, give me, give me. That attitude erodes ambition, crushes the human spirit, and creates dependency on a government colossus. Yes, some people need help, but we are on our way to a culture where giveaways mean more than accomplishments. Working is a key to a healthy life. Step up—be a man or a woman. You don't need handouts from Bernie Sanders.

- America is becoming a "godless" country. Why should you care? Well, social order, for one thing. Religion tamps down destructive behavior. The decline of spirituality in this nation is enormous, the concepts of right and wrong under siege. You don't have to be a member of the "God Squad," but you should respect the law and practice decent behavior.

- Generosity is the antidote to greed. There is far too much excess on display in America. If you can help others, do so. You're not always going to be rewarded, but so what? It's not about you. It's about trying to assist those who need it. No downside, right? Personal message to Jeff Bezos and his wife. You don't need to spend $70 million on a wedding. Got it?

- Mythologizing or demonizing our leaders is destructive. This has to change, because if it doesn't, we are going to get leadership that is corrupt. Americans can now be easily manipulated by social media and the greedy mainstream press. Very simple counter: Think for yourself.

- Self-respect is paramount. Alcoholism, drug addiction, violent behavior, treachery are all indicators that a person is simply self-destructive. You cannot respect yourself and then, at the same time, do harm. If you don't appreciate your own life, then nothing really matters, including other people. Take some time to figure out where you are in this equation.

- Don't have kids if you can't make them your top priority. That is very difficult for many parents to do. They put themselves and *their* needs first. They will never admit it, but the epidemic of selfishness is obvious. Children need *all* of your skill sets. Don't shortchange them. You will not be a person of respect if you do.

- Destroyers are everywhere. From the radical left George Soros to the insane-right Proud Boys and the racist Ku Klux Klan, America is filled with people who want to harm others. Evildoers have gravely damaged this country—they have divided us, encouraged sedition, and sanctioned violence. Stand against them. Call them out.

- America needs more "buccaneers." These flamboyant individuals make life more interesting; they break through boring convention. We need people who follow different pathways, who take risks, who have vision. They have contributed greatly to the nation's well-being.

- Beware the "bubble people." Some citizens are so uninformed it's scary. I'm sure you know a few of them. Living in a free society should demand some kind of information gathering. If you don't care about your freedom, you might very well lose it. Poverty and antisocial behavior are enslavement. Americans need to wise up, literally.

- Finally, your own legacy matters. Younger Americans tend to live in the moment. There's not a lot of vision for the future. The truth is this: What you do is on the record and will define you. This can either help or hurt your life. There is no statute of limitations. A good American wants to be remembered as a positive force. This takes thought and self-sacrifice, but when it's all over—do you want ten people at your funeral? Or a lasting legacy of respect and admiration?

You know the answer to that question.

Thanks for reading this book.

Notes and Sources

Chapter One: Money Matters—A Lot

According to data from the US Census Bureau and the IRS, income inequality in America has risen significantly over the past four decades, with wealth and income becoming heavily concentrated at the top. The top 1 percent of households held 31.7 percent of all US wealth in late 2025, with their income growing roughly 27 times faster than that of the bottom 20 percent between 1979 and 2021.

Modern Trends in Economics

- Growing Divide: Since the 1970s, income growth has favored the highest earners. By 2025, the top 1 percent held roughly the same amount of wealth as the bottom 90 percent combined.

- Income Disparity: In 2021, the top 1 percent of households earned over six times as much as the bottom 20 percent of households.

- Wealth Concentration: The top 10 percent of households own 70 percent of all wealth, while the bottom 50 percent own just 1.2 percent.

- Wages and Investment: The top 1 percent take home 21 percent of all income in the US.

- International Standing: The US has the highest level of income inequality among developed nations.

- Health Disparities: There is a ten- to-fifteen-year gap in life expectancy between the richest and poorest Americans.

- Living Costs: While top incomes have soared, the cost of essentials like healthcare and education has risen exponentially, leading to a "middle-class squeeze" where families struggle to afford a two-bedroom apartment or unexpected medical bills.

Taxation in America

- The Top 1 Percent: Taxpayers with an adjusted gross income (AGI) of $663,164 and above paid roughly 40.4 percent of all federal income taxes.

- The Top 10 Percent: Earners making at least $187,608 contributed approximately 71 to 72 percent of total federal income tax revenue.

- The Top 50 Percent: Collectively, the top half of earners (those making more than roughly $50,000) paid 97 percent of all individual income taxes.

- The Bottom 50 Percent: This group accounted for just 2.3 to 3 percent of federal income tax receipts.

✪ ✪ ✪

Chapter Two: The Race Dilemma

According to data from Pew Research and Gallup, as of 2026, race relations in the United States are marked by a deep contrast between increasing personal interracial connections and a growing political and systemic divide.

- State of Relations: Public opinion is divided; about 48 percent of Americans believe race relations have improved since the 1960s, while roughly 26 percent say they have worsened.

- Rollback of DEI Initiatives: The federal government has moved to dismantle diversity, equity, and inclusion (DEI) efforts. An executive order in 2026 threatened to terminate contracts for federal contractors engaging in what the administration termed "racially discriminatory" diversity practices.

- Economic Indicators: The Black unemployment rate reached 7.5 percent in 2026, its highest level since late 2021.

- Immigration and Policing: Increased surveillance and policing have heightened tensions in immigrant communities. High-profile concerns include the ending of Temporary Protected Status for Haitian nationals in early 2026 and intensified ICE activities in major cities.

✪✪✪

Chapter Three: It's Criminal

The Barack Obama Foundation,
"My Brother's Keeper Alliance"
http://www.obama.org/programs/my-brothers-keeper-alliance/

We believe communities are the unit of change to realize improved life outcomes for boys and young men of color. Research shows that the collective work of community leaders, members, and public and private agencies pursuing the same goals for boys and young men of color can lead to sustainable, place-based change.

President Obama launched the My Brother's Keeper program in February 2014, in response to the death of Trayvon Martin. The program sought to address the persistent opportunity gaps boys and young men of color face and to ensure all young people can reach their full potential.

We believe communities are the unit of change to realize improved life outcomes for boys and young men of color. Research shows that the collective work of community leaders, members, and public and private agencies pursuing the same goals for boys and young men of color can lead to sustainable, place-based change.

Bill O'Reilly on My Brother's Keeper in his 2017 book *Old School*

Without violating confidences, I was well on the way to setting up a huge rock concert complete with corporate sponsorship and a national TV airing. The money raised, tens of millions of dollars, would all go to My Brother's Keeper, and the concert would garner massive publicity for the noble effort.

Sensitive to any political stuff, I told the White House that I did not want any mention of my involvement. I'd get the venue and the talent gratis, and they could handle the rest.

The event never happened.

I don't know why.

Everything was set to go.

I strongly suspect that politics is the reason the show did not go on. President Obama could have made the concert a reality simply by snapping his fingers.

The Super Bowl Interviews

- O'Reilly interviewed Barack Obama at the White House on February 6, 2011.

- O'Reilly interviewed Barack Obama at the White House on February 2, 2014.

- An extended version was broadcast on *The O'Reilly Factor* on February 3, 2014.

Excerpt from February 2, 2014, interview

O'REILLY: Do you think I'm being unfair to you?

PRESIDENT OBAMA: Absolutely. Of course you have been, Bill. But, I like you anyway, Bill.

O'REILLY: Give me how I'm unfair. Come on, you can't make that accusation without telling me.

PRESIDENT OBAMA: Bill—we've just run through an interview in which you asked about health, uh, healthcare not working, IRS where-where we, uh, wholly corrupt, Benghazi—Here's what I would say. I think regardless of whether it's fair or not, uh, it has, uh, it has made FOX News very successful.

Data from the Department of Justice and the Federal Bureau of Investigation

The US criminal justice system is a decentralized network of federal, state, and local agencies categorized into three primary "pillars": law enforcement, the courts, and corrections. As of 2026, the system manages nearly two million confined individuals and millions more under community supervision.

Current Trends

- Rising Incarceration: After a decade of decline, prison populations rose for the second consecutive year as of late 2025, driven partly by a 58 percent surge in ICE detention.

- Policy Shifts: The Trump administration has prioritized a "tough on crime" agenda, directing prosecutors to pursue the most serious provable charges and ending the moratorium on the federal death penalty.

- Budgetary Changes: The 2026 federal budget proposed an $850 million reduction in Justice Department grant making, eliminating programs for community violence intervention and body cameras.

National Challenges

- Mass Incarceration: The US maintains the highest incarceration rate of any independent democracy, at roughly 580 per 100,000 residents.

- Racial Disparities: Black Americans are incarcerated at approximately five times the rate of White Americans. Black boys born today face a one-in-three chance of being imprisoned, compared to one-in-seventeen for White boys.

- Public Defense Crisis: Funding shortfalls for indigent defense programs continue to strain public defenders, potentially compromising the quality of legal representation for low-income defendants.

✪✪✪

Chapter Four: Are You a Patriot?

Data from Pew Research,
"6 Facts About National Pride in the U.S."
https://www.pewresearch.org/short-reads/2026/02/17/6-facts-about-national-pride-in-the-us/

In a 2025 survey, we asked people in 25 nations to say—in their own words—what makes them proud of their country. In several ways, Americans' answers stand out from those of people in other countries.

Americans are among the most likely to emphasize freedom as a source of pride. They are also more likely than people in many other surveyed nations to offer a negative sentiment when asked what makes them proud. And Republicans and Democrats tend to highlight different sources of pride—a partisan divide that is not as pronounced in most other countries.

Here is a closer look at national pride in the United States, including how it's similar to or different from national pride in other countries. The analysis includes direct quotes from some Americans to highlight key themes that were mentioned by multiple respondents. . . .

Freedom is the top source of pride in the U.S. Americans are most proud of their freedom: 22% name this as a reason they are proud of their country. Many people say this in other countries, too, particularly in the Netherlands, Sweden, and France. But the U.S. is the only surveyed country where freedom is the single most frequently mentioned source of pride.

✪✪✪

Chapter Five: Loyalty

National Institute of Health, "October 7th Mass Casualty Attack in Israel: Injury Profiles of Hospitalized Casualties" https://pmc.ncbi.nlm.nih.gov/articles/PMC11415105/

On Saturday, October 7th, approximately 3000 Hamas-led terrorists infiltrated Israel's southern border and attacked civilians and soldiers. Terrorists murdered close to 1200 people, abducted hundreds, and injured thousands. This surprise attack involved an unprecedented number of casualties.

A total of 630 hospitalized casualties (277 civilians and 353 soldiers) suffered from gunshot wounds (90%), explosion-related wounds (19%), and multiple injury mechanisms (16%). The median age for civilians was 33 years (ages <1–88) and 21 years for soldiers. The most frequently injured body regions were lower (49%) and upper (42%) extremities, abdominal (28%), and thoracic (23%) injuries. Four hundred thirty-one (68%) patients underwent surgery, of which 240 within 12 hours. Over half of the severe and critical (Injury Severity Score 16+) casualties were discharged to a rehabilitation center. In-hospital mortality rate was 2.5%.

Congressman Jared Moskowitz, "Moskowitz, Mills Lead Legislation Calling on U.S. Government to Ramp Up Efforts to Dismantle Illicit Drug Used by Hamas and Other Terrorist Organizations" https://moskowitz.house.gov/posts/captagon-hamas

Recent News Reports said Hamas used the drug during their terrorist attack in Israel; captagon is supplied to terrorist organizations across the Middle East by the Assad Regime in Syria.

Official Inquiry from the Israel Defense Forces https://www.idf.il/en/mini-sites/710-the-inquiries/all-of-the-710-inquiries/battle-of-kibbutz-beeri-the-inquiry/

The findings reveal that approximately 340 terrorists infiltrated the kibbutz, including about 100 Nukhba terrorist operatives of Hamas, who carried out murderous massacres, abductions of hostages, looting, and other brutal crimes. According to updated estimates from the inquiry team, about 100 terrorists were eliminated within the kibbutz. The houses in the kibbutz sustained heavy damage, and the recovery process for the kibbutz is expected to take a long time.

Information on Kate Steinle from the Department of Justice, "Jose Inez Garcia-Zarate Pleads Guilty to Federal Firearm Charges in Death of Kate Steinle" https://www.justice.gov/usao-ndca/pr/jose-inez-garcia-zarate-pleads-guilty-federal-firearm-charges-death-kate-steinle

Jose Inez Garcia-Zarate pleaded guilty today in federal court to being a felon in possession of a firearm and to being an alien unlawfully present in this country in possession of a firearm, announced United States Attorney Stephanie M. Hinds and Bureau of Alcohol, Tobacco, Firearms, and Explosives (ATF) Special Agent in Charge Patrick Gorman.

A federal grand jury indicted Jose Inez Garcia-Zarate on December 5, 2017. According to the indictment, on July 1, 2015, Garcia-Zarate, who is a citizen of Mexico and reportedly 51 years old, possessed a semi-automatic pistol and multiple rounds of ammunition in violation of 18 U.S.C. § 922(g)(1) (felon in possession of a firearm) and 18 U.S.C. § 922(g)(5) (possession of a firearm by an alien unlawfully present in the United States). In a public filing in the case, the government described that Garcia-Zarate was on Pier 14 of the Embarcadero in San Francisco on July 1, 2015. Also on the pier were Kathryn "Kate" Steinle, who was 32, her father James Steinle, and Frances "Kaye" Williams, a family friend. The three were sightseeing. At approximately 6:30 p.m., Garcia-Zarate possessed and fired a loaded semi-automatic pistol. The bullet hit Kathryn Steinle in her back, killing her. At the time of the shooting, Garcia-Zarate was a convicted felon and illegally in the United States, having previously been deported. He was also on federal supervised release from a 2011 Texas conviction.

On November 30, 2017, a prosecution by the San Francisco County District Attorney's Office resulted in a jury convicting Garcia-Zarate of one state violation—being a felon in possession of a firearm in violation of California state law—and acquitting him of homicide charges. On August 30, 2019, a California state Court of Appeals court overturned Garcia-Zarate's conviction based on the failure of the state trial court to instruct the jury on the state's affirmative defense of momentary possession. The ruling had no legal effect on the federal prosecution, which had already been initiated.

✪✪✪

Chapter Six: Always Faithful

In its four-thousand-year history, China has never known freedom or democracy. Order has been imposed by dictators, all of them using various titles.

- 2000 BC–AD 1200: Various dynasties (Shang, Qin, Han, Jin, Tang, Xia)
- 1200–1350: The Mongolian Khans
- 1350–1912: Various dynasties (Song, Yuan, Ming, Qing)

- 1912–1937: Military rule (Kuomintang and Chiang Kai-shek)
- 1937–1945: Empire of Japan (World War II)
- Total deaths during World War II: twenty million Chinese civilians
- 1945–1949: Civil war (Kuomintang versus Communists)
- 1949–Present day: Chinese Communist Party

China's Communist Revolution
Stanford University, "Introduction to the Cultural Revolution"
https://spice.fsi.stanford.edu/docs/introduction_to_the_cultural_revolution

The roots of the Cultural Revolution date back to the early 1960s. After the catastrophic Great Leap Forward, in which more than 20 million people died, Chairman Mao Zedong decided to take a less active role in governing the country. More practical, moderate leaders, such as Vice-Chairman Liu Shaoqi and Premier Zhou Enlai, introduced economic reforms based on individual incentives—such as allowing families to farm their own plots of land—in an effort to revive the battered economy. Mao detested such policies, as they went against the principles of pure communism in which he so firmly believed. Nevertheless, China's economy grew strongly from 1962 to 1965 with the more conservative economic policies in place.

The New York Times, "Mao's Cultural Revolution Explained"
https://www.nytimes.com/2016/05/15/world/asia/china-cultural-revolution-explainer.html

Gary J. Bjorge, *Moving the Enemy—Operational Art in the Chinese PLA's Huai Hai Campaign*
https://www.armyupress.army.mil/Portals/7/combat-studies-institute/csi-books/bjorge_huai.pdf

The Chinese Politburo

- Official title: Standing Committee of the Political Bureau of the Central Committee of the Communist Party of China.

- The committee consists of senior members of the Chinese Communist Party and other government officials.

- According to China's constitution, the party's Central Committee elects the politburo in so-called elections. In reality, the politburo is selected through secret negotiations.

- Since the Communist Revolution, membership has ranged from five to nine people.

Seven Current Members
(Ranked in Order of Importance)

- Xi Jinping—General secretary of the Communist Party

- Li Qiang—Premier of China

- Zhao Leji—Chairman of the National People's Congress (national legislature)

- Wang Huning—Chairman of the People's Consultative Conference (advisory body)
- Cai Qi—Director of the Communist Party
- Ding Xuexiang—Vice premier of China
- Li Xi—Secretary for discipline inspection (enforcer of the constitution)

Criminal Justice in China

- China's criminal justice system operates under the control of the Communist Party.
- It is characterized by a 99 percent conviction rate in criminal trials.
- Suspects have limited rights, such as no right to refuse interrogation, no presumption of innocence, and no right to confront accusers.
- Penalties include prison, public shaming, forced labor, and death.
- Crimes punishable by death in China: murder, drug dealing, corruption, bribery, fraud, crimes against the state, crimes against the Communist Party, crimes that jeopardize national security, and counterfeiting currency.
- Methods of execution: firing squad and lethal injection.
- China is the only country in the world with "execution vans." These vehicles are essentially converted ambulances that restrain people

to gurneys and administer lethal injections. According to Amnesty International, there are forty "execution vans" in operation.

- Number of executions each year: unknown.
- People currently in Chinese custody: 1.7 million prisoners.

✪ ✪ ✪

Chapter Seven: A National Dereliction

Data from American Addiction Centers, "Alcohol and Drug Abuse Statistics (Facts About Addiction)," https://americanaddictioncenters.org/rehab-guide/addiction-statistics-demographics, and the CDC, "Illicit Drug Use," https://www.cdc.gov/nchs/fastats/drug-use-illicit.htm

The drug abuse situation in the United States is considered one of the worst public health crises in its history, with roughly 48.4 million Americans (about one in six people) aged twelve and older struggling with a substance use disorder in 2024.

While drug-related deaths had been increasing rapidly, recent data indicates a potential turning point, with provisional data for 2024 showing a decline in fatal overdoses. Despite this, synthetic opioids—primarily fentanyl—remain the leading cause of death for Americans aged eighteen to forty-nine.

Key Aspects of the Current Situation (2024–2025 Data)

- Fatal Overdoses: Provisional data from 2024 shows a 25 percent decrease in fatal drug overdoses, representing roughly 30,000 fewer deaths than the previous year. However, the 2022 total was roughly 107,941 deaths.

- The Fentanyl Crisis: Fentanyl is involved in over 70 percent of all overdose deaths. In 2024, the DEA seized over 377 million lethal doses of fentanyl.

- Polysubstance Use: A significant trend is "polysubstance use," where users consume multiple substances simultaneously (e.g., mixing fentanyl with cocaine or stimulants), which increases the danger.

- Most Commonly Used Substances: Marijuana remains the most commonly used illicit substance, with roughly 64.2 million users in 2024, showing an upward trend.

- Age-Related Trends: While younger people are more likely to initiate drug use, rates of drug abuse are rising faster in people over forty. However, drug misuse still often starts during adolescence.

Drug Abuse (Data from the NIH)
https://nida.nih.gov/research-topics/trends-statistics

- 48.5 million (17 percent) Americans (aged twelve and older) battled a drug abuse disorder in the past year (this means they use drugs at least once a week).

- 7.5 million (3 percent) of Americans twelve and older struggled with both alcohol and drug use disorders simultaneously.

- 20.4 million American adults (8 percent) suffered from both a mental health disorder and a substance use disorder.

- 40 percent of young adults aged eighteen to twenty-five reported illicit drug use in the past month.

Impact on Law Enforcement/Crime (Data from the FBI)

- The federal government spends $40 billion each year to wage the "war on drugs."

- State and local governments spend an additional $30 billion.

- About 60 percent of people arrested for crimes test positive for illegal drugs.

- Around 80 percent of incarcerated people have a history of drug abuse.

- Each year, nine hundred thousand people are arrested in the US for drug possession, manufacture, or dealing.

Impact on Children (Data from the NIH)

- 20 million US children—or one in four—live with at least one parent who has a substance use disorder.

- Over 7.5 million of these children live with a parent whose addiction is classified as moderate to severe.

- More than 6 million children have a parent with both a disorder and a coexisting mental illness, such as depression.

Impact on Society

- According to data, 65 percent of homeless people are addicted to drugs.

- In addition, 65 percent of on-the-job accidents are drug or alcohol related.

- Around 40 percent of unemployed adults have a substance disorder.

What Cities Tolerate Drug Use?

- Beginning in 2010, many US cities changed their drug-enforcement policies toward "harm reduction." This means legal injection sites, free needles and crack pipes, the "decriminalization" of narcotics, and refusal to arrest in most circumstances not involving violent crime.

- The following major cities no longer prosecute drug abuse: New York, San Francisco, Portland, Philadelphia, Boston, Seattle, Denver, Oakland, Washington, DC, Baltimore, and Los Angeles.

History of Narcotics in America

In the nineteenth century, opiates like morphine and laudanum, along with cocaine, were freely available and widely used with little regulation. Addiction rates soared, particularly following the Civil War. The pivotal Harrison Narcotic Act of 1914 regulated and taxed opiates and cocaine, making nonmedical use illegal. This led to a black market and the rise of a punitive approach to drug use.

The 1960s saw a significant rise in drug use, driven by counterculture movements that embraced psychedelic drugs like LSD and marijuana as tools for spiritual and social exploration. This era coincided with increased social unrest, and drug use became a prominent symbol of rebellion against traditional norms and authority. The growing presence of drugs led to governmental responses, including the formation of the Bureau of Narcotics and Dangerous Drugs in 1968. This period marked a cultural shift where drug use was no longer just a fringe activity but a visible and debated, and often celebrated, part of society.

✪ ✪ ✪

Chapter Eight: Fake News

Congress, "False Speech and the First Amendment: Constitutional Limits on Regulating Misinformation" https://www.congress.gov/crs-product/IF12180

The First Amendment and Fake News

- Broad Protection: The Supreme Court in *United States v. Alvarez* (2012) held that false statements, in general, are protected, as the government cannot pass laws merely because a statement is false.

- Exceptions:
  Misinformation can be regulated if it falls under specific legal exceptions:
  - Defamation: False statements that harm a person's reputation
  - Fraud: False statements made to gain money, property, or legal advantage
  - Impersonation: Falsely acting as a government official
  - Perjury: Lying under oath

- Political Speech: Deliberate lies about the government or politics are generally protected under the "marketplace of ideas" concept, which holds that counter speech, not censorship, is the remedy.

- Professional Context: While general speech is protected, professionals like doctors may face discipline for spreading medical misinformation within their professional practice.

- Private Platforms: Social media companies are private entities and can enforce content moderation policies against misinformation without violating the First Amendment, which restricts only government action.

✪ ✪ ✪

Chapter Nine: Working for a Living

The American Entitlement System
House Committee on the Budget, "What You Need to Know About Means-Tested Entitlements"
https://democrats-budget.house.gov/publications/report/what-you-need-know-about-means-tested-entitlements

Key Components and Types

- Social Security and Medicare: Financed by payroll taxes, these are "contributory" programs that provide retirement and health benefits, regardless of income.

- Means-Tested Programs: Provide assistance based on income level and include Medicaid, Supplemental Security Income (SSI), Supplemental Nutrition Assistance Program (SNAP/food stamps), and Temporary Assistance for Needy Families (TANF).

- Unemployment Insurance: Provides temporary financial assistance to eligible workers.

Characteristics

- Mandatory Spending: Entitlement programs make up over 60 percent of the federal budget, costing roughly $2.8 trillion, and they are authorized permanently by law rather than annually.

- The government must pay out benefits to all who qualify, meaning expenditures can exceed forecasts if more people become eligible.

- Safety Net: Primarily designed to support the elderly, the disabled, and low-income populations.

Controversies

- Poverty Reduction: Programs significantly reduce poverty, especially among seniors and low-income families, with Social Security keeping millions above the poverty line.

- Fiscal Growth: Entitlement spending has shown steady growth, often cited as a significant contributor to long-term federal budget pressures.

- Debate over Dependency: Critics sometimes argue that some programs create disincentives for self-sufficiency, while proponents argue they provide necessary support for working households, the elderly, and the disabled.

✪ ✪ ✪

Chapter Ten: God Help Us

Intelligent Design (from Oxford Dictionary): The theory that life, or the universe, cannot have arisen by chance and was designed and created by some intelligent entity.

Artificial Intelligence (from Oxford Dictionary): The application of computer systems able to perform tasks or produce output normally requiring human intelligence, especially by applying machine learning techniques to large collections of data.

Religion Around the World in 2025
Major Religious Groups
(Approximate Figures and Shares)

- Christianity: 2.4–2.6 billion (around 31–33 percent)
- Islam: 1.9–2 billion (around 24–25.6 percent)
- Hinduism: Over 1.2 billion (around 14.9–15 percent)
- Buddhism: Around 500 million (around 7 percent)
- Unaffiliated (No Religion): Roughly 1.3–1.8 billion (around 24.2 percent)
- Folk Religions (Chinese Folk, African Traditional, Etc.): Hundreds of millions
- Sikhism: Around 29 million
- Judaism: Around 15 million (0.2 percent)

Religion in the United States: 2000 vs. 2025
(Data from Pew Research)
https://www.pewresearch.org/religious-landscape-study/

Christianity

2000: Protestants were over 50 percent of the adult population, and Christians (including Catholics and Mormons) generally made up around 80 percent.

2025: Christianity dropped to 60 percent.

Religiously Unaffiliated ("Nones")

2000: About 15 percent of the US population identified as atheist, agnostic, or "nothing in particular."
2025: This group grew substantially, reaching around 30 percent, with Gen Z and millennials leading this trend.

Non-Christian Religions

Numbers remain relatively unchanged between 2000 and 2025.
Jewish (2 percent), Muslim (1.2 percent), Buddhist (1.1 percent), and Hindu (0.9 percent).

The Founding Fathers and Religion

Benjamin Franklin: Ben Franklin held a pragmatic, Deist-leaning view of religion, believing in one God, divine Providence, the immortality of the soul, and the supreme importance of doing good to others as the best worship, while rejecting rigid dogma, miracles, and sectarian disputes. He embraced religious freedom, saw virtue as the core of faith (not just belief), and admired Jesus's morals, though he questioned his divinity, ultimately focusing on practical morality over strict orthodoxy.

Thomas Jefferson: Thomas Jefferson believed religion was a personal matter between an individual and God, advocating for a strict "wall of separation between church and state" to protect freedom of conscience, but personally embraced Jesus's ethical teachings while rejecting Jesus's divinity, creating his own Bible to focus on morality, not miracles. He saw a government-free religious sphere as crucial for both true faith and a functioning republic, opposing forced worship or government endorsement.

James Madison: James Madison believed religion was a sacred, individual matter of conscience, not the government's business, advocating for a strict separation of church and state to protect true religious freedom from state control, which he saw as corrupting to both faith and liberty.

Patrick Henry: Patrick Henry saw religion, specifically Christian virtue, as essential for a healthy republic, supporting a "general assessment" to fund Christianity but also advocating for broad religious freedom, even proposing an amendment guaranteeing free exercise of conscience; he believed faith fostered morality, but his support for state funding clashed with Madison and Jefferson, who championed full separation between church and state.

John Hancock: John Hancock was a devout, lifelong Congregationalist who saw Christian piety and virtue as essential for a stable republic, frequently invoking God and biblical principles to justify American liberty, guide policy, and encourage public morality, even supporting the establishment of Congregationalism in Massachusetts.

George Washington: Washington saw religion and morality as essential for a prosperous nation, believing they fostered public virtue, but he championed religious freedom and tolerance, stating the government shouldn't dictate belief, only demand good citizenship. He viewed God as a divine protector of America, though his personal practices leaned toward Anglicanism while supporting diverse faiths.

Other American Leaders' Thoughts on Religion

Abraham Lincoln: Abraham Lincoln's religious views were complex, evolving from early skepticism to a profound, though unconventional, faith, characterized by deep Bible knowledge, respect for moral law, and belief in a guiding Providence, but a rejection of specific creeds or church membership, deepening especially during the Civil War's tragedies. He found organized religion divisive but was deeply influenced by Christian themes, often quoting scripture and expressing a reliance on God's will for the nation, while never joining a church.

Franklin Roosevelt: FDR was a devout, practical Episcopalian whose faith focused on the Social Gospel, emphasizing action, social justice, and service. He drew strength from biblical principles for public life, though he rarely discussed personal theology, instead promoting a shared Judeo-Christian ethic for national unity, particularly during crises like the Depression and World War II.

Criminality and Religion

Research suggests a significant, generally inverse connection between religiosity and criminality, meaning higher religious involvement often correlates with lower crime rates, acting as a protective factor against delinquency.

Key Findings from Research

- Negative Correlation: The majority of studies show that increased religious commitment (prayer, church attendance, belief) is linked to reduced offending and antisocial behavior.

- More Religion / Less Crime: Communities with strong religious backgrounds—i.e., the Amish, Mormons, and Catholics—have the lowest levels of crime, particularly violent crime.

- Social Control: This relationship is often explained by social control theories, where religious communities provide moral guidance, social support, and monitoring, deterring crime.

✪✪✪

Chapter Eleven: Never Too Much

Income in America—Data from the US Census Bureau and the US Department of Labor

https://www.census.gov/topics/income-poverty/income.html

- The average annual salary in the United States is $66,622.

- Thirty-six million Americans (11 percent) live beneath the poverty line. The poverty line is defined as individuals earning less than $31,000 per year.

- Around 80 percent of US households owe more than $10,000 in debt.

- In total, Americans owe $18 trillion in credit card debt, mortgages, auto loans, and student loans.

- The average American under the age of forty has less than $5,000 in savings. That figure goes up to $15,000 for folks over sixty-five.

Salary Brackets in America

- Around 60 percent of Americans earn more than $50,000 per year.

- About 18 percent of households earn more than $100,000 per year.

- Only 2 percent earn more than $500,000 per year.

Wealth in America

- There are twenty-three million millionaires in America (9 percent of the adult population). More than anywhere else in the world. For example, there are two million millionaires living in France, which is 2.5 percent of that nation's population.

- There are one thousand billionaires in America (0.0003 percent of the adult population). More than anywhere else in the world. The second most live in China, with four hundred billionaires.

Buffet vs. Bezos

Warren Buffet

- Origin: His conglomerate corporation, Berkshire Hathaway, grew from a textile mill into a $1 trillion company.

- Total net worth: $150 billion.

- Charity: Buffet has given $208 *billion* in stocks and other charitable donations over his lifetime. He plans to donate most of his entire net worth upon his death.

- Lifestyle: Buffet lives a remarkably humble life.

- He has resided in the same house in Omaha, Nebraska, since 1958. The home is a modest five-bedroom, two-and-a-half-bathroom property that he purchased for $30,000. The car he drives is a 2006 Cadillac. He has received the same fifteen dollar haircut for six decades.

Jeff Bezos

- Origin: Founder and executive chairman of Amazon, the world's largest e-commerce and cloud-computing company.

- Total net worth: $240 billion.

- Charity: Bezos has donated $10 billion to charities that focus on climate change, including his own operation, the Bezos Earth Fund. He has also given $200 million to the Smithsonian Institute.

- Lifestyle: Bezos's life is defined by extravagant luxury.

- Transportation: Owns multiple private jets (like the Gulfstream G700) and the massive sailing yacht *Koru*.

- Real Estate: Extensive properties in Beverly Hills, Washington, DC, New York City, Miami, and Hawaii, as well as a Texas ranch.

- Vanity Projects: Building a ten-thousand-year clock in Texas and owns a robot dog.

✪✪✪

Chapter Twelve: Mythology in America

Theodore Roosevelt and His Daughter

National Archives

Teddy Roosevelt and his eldest daughter, Alice, had a tumultuous relationship from the start, when he was unable to take care of her due to the childbirth death of his first wife, also named Alice. A headstrong, privileged child, Alice's youthful antics soon turned into newspaper fodder as an adult.

She hardly ever resigned herself to follow the strict rules White House officials deemed appropriate for a First Daughter and conducted her life as she wished, the result usually ending up on the front of every tabloid in America and overseas.

Alice Roosevelt's Exploits

- She publicly pronounced herself to be a pagan, calling Christianity "sheer voodoo."

- She raced cars through the streets of Washington accompanied by unmarried young men.

- She smoked cigarettes in public and, on occasion, on the roof of the White House.

- Alice often placed bets on sporting events or horse races.

- In 1909, when the Roosevelt family prepared to move out of the White House, Alice buried a voodoo doll of new First Lady Nellie Taft in the front yard, an act that got her banned from the Taft White House.

- She had a snake named Emily Spinach that could often be found on her person.

- During a fifteen-month stay in Paris, one French newspaper reported Alice was in attendance at 407 dinners, 350 balls, and at least 300 parties.

Joe Biden Myths

The Myth of "Middle-Class" Joe: Biden was praised in the media for his "humble" lifestyle and called "Scranton Joe." Biden often claimed his father struggled to "put food on the kitchen table."

Fact: While Biden was generally less wealthy than most other US senators during his long tenure, he consistently had a high income, and his earnings skyrocketed after leaving the vice presidency through book deals and speaking fees. In 2024, Biden's net worth topped $10 million. He owns at least three homes, including a beachfront mansion in Delaware.

The Myth of Biden's Civil Rights Record: Democrats and media figures hailed Biden's work during the civil rights era. Joe routinely tells stories of marching in Selma, Alabama, or being arrested in South Africa while protesting apartheid.

Fact: No evidence exists that Biden was ever detained in South Africa. Aides later admitted Biden never marched in any significant events like those in Selma. Though he claims he "came out of the civil rights movement," his 2007 memoir states, "I had no real relationship with Black people" at that time.

The Myth of Beau Biden: Biden has repeatedly made exaggerated claims about his family, including his son Beau dying in Iraq.

Fact: In 2023, Biden told reporters, "My son lost his life in Iraq." Beau Biden died in Bethesda, Maryland, in 2015 after a five-year battle with brain cancer.

✪✪✪

Chapter Thirteen: A Matter of Respect

Famous Quotes About Respect

Jackie Robinson: "I'm not concerned with your liking or disliking me . . . all I ask is that you respect me as a human being."

Abraham Lincoln: "If once you forfeit the confidence of your fellow citizens, you can never regain their respect."

Tecumseh: "Show respect to all people but grovel to none."

Confucius: "Respect yourself, and others will respect you."

Andrew Jackson vs. Charles Dickinson (1806)

- Background: Charles Dickinson, a Nashville attorney, accused Andrew Jackson of reneging on a horse bet, calling Jackson a coward and an equivocator. Dickinson also called Rachel Jackson a bigamist and a prostitute. (Rachel had married Jackson not knowing her first husband had failed to finalize their divorce.)

- In response, Jackson challenged Dickinson to a "duel to the death." The shoot-out took place at Harrison's Mill (also known as the Jeff Burr farm) near Nashville, in Logan County, Kentucky. Dickinson, a renowned marksman, shot Jackson first, hitting him in the chest. Jackson's first shot misfired, but he cocked his pistol and fired again, killing Dickinson instantly. Jackson survived but carried a bullet in his chest for the rest of his life, a reminder of the duel.

- Historians estimate Jackson took part in five to one hundred duels throughout his life.

Republican Congressman Yells "You Lie!" at Obama's Congressional Speech (2009)

- Background: On September 9, 2009, President Obama was delivering a speech before a joint session of Congress when he discussed details for his "Affordable Care Act."

- Said Obama, "There are also those who claim that our reform effort will insure illegal immigrants. This, too, is false—the reforms I'm proposing would not apply to those who are here illegally."

- Suddenly, South Carolina Congressman Joe Wilson yelled, "You lie!"

- The aftermath: Wilson quickly issued a statement apologizing for his "lack of civility" and called the White House to apologize to the president's chief of staff. President Obama accepted the apology. The House of Representatives formally rebuked Wilson with a "resolution of disapproval" for his breach of decorum in a near party-line vote of 240–179.

Hillary Clinton Disrespects "Deplorable" Trump Voters (2016)

On September 9, 2016, Hillary Clinton was speaking with supporters at an LGBTQ event in New York City.

CLINTON: You could put half of Trump's supporters into what I call the basket of deplorables. *(Laughter/applause)* Right? *(Laughter/applause)* They're racist, sexist, homophobic, xenophobic, Islamophobic—you name it. And unfortunately, there are people like that. And he has lifted them up. He tweets and retweets their offensive hateful mean-spirited rhetoric. Now, some of those folks—they are irredeemable, but thankfully, they are not America.

Hillary Clinton apologized on Twitter the next day: "Last night I was 'grossly generalistic' and that's never a good idea. I regret saying 'half'—that was wrong. . . . It's deplorable that Trump has built his campaign largely on prejudice and paranoia and given a national platform to hateful views and voices. . . . As I have said, many of Trump's supporters are hard-working Americans who just don't feel like the economy or our political system are working for them. I'm determined to bring our country together."

✪ ✪ ✪

Chapter Fourteen: It's a Family Affair

The Average "American Family"

1960: Two parents, three children, one household pet
2025: One parent, one child

Average Age at Marriage

1960: Twenty-two years old for men, twenty for women
2025: Thirty-one years old for men, twenty-nine for women

Marriage Rate (Adult Population over the Age of 25 Who Are Married)

1960: 79 percent
2025: 40 percent

Nuclear Families (At Least One Child Living in a Two-Parent Household)

1960: 87 percent
2025: 22 percent

Divorce in America (Percentage of Marriages That End in Divorce)

1960: 14 percent
2025: 50 percent

Traditional vs. Liberal Philosophy

The liberal definition of family emphasizes function and chosen bonds over traditional structures, viewing family as any group providing love, support, and care, including non-nuclear setups, same-sex couples, multi-generational households, and even close friends, focusing on the commitment and nurturing roles rather than just blood, marriage, or legal ties. It values inclusivity, individual choice in forming relationships, and the evolving nature of family to reflect diverse realities, recognizing that family can be defined by shared lives and emotional connections.

Traditional philosophy of the "family" defined by New York University:

A traditional family typically means a married mother and father with their biological children, often with the father as the income-earner and the mother as the caretaker. Cornerstones of the family unit are traditional beliefs like religion, patriotism, and discipline. Other values include fidelity, hard work, family unity, loyalty, and adherence to the truth.

Youth Crime Statistics

Juvenile Court Cases Nationwide

1960: 405,000
2025: 1.1 million (an increase of 171 percent)

Youth Crime Rate

1960: 1,600 per 100,000 youths were arrested for a felony.
2025: 2,200 per 100,000 youths were arrested for a felony (an increase of 38 percent).

Other Stats for 2025

- According to data, 8 percent of arrests for violent crimes in America are committed by people under the age of eighteen.
- Around 10 percent of homicides in America are committed by people under the age of eighteen.
- Around 15 percent of drug-related crimes are committed by people under the age of eighteen.
- About 40 percent of car thefts are committed by people under the age of eighteen.
- In addition, 20 percent of property crimes are committed by people under the age of eighteen.

✪ ✪ ✪

Chapter Sixteen: The Buccaneers

Definition: A daring, adventurous, and sometimes reckless person, especially in business.

From the French *boucanier*, seventeenth-century European hunters in the Caribbean who smoked meat on a wooden rack called a *boucan*. When unable to find food, they resorted to thievery and murder to secure provisions.

Donald Trump—The Ultimate Buccaneer

- Member of the WWE (World Wrestling Entertainment) Hall of Fame: Trump is a member of the WWE Hall of Fame and once participated in a "Battle of the Billionaires" match at WrestleMania 23, where he shaved WWE owner Vince McMahon's head in the ring.

- The $110,000 Pension: Despite his wealth, Trump is a member of the Screen Actors Guild and receives an annual pension of over $110,000 for his various film and TV appearances.

- A "Fast Food" Fan: He famously served McDonald's and Wendy's to a championship college football team at the White House in 2019, stating his preference for the "great American food."

Billy Joel

- The Professional Boxer: Long before he was the "Piano Man," Joel was a successful teenage boxer in the Golden Gloves. He won twenty-two of his twenty-eight bouts, but he quit the sport for good after a particularly brutal fight resulted in a shattered nose, which is why his nose looks slightly flattened in early album photos.

- The $90 Million Fraud: In 1989, Joel discovered that his brother-in-law and manager, Frank Weber, had reportedly mismanaged or stolen $90 million of his earnings. Joel filed a massive lawsuit, but much like Doris Day, he had to tour relentlessly for years just to dig himself out of a financial hole he hadn't known he was in.

- The Soviet Tour: In 1987, Joel became the first American pop star to bring a full-scale rock production to the Soviet Union. He famously had a meltdown on stage in Moscow, flipping his electric piano in frustration over the lighting crew.

- High School Graduate (Thirty-Five Years Late): Joel missed his high school graduation because he was exhausted from playing a gig the night before and failed an English exam. He didn't bother to make up the credits, famously saying, "I'm not going to Columbia University, I'm going to Columbia Records." He finally received his diploma in 1992 at the age of forty-three.

- The Heavy Metal "Attila" Phase: In 1970, Joel was in a psychedelic heavy metal duo called Attila. They released one album where Joel played a distorted Hammond organ like a lead guitar. The album cover famously featured Joel and his bandmate dressed as Huns in a meat locker. Joel later called it "psychedelic bullsh*t."

Jack Nicholson

- The "Sister" Secret: Nicholson grew up believing his mother, June, was his older sister and his grandparents were his parents. He only discovered the truth in 1974, at age thirty-seven, when a *Time* magazine researcher uncovered his birth certificate while preparing a cover story.

- The "Bad Boy Drive" and Tunnels: Nicholson lived on Mulholland Drive next to Marlon Brando and Warren Beatty, earning the street the nickname "Bad Boy Drive." Rumors long persisted—and blueprints later confirmed—that an underground tunnel connected Nicholson's home to the Playboy Mansion.

  Fact Check: An underground maintenance tunnel *does* run from Nicholson's home to the Playboy Mansion. But no proof exists it was ever used by the actor.

- Extreme Method Acting: To prepare for his role in *The Postman Always Rings Twice*, Nicholson reportedly spent three months walking around his house completely nude, regardless of who came by, to feel "comfortable" in his own skin for sex scenes.

Clint Eastwood

- The Shark-Infested Plane Crash: In 1951, at age twenty-one, Eastwood was hitching a ride on a Navy torpedo bomber that ran out of fuel and ditched into the Pacific Ocean near Point Reyes. He and the pilot were forced to swim over two miles through frigid, rough waters to reach the shore. It wasn't until years later that Eastwood discovered he had been swimming through a major great white shark breeding ground.

- Turning Down Bond and Superman: Eastwood is one of the few actors to have turned down both James Bond and Superman. He was offered the role of 007 after Sean Connery left the franchise but declined because he believed Bond should be played by an English actor. He turned down *Superman* (1978) because playing a superhero simply didn't appeal to his nature.

- The $15,000 "Man with No Name": Eastwood almost missed out on his breakout role in *A Fistful of Dollars*. The role was only offered to him after James Coburn and Charles Bronson turned it down. Eastwood agreed to the part for just $15,000—a massive pay cut from his TV salary at the time. To save money, he even supplied his own signature poncho, which he reportedly never washed across the entire *Dollars* trilogy to maintain its weathered look.

Jonathan Winters

- The "Wristwatch" Start: Winters didn't plan to become a comedian; he just needed a new watch. In 1948, after losing his wristwatch and being unable to afford a replacement, his wife Eileen encouraged him to enter a local talent contest where the first prize was a watch. He won the contest, which led to a job as a disc jockey and eventually launched his entire career.

- The "Man in the Moon" Incident: In 1959, the pressure of his rising fame led to a public breakdown. Winters was found by San Francisco police climbing the rigging of the historical ship

Balclutha, claiming he was "from outer space" and was the "Man in the Moon." This led to his first of two voluntary institutionalizations, which he later fearlessly incorporated into his stand-up routines, referring to the mental hospital as "the zoo."

- A Teenage World War II Gunner: Long before he was a "cherubic madman" on TV, Winters was a teenage marine. He quit high school at seventeen to enlist and served as a gunner on the aircraft carrier USS *Bon Homme Richard* in the Pacific Theater during World War II.

Doris Day

- A Train Crash Ended Her First Dream: Doris Day never intended to be a singer or actress; she was a prodigious dancer with a contract to move to Hollywood at age fifteen. On her final night in Cincinnati, the car she was in was struck by a freight train, shattering her right leg. It was during her grueling yearlong recovery in a wheelchair that she began singing along to the radio, discovering the voice that would eventually make her a star.

- The Manson Family Connection: Her only son, record producer Terry Melcher, was a primary target of Charles Manson. Manson had been to Melcher's home on Cielo Drive several times to pitch music. Frightened by Manson's "scary antics," Day insisted her son move out of the house just months before the infamous Tate-LaBianca murders occurred at that exact address.

Kirk Douglas

- Breaking the Hollywood Blacklist: Douglas is widely credited with dealing a death blow to the Hollywood blacklist in 1960. While producing and starring in *Spartacus*, he insisted that the blacklisted writer Dalton Trumbo receive official on-screen credit.

- The $50,000 Single-Word Payday: In one of the most lucrative "easy" jobs in history, Douglas was once paid $50,000 for a Japanese television commercial. His entire performance consisted of saying just one word in English: "Coffee."

- Two Bar Mitzvahs (Seventy Years Apart): Though he had his first bar mitzvah at age thirteen, Douglas celebrated a second bar mitzvah at age eighty-three. After his 1991 helicopter crash and a subsequent stroke in 1996, he rededicated himself to his heritage, stating, "I was spared because I had never come to grips with what it means to be Jewish."

Charlton Heston

- Q-Level Security Clearance: For six years, Heston held a Q clearance (the nation's highest security level, equivalent to Top Secret) to narrate highly classified instructional films for the military and the Department of Energy regarding nuclear weapons.

- Resemblance to Art: Director Cecil B. DeMille cast Heston as Moses because he believed the actor bore an uncanny physical resemblance to Michelangelo's statue of Moses. Heston's three-month-old son, Fraser, also played the baby Moses floating in the basket in the same film.

- The "Eagle Profile": Heston broke his nose playing football in high school. He later claimed this was a professional blessing, as the injury gave him what he called "the profile of an eagle," which helped him land noble, heroic roles.

- Civil Rights Pioneer: Long before it was considered fashionable in Hollywood, Heston was a staunch advocate for civil rights. He picketed segregated restaurants in Oklahoma in 1961 and marched alongside Martin Luther King Jr. during the 1963 March on Washington.

David Letterman

- Wacky Weatherman Antics: As an Indianapolis weatherman, he once congratulated a tropical storm for being upgraded to a hurricane and reported that the border between Indiana and Ohio had been "erased" due to political dealings.

- The "C-Student" Scholarship: A self-described average student, he endowed a scholarship at Ball State University (his alma mater) specifically for students with average grades, which he nicknamed the scholarship for "C students."

- Late-Night Record Holder: With 6,080 total episodes hosted, Letterman is the longest-serving late-night talk show host in US history, surpassing Johnny Carson.

✪ ✪ ✪

Chapter Seventeen: The Deceivers

Bernie Madoff Case: Inside History's Biggest Financial Crime

https://www.fbi.gov/history/cases-and-criminals/bernie-madoff

Bernie Madoff orchestrated the largest Ponzi scheme in history, defrauding thousands of investors of approximately $65 billion in fabricated wealth.

Background

Founded in 1960 in Queens, in New York City, with $5,000 earned from Bernie's work as a lifeguard and sprinkler installer, Bernard L.

Madoff Investment Securities LLC initially gained a reputation as a scrappy, innovative market maker.

Madoff gained prominence by pioneering electronic trading technologies in the 1970s and 1980s, helping to establish the NASDAQ stock exchange, where he later served as chairman for three terms.

Parallel to his public brokerage, Madoff ran a private investment advisory business that began in the early 1960s with referrals from his father-in-law, a successful accountant. By cultivating an image of exclusivity, Madoff created a "prestigious" allure, often making investors feel privileged to invest with him, thereby preventing them from asking too many questions.

The scheme, believed to have accelerated in the 1980s or early 1990s, promised steady, high returns of 10–12 percent annually, even during market downturns. Madoff paid early investors with money from newer investors, fabricating account statements to show nonexistent gains. He leveraged his reputation as a "Wall Street wizard" to lure wealthy individuals, charities, and celebrities.

The Fraud

Instead of investing client funds, Madoff deposited them into a Chase Manhattan bank account, paying returns to early investors using money from new clients. The scheme required a constant inflow of new capital to work. To conceal the fraud, Madoff and his employees fabricated phony account statements, showing gains that never existed.

Despite early warnings, the Securities and Exchange Commission (SEC) failed to uncover the massive fraud. The scheme began to unravel during the 2008 financial crisis when investors requested roughly $7 billion in redemptions, a sum Madoff could not produce.

Madoff Confesses

On December 10, 2008, Madoff confessed to his sons that his business was "one big lie" and a giant Ponzi scheme. His sons reported him to authorities, and he was arrested on December 11, 2008. In March 2009, Madoff pleaded guilty to eleven federal crimes, including securities fraud, money laundering, and perjury. He was sentenced to 150 years in prison.

Fate of the Madoff Family

- Bernie Madoff: Died in federal prison on April 14, 2021, while serving a 150-year sentence. The cause of death is listed as kidney failure. He was eighty-two years old.

- Mark Madoff (Son): Hanged himself on December 11, 2010, exactly two years after his father's arrest, reportedly unable to escape the stigma.

- Andrew Madoff (Son): Died of lymphoma on September 3, 2014, at age forty-eight, after blaming the stress of the scandal for his cancer's return.

- Ruth Madoff (Wife): Divorced herself from Bernie, gave up millions in assets to avoid prosecution, and lives quietly, avoiding the public eye. Ultimately, Ruth was forced to forfeit assets totaling $80 million, including her home. Afterward, she was allowed to keep $2.5 million. She currently lives in a $3.8 million waterfront mansion in Connecticut. The property is owned by the widow of her son Mark.

- Peter Madoff (Brother): Served a ten-year prison sentence for his role in the firm's compliance failures.

- Shana Madoff (Niece/Compliance Officer): Daughter of Peter, she was investigated but avoided criminal charges, leaving the financial industry.

- Sondra Wiener (Sister): Died in an apparent murder-suicide with her husband in Florida in February 2022.

The Victims (Foundations and Groups)

- Grupo Santander (Spanish Bank): $7.5 billion
- Kingate Management (Bermuda hedge fund): $3.5 billion
- Bank Medici (Austrian Bank): 3.5 billion
- HSBC: $1 billion
- Yeshiva University: $140 million
- Hadassah Jewish Charity: $90 million
- LA Jewish Community Foundation: $18 million
- America-Israel Cultural Foundation: $15 million
- Elie Wiesel (Author and Holocaust Survivor) and His Charity: $30 million

The Victims (Celebrities)—Actual Financial Figures Not Available

- Kevin Bacon and his wife Kyra Sedgwick
- John Malkovich
- Steven Spielberg

- The Wilpon Family (owners of the New York Mets)
- Larry King
- Sandy Koufax (former Dodgers pitcher)
- Jeffrey Katzenberg (Hollywood executive and Biden campaign co-chair)

Deception in America

Cass R. Sunstein, *Liars: Falsehoods and Free Speech in an Age of Deception*

https://hls.harvard.edu/bibliography/liars-falsehoods-and-free-speech-in-an-age-of-deception/

- Perjury: Ten thousand people are convicted of perjury at the federal and state level each year.
- Average Frequency: Most Americans tell 1.65 to 2.03 lies per day.
- The "Honest Majority": Approximately 75 percent of people report telling 0 to 2 lies daily.
- Prolific Liars: A small group (about 1 percent of the population) averages roughly 17 lies per day, and just 5 percent of people are responsible for half of all lies told.
- Conversation Spans: Research indicates that 60 percent of adults cannot have a ten-minute conversation without lying at least once, averaging 2 to 3 lies in that time frame.
- Gender Differences: Studies suggest men lie about 6 times per day, while women lie roughly 3 times.

- Romantic Relationships: 92 percent of individuals admit to lying to a partner.
- Online Dating: 90 percent of users admit to some form of deception on their profiles.
- Professional: 70 percent of job applicants admit to lying or embellishing their résumés.
- Family Dynamics: 86 percent of lies are told to parents, making them the primary targets of domestic deception.
- Job Interviews: 80 percent of workers admit to having lied during a job interview.

✪✪✪

Chapter Eighteen: The Bubble People

"Bubble people"

The phenomenon where individuals, communities, or political actors exist within highly insulated social, geographic, or digital environments, interacting primarily with those who share their exact political views and consuming media that reinforces their pre-existing beliefs. This environment creates a skewed perception of reality, where one's own political, social, or cultural perspective is overestimated, leading to increased polarization, reduced empathy for opposing views, and "information gerrymandering," where only specific viewpoints are consumed.

Key Data on Political Bubbles

- Media Consumption: Approximately 20 percent of Democrats and 18 percent of Republicans consume news only from sources aligned with their party.

- Social Media Echo Chambers: A study of Twitter users indicated that 84 percent of the most liberal users and 78 percent of the most conservative users live in ideological "bubbles."

- Asymmetry in Media: While 32 percent of Fox News viewers are strong Republicans, 42 percent of them are less partisan, whereas 36 percent of CNN/MSNBC viewers are strong Democrats.

- Distrust of Opposite Views: Republicans show greater distrust of mainstream media, with only seven out of thirty surveyed outlets generating more trust than distrust, compared to twenty-two for Democrats.

- Urban-Rural Divide: Democrats are more likely to live in high-density areas with little exposure to opposing views.

- Rising Polarization: The gap between the two major parties has increased steadily since the 1990s, with party identification aligning closely with underlying cultural values.

- Asymmetric Behavior: Studies show that conservatives are more likely to consume some left-leaning media (e.g., following accounts to the left of MSNBC) than liberals are to consume right-leaning media.

Smartphone Addiction

- 57 percent of Americans are addicted to their devices (they check more than five times per hour).

- 24 percent of Americans suffer from severe addiction (are on the devices more than six hours per day)

- The average American checks their phone 224 times per day.

- Gen Z (fourteen- to-twenty-nine-year-olds) spend an average of 6 hours and 37 minutes on their phones each day.

The Consequences of Living in a Bubble

- Governmental Knowledge: Only 34 percent of people can identify the three branches of government, and 70 percent cannot name their state's senators.

- Historical/Civic Literacy: 63 percent of millennials in one study did not know that six million Jews were killed in the Holocaust.

- Political Participation: Over one-third of Americans do not feel informed enough to participate in the political process.

- News Consumption: With the abundance of information online, 58 percent of US adults believe it is harder now to be well informed.

✪✪✪

Chapter Nineteen: Asides

The Michelle Obama "Proud" Controversy

In February 2008, during Barack Obama's first presidential campaign, Michelle Obama sparked controversy by stating, "For the first time in my adult lifetime, I am really proud of my country."

She made the comment at a Milwaukee rally, attributing this renewed pride to the massive grassroots engagement, hope, and desire for change she witnessed, rather than just her husband's political success.

- The Backlash: Critics, including Cindy McCain (wife of Republican nominee John McCain), used the statement to paint her as out of touch. The remark prompted concerns that it reflected "anger" or a negative view of America, as analyzed by NPR and Fox News.

- The Clarification: She quickly clarified that she did not mean she was previously *ashamed* of the US but rather that the level of political involvement in 2008 was unprecedented for her. She stated she has "absolutely" always been proud of her country, according to reports from 6ABC and *The New York Times.*

- Political Impact: The comment was seen as a key moment in the campaign's need to "reintroduce" her and manage the narrative, as discussed in *PBS News Hour* coverage of the election.

Ultimately, the remark was viewed by supporters as an awkward phrasing of her enthusiasm for political change. Her political opponents continued to cite it as evidence of a deeper dislike for the country, a debate that persisted throughout the 2008 presidential campaign.

Acknowledgments

All books are collaborations. The following folks helped me a lot in putting this one together: Josh Hammer, Makeda Wubneh, Jon Leibner, George Witte, Therese Janow, Dr. Ira Jacobson, Dr. Florence Barracelli, and Dr. Ryan Hickey.

Bill O'Reilly

For my nephew and niece, the future is yours. Special thanks to the intrepid Bill O'Reilly, who works tirelessly every day to make America a better place.

Josh Hammer

Index

About the Author

BILL O'REILLY is a trailblazing television journalist and the author of twenty #1 *New York Times* bestsellers, including the twelve books in the *Killing* series of narrative histories, as well as *Confronting the Presidents* and *Confronting Evil*. He lives on Long Island, New York.

JOSH HAMMER studied political theory at The George Washington University and international politics at the University of Edinburgh, Scotland. He writes and produces some of the most successful programs in America, including *The O'Reilly Update* with Bill O'Reilly. He lives in Brooklyn, New York.